WHAT ARE YOU SO AFRAID OF?

(Second Edition)

ROMAIN MUHAMMAD

Copyright © 2025 by Romain Muhammad Limited. All rights reserved.

No part of this publication may be reproduced, distributed, or transmitted in any form or by any means, including photocopying, recording, or other electronic or mechanical methods, without the prior written permission of the publisher, except in the case of brief quotations used in critical reviews or non-commercial uses permitted by copyright law.

For permission requests, write to the publisher, addressed "Attention: Permissions Coordinator," at the address Contact Information: hello@romainmuhammad.co.uk

Note on the Second edition

This second edition represents both a refinement and an expansion of the original work. Since the book's first release, countless conversations, coaching sessions, and reader reflections have deepened my understanding of how fear shapes our personal, professional, and collective lives. It felt only right that this edition reflected that growth, both mine and yours.

You'll find several revised and expanded chapters, written with greater clarity, nuance, and heart. There are new sections rich with lived experience, additional stories, personal reflections, and real-world case studies that bring the ideas to life in practice. These additions move the book beyond theory, illustrating how fear, courage, and transformation unfold in everyday moments, in boardrooms, relationships, and within ourselves.

A brand-new chapter explores dimensions of fear and freedom that weren't present in the first edition, bridging personal psychology with cultural and generational context. You'll also find a curated glossary of key terms, a comprehensive bibliography/and a "Further Reading" section, designed for those who wish to continue the work of reflection, research, and growth long after the final page.

This edition exists because fear evolves, and so must our understanding of it. My hope is that these revisions make the book not only more complete, but more intimate; not just instructive, but transformative.

Thank you for returning to this work or discovering it for the first time. Either way, I hope these pages meet you exactly where you are, and remind you that fear, when faced with awareness and compassion, can become one of our greatest teachers.

Disclaimer

What Are You So Afraid Of? is a book about courage, fear, and the subtle ways we learn to doubt ourselves. It is a reflective guide rooted in lived experience, social context, and compassionate insight. While it engages with psychology, sociology, and personal storytelling, it is not a substitute for medical, legal, therapeutic, or career advice.

I am not a psychologist, psychiatrist, or clinical therapist. I do not diagnose, treat, or claim to offer medical or psychological intervention. What I *am* is an expert in People & Culture, workplace behaviour, and Diversity, Equity & Inclusion. These are areas in which I have built deep, evidence-based expertise over more than 15 years. My reflections in this book come from thousands of hours of research; from my academic background in history, identity, and belonging; and from my lived experiences navigating systems that were never designed with people like me in mind.

This work also reflects my professional journey as a corporate leader, entrepreneur, business owner, coach, and consultant who has worked with hundreds of companies and taught or coached thousands of people across industries and continents. The insights shared here arise from years spent supporting individuals and organisations through complex issues of confidence, identity, leadership, self-doubt, belonging, and systemic barriers.

This book was written to shine a light on the quiet ways fear arrives in our lives, through childhood experiences, cultural expectations, workplaces that undervalue us, and societies that demand conformity at the expense of authenticity. It explores how imposter syndrome, far from being a personal flaw, often emerges as a survival response: a way of navigating environments that fail to fully recognise or affirm our worth.

What you will find here are ideas, reflections, and strategies: ways to notice your internal patterns, to question the stories you have inherited, to record your successes instead of minimising them, and to build resilience through practice rather than perfection. These are not "quick fixes" or universal solutions. They are tools to try, perspectives to sit with, and reminders that you are not alone in your struggle with self-doubt.

The stories included in this book are drawn from my own life and, where relevant, from experiences that have been anonymised or adapted for storytelling purposes. Any resemblance to real individuals is coincidental unless specifically acknowledged.

Because fear and self-doubt are deeply human experiences, some of the reflections in these pages may resonate strongly. They may also surface memories or emotions you have carried quietly for years. If you find yourself overwhelmed or in need of deeper support, I encourage you to seek help from qualified professionals such as therapists, counsellors, medical practitioners, or specialised coaches. There is courage in reaching for support, it is a sign of strength, not weakness.

Ultimately, this book is not a manual, a diagnosis, or a step-by-step formula. It is a companion for your journey. It will not tell you what to fear or what not to fear. Instead, it will help you recognise the role fear has played in your life and invite you to choose differently.

This is an invitation: to confront what has held you back, to reclaim your voice, to live with clarity and courage, and to redefine success on your own terms. These pages are not about silencing fear, fear is part of being human but about learning to understand it, navigate it, and move forward anyway.

Dedication

To my girls, Lailah & Mia

I didn't grow up with a blueprint.
Just questions.
Questions that felt bigger than the walls I grew up in.
Questions that children shouldn't have to carry,
but somehow I did.

How do you protect what you never had?
How do you guide when no one showed you the way?
How do you learn the language of love
when your dictionary never had the right words?

I learned early that some lessons come through absence,
through what you didn't receive,
through the gaps you had to fill on your own.

And maybe that's why fatherhood hit me the way it did.
It didn't scare me because I wasn't ready
it scared me because I wanted it to look nothing like what came
before me.
Because I knew love could be rewritten
if someone was willing to try.

When you were born, something in me shifted.
It was like standing in front of a mirror for the first time,
seeing the reflection of a man I hadn't met yet.
A man rising from the history he refused to continue.
A man determined to build a world for you
that didn't come with the same shadows mine did.

Every bedtime story I tell,
every school run,
every scraped knee I kiss,
every "How was your day?"
every check-in when something feels off,
every "I'm proud of you,"
every "I love you" before sleep
it's more than routine.
It's a rebellion.
It's me choosing presence
over the silence that shaped me.
It's me proving that cycles break
when someone is brave enough to stand in the middle
and say, "It ends here."

I'm not just raising daughters.
I'm raising two lights
in a world that sometimes forgets how to treat gentle souls.
Two girls who will grow into women
who know their worth without needing to search for it in anyone else's hands.
Two stories that will never doubt their own pages.

And yes, I haven't been perfect.
I've made mistakes.
I've learned on the go.
Some days, I parented from love;
other days, I parented from fear, fear of failing you,
fear of repeating things I swore I'd never repeat,
fear of not being enough.

If life gave me a chance to rewind,
there would be moments I'd handle with softer hands,
words I'd slow down before saying,
arms I'd open sooner,
tears I'd wipe quicker,
and memories I'd hold tighter.

But hear me clearly
You will never have to question
if you're enough,
if you're seen,
if you matter,
if you are loved with a love
that doesn't shrink, hide, or hesitate.

You are both the reason I healed,
the reason I softened,
the reason I grew into someone I once doubted I could be.
In giving you what I missed,
I became the man I needed when I was young.
Present.
Patient.
Learning.
Healing.
Whole.

One day, when you read this,
I hope you see not just the father I am,
but the boy I was
the boy who turned his broken pieces
into building blocks for your future.

The boy who promised himself
that if he ever had children,
they would never inherit the storms he survived.

I love you both, loudly, endlessly, without condition.
My girls.
My teachers.
My mirrors.
My purpose.

Yours forever,
Dad x

Acknowledgements

To my grandmother, Clarista James: My leader, my hero, my mentor, my role model, my inspiration, my father figure: the person who came here to build a new life and the person in whose honour I do this. Your courage crossed an ocean and laid the first brick. Every step I take is a continuation of your journey. You being proud of me is why I do this. May this book stand as a small return on the debt I owe to your grit, your grace, and your unwavering belief.

To my mother, Monica James: My first home and constant compass. Thank you for the sacrifices nobody saw, the prayers that carried me, and the fierce love that set a standard for how to live with integrity. You taught me to work hard without hardening, to speak truth with tenderness, and to keep moving when the way wasn't clear. Everything good in these pages has your fingerprints on it.

To my children: Who taught me that love is not a theory but a daily practice. Your curiosity and courage are the reason I wrote this book and the reason I keep going.

To my family: Here and across the Atlantic, who carried history on their backs and still chose hope. I stand on your prayers, sacrifices, and stubborn faith.

To the Windrush generation and our elders: You rebuilt a country that did not always know how to hold you. Your quiet excellence is the foundation under every chapter.

To my clients, students, leaders, and teams: Across sectors who let me into your boardrooms, away-days, and living rooms thank you for your trust, your candour, and your willingness to do the hard work when cameras aren't rolling.

To mentors, peers, and collaborators: Who challenged my thinking, sent late-night voice notes, and asked the uncomfortable questions: you sharpened this work. Special thanks to the colleagues who opened doors and the friends who reminded me who I am.

To the readers and community: Who shared stories of doubt, belonging, and becoming, his book is for you. May it be a companion when the room feels cold and the voice in your head gets loud.

And to the most important one of all, the creator, the One who sees what is unseen and knows what is possible. Every gift and blessing returns to You.

Table of Contents

Introduction: The Quiet Arrival of Fear 1

Chapter 1: Unmasking Your Hidden Fears 7

Chapter 2: The Anatomy of Fear: How Fear Thinks, Hides, and Heals 77

Chapter 3: Fear and Intersectionality - The Masks and Architectures of Survival 188

Chapter 4: Courage in Action: Navigating Discomfort 249

Chapter 5: Leading with Courage: Actionable Habits 304

Chapter 6: Conclusion - The Only Way Out Is Through 348

Glossary of terms 367

Bibliography & Further Reading 381

INTRODUCTION

The Quiet Arrival of Fear

Fear rarely walks into the room announcing itself. It doesn't slam doors or shout its name. It arrives quietly, dressed in more respectable clothes. It disguises itself as caution, as professionalism, as ambition. It whispers what we may perceive as logic: "Wait until you're ready. Don't rush. Play it safe."

That's the thing fear doesn't always look like panic or trembling hands. Sometimes it looks like the polished CV you never send. The meeting where you nod along, heart racing, but swallow the point you wanted to make. The bold idea you rehearse in your mind but never share because the timing doesn't feel "right." The opportunity you scroll past because you've convinced yourself someone else is better suited.

Fear is clever. It will let you stay busy, respectable, competent while keeping you small.

And I know this voice well. I've walked into rooms where, on paper, I had every right to be there degrees, experience, achievements lined up yet still felt like an intruder.

I've held ideas that could have changed a conversation, only to keep them hidden because fear convinced me silence was safer.

The Real Question

This book is not about becoming fearless. That's a myth. Fear will always be with us, and that is okay, it's part of being human. The real question is not "How do I get rid of fear?" The real question is **"What will I do, even though I am afraid?"**

If you've ever felt paralysed by self-doubt, silenced in rooms where you had something to say, or caught in that strange tension of fearing both failure and success, this book is for you.

Who I'm Speaking To

I'm writing for the quiet warriors. The hesitant dreamers. The professionals who know they're capable of more yet find themselves inexplicably holding back.

This is for the leader who bites their tongue instead of voicing their vision.

The entrepreneur who delays launching the campaign they know could shift their business.

The artist who hides their masterpiece in the drawer, waiting for the mythical moment of "perfection."

The employee who avoids the difficult conversation, telling themselves it's not worth the conflict.

And maybe it's for you, the person who has always been told you're talented, smart, capable, but who lies awake at night wondering why you haven't quite stepped into the life you know is possible.

Why We Hide?

We live in a culture that celebrates the fearless.

We idolise boldness, confidence, the people who seem to stride through life untouched by doubt. The ones who "just go for it."

But that's not most of us.

For most of us, fear isn't a dramatic storm.

It's a quiet undertow.

It hums beneath the surface of our lives, shaping our choices in ways we barely notice.

It looks like procrastination.

It looks like perfectionism.

It looks like staying busy with the small things, so we never have to face the big thing.

Fear convinces us that staying put is safer than stepping forward. That silence is better than risk.

That invisibility is protection.

And sometimes, it's not even *our* fear. Sometimes it's inherited passed down through families, cultures, histories. Whispers of caution from people who wanted to keep us safe: **"Keep your head down. Don't draw attention. Don't take risks."**

Lessons that may have once been survival strategies, but which now keep us stuck.

Why This Book Exists?

What Are You So Afraid Of? was born from my own wrestling with fear. I've seen how it silences people clients, colleagues, even leaders at the top of their game. And I've seen how learning to name it, to face it, to act with it instead of against it, can completely shift a person's trajectory.

I've had moments in my life where fear cost me opportunities.

Roles I never applied for.

Rooms I stayed quiet in.

Dreams I convinced myself weren't realistic.

I've also had moments where I stepped forward despite it and those are the moments that changed everything.

What We'll Do Together

Across the chapters ahead, we'll explore the many disguises of fear. We'll look at:

- The fears we don't admit, and how they quietly shape our lives.
- Why we fear both failure *and* success, and how both can hold us hostage.
- How the fear of rejection keeps us silent and small.
- Why authenticity feels risky, and how to find freedom in being seen.
- The fears we inherit from families and cultures, and how to decide which ones to carry forward.
- How to repurpose fear into fuel, turning anxiety into energy.
- What it means to lead, not without fear, but despite it.

This is not theory alone. You'll find reflection prompts, practical exercises, and strategies that you can apply immediately. Because awareness is only half the work the other half is action.

An Honest Acknowledgment

I need to be clear: this book won't make you fearless. I wouldn't trust a book that claimed it could. Fear is stitched into us and as I mentioned its what makes us human beings.

It shows up in new guises every time we stretch into something bigger.

But here's what I can promise: by the end of this book, you'll be **fear aware**. You'll know how to recognise fear's disguises, how to separate its lies from its truths, and how to keep moving anyway.

You'll understand that courage isn't waiting until the fear disappears. It's deciding to act while the fear is still in the room.

An Invitation to Begin

If you picked up this book, something in the title spoke to you.

Maybe you're tired of talking yourself out of opportunities.

Maybe you're done with procrastination and perfectionism.

Maybe you're simply curious about what life could look like if fear stopped running the show.

So let me ask you the same question I asked myself when I started writing:

What are you so afraid of?

Sit with that for a moment.
Name it honestly.
Don't dress it up.
Don't rationalise it.
Just say it.
Because once you name it, you take back some of its power.

And then, as you move through these pages, you'll learn how to live not in fear's absence, but in its presence. To act powerfully, even when afraid.

So, let's begin. Together.

CHAPTER 1

Unmasking Your Hidden Fears

Every journey of transformation begins with honesty, not about who we wish to be, but about what stands in the way of becoming that person. Before courage can grow, fear must be seen. Not judged, not denied seen, because what we refuse to face will always find a way to guide us from the shadows.

Fear is one of the most powerful forces in our lives, yet one of the least understood. It shapes the choices we make, the dreams we postpone, the boundaries we build around what feels safe. Sometimes it's obvious, the panic before a big decision, the dread of failure or rejection. But most of the time, it's subtle. It hides behind confidence, discipline, even kindness. It wears masks so convincing that we start mistaking fear for personality.

This chapter is about learning to see through those masks, to recognise the disguises fear wears and the ways it quietly shapes our behaviour. It's the first step in reclaiming the energy we've spent on avoidance and redirecting it toward awareness, purpose, and power.

Because before we can outgrow fear, we must first learn to recognise its voice.

Fear Doesn't Always Look Like Fear

Fear doesn't usually arrive kicking down the door. It's smarter than that. It slips in quietly, wearing the clothes of everyday life. It hides in the habits we justify, the excuses we recycle, the silences we keep.

Most of the time, we don't meet fear as a dramatic crisis. We meet it in the small, ordinary moments where we feel ourselves holding back. That's where the real work begins, not with the lion's roar, but with the faint rustle in the background. The subtle tightening in your chest before you speak. The hesitation before you press "send." The thought you swallow because it might make things awkward.

That's fear, not the loud kind that screams danger, but the quiet kind that whispers, *stay small.*

Over time, I learned something crucial: fear isn't always a warning. Sometimes, it's a compass. The things we fear most often point to what we value most. Fear can illuminate where growth lies, where meaning and fulfilment are waiting on the other side of risk.

This book, and this work, is an invitation to stop treating fear as the enemy and start treating it as information. Fear is a messenger, carrying clues about where we've been hurt, what we hope for, and what still matters deeply to us.

But fear is clever. It rarely announces itself plainly. Instead, it adapts. It shape-shifts. It learns how to blend in. Fear doesn't always look like fear, it's cleverer than that. It dresses itself in traits that the world rewards: professionalism, composure, preparation, intellect. It wears masks that look like strength.

The Core Masks of Fear

These are what I call the *core masks of fear:* **perfectionism, procrastination, people-pleasing, cynicism, Busyness and control.**

They appear polished, even admirable.
A perfectionist is seen as someone who cares about detail.
A people-pleaser seems agreeable and kind.
The overthinker looks analytical and measured.
The cynic sounds smart.
The controller looks reliable.
The busy body seems productive and successful.

We're praised for these traits, rewarded for them, even, which makes them harder to recognise for what they really are. Because under each of these masks lies something more fragile: fear.

Fear of not being enough.

Fear of being exposed.
Fear of being rejected, humiliated, or wrong.
Fear of being too visible, or not visible enough.

Each mask begins as protection, a kind of emotional armour we put on to stay safe in a world that can be quick to judge and slow to understand. They start as coping mechanisms, intelligent responses to uncertainty and pain. But over time, those same masks stop protecting us; they start restricting us.

We wear them so long that we forget who we are underneath. We start mistaking the mask for our identity. The perfectionist becomes "high achieving." The people-pleaser becomes "collaborative." The cynic becomes "realistic." The controller becomes "dependable." And the busy one? The busy one becomes "driven."

But the truth is quieter, and more complex. These aren't signs of confidence; they're symptoms of caution. Fear has simply found a socially acceptable costume.

And that's why it's so hard to spot. Because fear in disguise doesn't look weak, it looks polished. It wins awards, earns promotions, garners praise. But what it doesn't do is allow expansion. Fear keeps you competent, but not creative. Busy, but not brave. Liked, but not known.

The moment you start to see these masks for what they are, not failures, but signals you reclaim power. Because when you can name fear's disguise, you can begin to dismantle it.

Every mask has a message:

- **Perfectionism** says, "If I do everything right, I'll finally be safe."
- **Procrastination** says, "If I wait long enough, I can avoid getting it wrong."
- **People-pleasing** says, "If everyone likes me, I'll never be rejected."
- **Cynicism** says, "If I expect disappointment, I can't be hurt by it."
- **Control** says, "If I manage every variable, nothing can fall apart."
- **Busyness says,** If I fill every minute, I won't have to sit with myself and face the silence"

Each one begins as a form of care an attempt to protect the self. But every mask that fear wears buys temporary safety at the cost of long-term freedom.

The work, then, isn't to shame these patterns. It's to understand them, to see how fear hides behind competence, to notice how safety and stagnation sometimes look the same, and to ask gently: *"What am I really protecting myself from?"*

Because courage doesn't begin with action; it begins with awareness. And the moment you can see fear clearly, not as an enemy but as a messenger, is the moment you start to reclaim your freedom from it.

That's where real transformation begins not in slaying fear, but in recognising the thousand quiet ways it tries to keep you small, and choosing, moment by moment, to grow anyway.

The Layers Beneath: Fear's Sub-Masks

Fear is layered. It doesn't stop with the obvious masks; it hides inside smaller, subtler ones, habits that seem harmless, even responsible. These are what I call the *sub-masks of fear:* the everyday behaviours that keep us in motion without progress.

They look like:

- Overthinking decisions until the moment for action passes.
- Redrafting an email twenty times because "it has to sound right."
- Using sarcasm or cynicism to hide vulnerability.
- Staying busy to avoid stillness.
- Complaining instead of creating.
- Calling yourself "realistic" when what you really mean is "afraid."

These aren't flaws of personality, they're strategies of protection. The mind's way of saying, *"I'm not ready to be hurt again."*

Fear in Disguise: Six Everyday Masks

One of the most pervasive and insidious disguises fear wears is **Procrastination**, we all know the feeling. There's a big deadline around the corner, a phone call we keep meaning to make, or an email that needs a proper, thoughtful response. And instead of just getting it done, we find ourselves wiping down the kitchen counter, scrolling through Instagram again, or suddenly convinced now is the perfect time to reorganise the wardrobe. We tell ourselves, "I'm not in the right headspace today," "I'll do it tomorrow" or "I'll do it once I've gathered my thoughts." But often, what's really going on is fear.

Not laziness, fear.
Fear of messing it up.
Fear of what people might think.
Fear of failing.
Sometimes even fear of succeeding and having to carry the weight that comes with it.

Take the friend who's been talking for months about starting their podcast. The equipment's bought, the ideas are mapped out, the cover art is designed. On paper, everything's ready. But when it comes to actually hitting *record*, they keep finding "technical issues" to fix, the mic quality isn't quite right, the intro music doesn't feel professional enough, the lighting isn't ideal. They keep tweaking, adjusting, planning.

But the problem isn't the mic; it's the mind.

What's really holding them back isn't the software or the setup, it's the quiet storm of *what-ifs* beneath the surface: *What if no one listens? What if people laugh? What if my voice sounds awkward? What if I fail publicly?*

That's the cleverness of fear, it hides beneath logic, dressing itself up as caution, as preparation, as "being realistic." It whispers, *"You're just not quite ready yet."* And because that voice sounds reasonable, we obey it.

Procrastination, in this way, becomes the brain's subtle form of protection, a way of saying, *"Let's just wait. Let's not risk it yet."* But waiting doesn't dissolve fear; it deepens it. The longer we delay, the more we feed the illusion that we need perfect conditions before we can begin, and perfect conditions never come.

Fear of starting often disguises itself as fine-tuning, you tell yourself you're improving something, when really, you're protecting something: your ego. Because as long as the work isn't finished, it can't be judged; as long as you're still preparing, you're safe.

But that safety has a cost. You stay suspended between potential and proof, where your ideas never get to breathe.

The truth is, courage doesn't appear before the action; it arrives through it. Fear will always tempt you to wait for readiness, but readiness is built by doing. The first attempt, however imperfect, is where growth begins.

Fear may protect you from embarrassment, but it also protects you from expansion, and every time you choose movement over delay, you weaken its grip a little more.

Perfectionism: Fear Disguised as Excellence

Closely tied to procrastination, almost like its twin is perfectionism.
Not the healthy kind that pushes you to take pride in your craft, but the exhausting, never-ending chase for flawless. It's that whisper that says, *"good" isn't good enough*, that unless it's perfect, it doesn't count, and instead of driving you forward, it quietly paralyses you.

At first glance, perfectionism looks admirable. It wears the polished face of discipline and ambition. It's praised in workplaces, celebrated in schools, and reinforced by a culture that equates flawlessness with value. We're told to "do it properly," to "never settle," to "strive for excellence." But there's a fine line between striving and suffocating. And perfectionism crosses it quietly.

It begins innocently, the desire to do well. But underneath that drive, something else takes root: fear.

Fear of being exposed as not enough.
Fear that one mistake will confirm all the quiet doubts you've tried to bury.
Fear that your best still won't be good enough for the world, or for yourself.

I've seen it in clients, in colleagues, and in myself.
The writer who endlessly rewrites the first chapter of their book, never reaching chapter two.

15

The entrepreneur who won't launch until the brand looks like Apple.
The student who keeps redrafting an essay long past excellence, trying to outrun their insecurity.

Each of them believes they're working toward mastery, but really, they're working for safety.

I remember a time about 7 years ago, when I was building my first leadership workshop. I'd done the research, tested the material, and received brilliant feedback from pilot sessions. But when it came time to launch it formally, I stalled. I told myself I needed to "make it perfect" better slides, tighter language, more data. I reworked the content until it lost its flow. But it wasn't about refinement. It was about fear, fear that if I launched and it wasn't flawless, people would question my credibility. Fear that if someone found a gap, it would undo everything I'd built.

That's the hidden logic of perfectionism:
If I don't finish, I can't fail.
If I don't release it, no one can judge it.
But the irony is, nothing gets finished. Nothing gets released, and in the silence that follows, self-doubt grows stronger.

Perfectionism pretends to be about standards, but it's really about safety.
It doesn't protect your work; it protects your image.
It keeps you in a loop of refining instead of revealing, rehearsing instead of risking.

It's not about mastery, it's about control.

And control always has a cost.

It costs creativity because perfectionism leaves no room for experimentation or mistakes. It costs connection because the more polished you become, the less human you appear. It costs peace because your mind is never done; there's always something left to fix.

The perfectionist's paradox is this, you're not chasing excellence; you're avoiding exposure.
You want to be respected, not rejected. But in trying to eliminate all possibility of rejection, you eliminate all possibility of growth.

We live in a culture that rewards performance more than process, and perfectionism thrives in that environment because it disguises itself as commitment. You'll hear it in phrases like, "I just want it to be the best it can be," or "It's not quite ready yet." What we rarely admit is the truth beneath those words: "I'm scared of how it will be received."

I've seen this play out in leadership too.
In boardrooms where decisions drag on because no one wants to make the first imperfect move.
In teams where projects stall under the weight of revisions.
In individuals who hold back their best ideas until the "right moment," which never arrives.
The result is often the same, stagnation disguised as strategy.

But here's what perfectionism doesn't tell you:

Excellence isn't the absence of mistakes it's the presence of growth.

Perfectionism seeks control whilst excellence seeks progress, and progress itself, is built on imperfection, on feedback, adjustment, and courage.

Every imperfect action is a declaration of faith: faith that learning is more valuable than image, that trying matters more than approval.

In my coaching work, I often tell clients this truth, **perfectionism is not a strength, it's a strategy.**

A strategy to stay safe. To stay unseen. To stay comfortable in competence rather than vulnerable in growth, but here's the reframe: what if "not ready" is actually ready enough?

Because readiness isn't a feeling; it's a decision, and courage doesn't wait for perfect timing, it *creates* it. So much of what holds us back under the name of perfection is really the fear of being seen unfinished, but the truth is, you are *supposed* to be unfinished. You're supposed to evolve, to refine through experience, to grow by doing.

When you release something imperfect into the world, a project, an idea, a conversation, you don't lower your standards; you raise your resilience. You teach yourself that you can handle imperfection, that mistakes don't define you, that feedback doesn't diminish you.

Perfectionism whispers, *"If it isn't flawless, it isn't worth doing."*

But courage replies, *"If it's honest, it's already enough."*

And perhaps the most freeing truth of all is this: the world doesn't need your perfect; it needs your real.

Your presence.
Your ideas.
Your imperfect contribution that moves things forward instead of keeping them trapped in your drafts folder.

Perfectionism is fear wearing a polished mask, the kind that looks professional, responsible, even admirable, but the moment you see it for what it is, fear of exposure, you take its power away.

Because perfection is not the goal.
Progress is.
And every imperfect step forward is evidence that you're growing, learning, and leading, not in spite of the fear, but through it.

Busyness: Fear in Motion

Another mask fear often wears is **busyness**, not the natural kind that comes with living a full life, but the kind that consumes you. The calendar that's crammed, the to-do list that regenerates faster than you can tick it off, the feeling of being permanently "too busy" to stop.

In today's productivity-obsessed culture, constant motion is glorified. We wear exhaustion like a medal, answer emails at midnight as proof of dedication, and treat rest as a luxury reserved for the unambitious. Busyness has become one of fear's most socially rewarded disguises.

On the surface, it looks like commitment, responsibility, even excellence.
But beneath it, busyness often means **avoidance**, avoidance of silence, of reflection, of truth.
Because silence is dangerous to the ego.
In the quiet, the questions we've been outrunning start to surface:
Am I fulfilled?
Do I even want this?
Who am I when I'm not achieving?

I know this mask well.
There was a time in my career when I mistook movement for meaning, for success.
If my diary was full, I felt important. If I was exhausted, I felt successful, but beneath the grind was fear, fear of stillness, fear of inadequacy, fear of what might rise if I ever slowed down enough to listen.

I wasn't chasing purpose; I was running from discomfort, and the world made it easy. We're conditioned to equate worth with output and stillness with laziness. Entire systems depend on our inability to pause, economies built on endless productivity, cultures addicted to the illusion of control. We celebrate busyness as ambition but more often, than not, it's **fear in costume**, whispering: **"As long as you keep moving, you won't have to feel."**

You've seen it, maybe even lived it. The colleague who volunteers for every extra project, even though they're already at breaking point. The friend who insists they "can't stop," always chasing the next thing because standing still feels unbearable. They're not addicted to work, they're addicted to avoidance, because the moment the noise stops, the truth gets loud.

That's the part we rarely talk about, the echo of silence. We try to keep busy, whether that's with *someone* or *something*, because the silence can be deafening. Stillness holds up a mirror, and in that reflection are the truths we've been avoiding, the questions, the doubts, the discomfort we've buried under busyness. The quiet can feel unbearable because it strips away distraction. It forces us to confront what we already know but haven't wanted to admit, that something isn't working, that we're lonely, that we've been running not toward purpose, but away from pain.

So, we fill the space.
We scroll. We call. We commit.
We overwork, over give, overpromise.
We tell ourselves it's productivity, but it's really protection, protection from hearing what the silence is trying to tell us.
Because the silence speaks.
It whispers the things our busyness refuses to hear: *You're tired. You're afraid. You're disconnected from what matters.*

Sometimes that busyness takes subtler forms. It can show up as scrolling, shopping, drinking, or clinging to relationships that distract more than they nourish. Sometimes it's framed as "hustle" or "high standards," when really, it's just a clever way of not feeling the ache of emptiness or uncertainty. The fear isn't that we'll run out of time, it's that if we slow down, we might have to confront the parts of ourselves we've neglected.

I've seen this pattern in countless coaching sessions, executives, founders, parents, leaders, all convinced that if they stop, everything will fall apart. When we explore what's really behind that belief, what emerges isn't ambition, it's anxiety. It's the quiet fear of being unneeded. The fear that their value lives only in their utility.

One client once told me, "If I stop, I'm scared I won't know who I am." I understood that deeply, because busyness doesn't just drain energy; it **erodes identity**. When you define yourself solely by what you do, stillness feels like disappearance.

But here's the truth:
You are not your calendar.
You are not your inbox.
You are not your productivity.
You are a human being, not a human doing.

Busyness drowns out that truth. It keeps you efficient but disconnected, accomplished but anxious.
It keeps you competent but not creative, busy but not brave, liked but not known.

Real courage sometimes looks like doing less.
It's saying no when your ego wants to say yes.
It's closing the laptop while others keep typing.
It's giving yourself permission to rest, to reflect, to breathe, not as a reward, but as a right.

Stillness is not weakness; it's wisdom.
It's where clarity gathers.
It's where intuition whispers.
It's where courage begins to form.

Because the silence you fear isn't empty, it's full of information. It's in stillness that you reconnect with what matters, what's true, and what you've been running from.

So next time you find yourself filling every minute, stop and ask:

- What am I trying not to feel right now?
- What truth am I afraid will surface if I pause?
- What might I gain if I stopped proving and started being?

That's where the real work begins, because courage isn't found in constant motion, it's found in conscious pause. When you learn to stop, to breathe, to listen, you discover something powerful:
You were never running out of time.
You were just running from yourself.

Reflection Exercise: The Busyness Audit: Where Are You Avoiding Stillness?

Busyness can feel like control, but it's often just noise, a way of avoiding what silence might reveal. This reflection is designed to help you notice where fear may be hiding behind your productivity.

Take a moment.
Find somewhere quiet.

Put your phone away.
Breathe.
And ask yourself these questions, honestly, without judgment.

1. When do I feel most uncomfortable being still?

- Is it in the evenings when things quiet down?
- On weekends with no plans?
- During holidays when there's nothing urgent to do?
  What emotions rise in those moments, restlessness, guilt, anxiety, boredom? What might they be pointing to?

2. What do I fill my time with when I feel uneasy?

- Do I reach for work, my phone, other people, or distractions?
- What am I trying not to think or feel in those moments?

3. What stories do I tell myself about being busy?

- "If I stop, I'll fall behind."
- "If I rest, people will think I'm lazy."
- "If I slow down, I'll lose my edge."
  Whose voice is that, yours, or the culture that taught you your worth is measured in output?

4. What am I afraid might surface in stillness?

- Is it grief? Regret? Loneliness? Uncertainty about what's next?
  Write it down. Name it. Awareness is the first act of courage.

5. What might become possible if I slowed down?

- What clarity might emerge if I allowed silence to speak?
- What creativity, connection, or courage might return if I made room for it?

Now, take one small action to reclaim stillness:

- Block fifteen minutes in your day with no task attached.
- Go for a walk without your phone.
- Sit in silence and breathe, even if it feels uncomfortable.

Remember: stillness isn't the absence of progress, It's the space where real progress begins.

Because every courageous act starts in pause, the moment you stop reacting long enough to hear what your life is trying to tell you.

Avoidance: Fear's Quiet Refuge

Avoidance is perhaps the most direct manifestation of fear's subtle tactics. It's fear's most straightforward strategy, and yet its most deceptive. Because it doesn't feel like fear, it feels like relief. Like logic. Like self-protection.

While procrastination and busyness are quieter, more socially acceptable forms of avoidance, this one is more explicit, the conscious turning away from what makes us uncomfortable. We avoid the things that stretch us because they threaten our sense of control, our predictability, our emotional safety.

We avoid social gatherings because we fear judgment.
We avoid difficult conversations because we fear conflict.
We avoid applying for new jobs because we fear rejection, or worse, success, and all the unfamiliar expectations that might follow.

Avoidance offers short-term comfort but long-term cost. It's a psychological trick that trades peace of mind for a smaller life. It gives you a momentary sense of safety, the satisfaction of escape, but quietly builds invisible walls around your freedom. Every time you avoid something, your world contracts a little more. What once felt like a healthy boundary becomes a border. What began as protection slowly becomes a prison.

Here's the cruel irony: avoidance often feels empowering at first. Saying *no* to a risk feels like control. Walking away from discomfort feels like wisdom, you tell yourself you're "trusting your gut," but really, you're obeying your fear. You've mistaken the absence of anxiety for the presence of peace.

Fear doesn't need to shout when it's mastered the art of subtlety. It doesn't need to tell you "don't do it", it simply teaches you to delay, to disguise retreat as reason. You start to believe your own excuses:
"Now's not the right time."
"I just need to think it through."
"I'll do it when I'm ready."

But readiness never arrives. Readiness is the mirage fear builds to keep you waiting. The longer you delay, the deeper the roots of fear grow. Avoidance doesn't erase anxiety, it fertilises it. It tells fear, "You're right. I can't handle this," and fear listens.

It learns.

It takes notes.

Every time you sidestep a conversation, a challenge, or an opportunity, fear learns exactly how to stop you next time.

It learns which excuses work best.
It learns the tone of your hesitation.
It learns the moments when your conviction is weakest.

Avoidance is fear rehearsing your limitations. It becomes a choreography between you and your comfort zone, the same dance, repeated until it feels like safety. You think you're protecting yourself, but you're training yourself to shrink.

And avoidance wears many masks. It sounds like wisdom, responsibility, and restraint. It can look mature, even virtuous. We tell ourselves stories to justify it: "I'm being strategic," "I'm protecting my energy," "I'm focusing on what matters." Sometimes that's true but more often, it's not protection; it's postponement.

The tragedy of avoidance is that it shrinks the very life it's trying to preserve. It narrows your world inch by inch until even joy feels risky.

Your confidence fades because courage requires practice, and avoidance starves courage of opportunity.

You start to mistrust yourself, to lose faith in your own ability to cope, because you've stopped giving yourself chances to prove that you can.

Avoidance feels like control, but it's really control in reverse, your fear controlling you. It doesn't keep you safe from failure; it keeps you safe from growth.

And that's the quiet heartbreak of it:
the longer you avoid, the smaller your life becomes.
Your possibilities narrow.
Your voice quietens.
Your dreams grow faint at the edges.
You start to confuse safety with purpose, stillness with peace, hesitation with humility.

Avoidance doesn't shout "stop."
It whispers "later."
But if you listen carefully, you'll notice that *later* rarely comes.

Avoidance in Disguise

Avoidance rarely announces itself.
It doesn't arrive with drama or panic, it slips in quietly, dressed in reason.
It hides behind familiar phrases that sound responsible, even wise:
"I'm just being cautious."
"I'm not sure it's the right fit."
"I'm waiting for the perfect moment."

But if you listen closely, beneath those words is the same old whisper repeating the same old lie:
"You're not ready."

Avoidance is the most persuasive conversation, fear ever learned to have with us. It speaks in a calm, logical tone, never shouting, always reasonable. It sounds like self-care, strategy, or emotional intelligence. But what it really says is: *"Stay where it's safe. Don't risk being seen. Don't risk getting hurt"*. It's a quiet art of self-deception, a negotiation between your desire to grow and your instinct to stay comfortable.

It sounds something like this:
"I'll start when I have more time."
"I'll speak up when I know the perfect words."
"I'll leave when things get a little clearer."
And fear smiles, satisfied, because those moments never come.

Avoidance is the master of delay, and delay is fear's most faithful servant. We avoid protecting ourselves from pain, but avoidance is *pain in slow motion*. It doesn't eliminate discomfort, it simply spreads it out over time. Every time you avoid a difficult truth, a hard conversation, or a meaningful risk, you create a longer shadow to live under. The fear you refuse to face today becomes the barrier you trip over tomorrow. The silence you maintain in the name of peace eventually becomes the noise in your mind you can't quiet.

Avoidance gives you the illusion of control, but it's really control that's controlling you. You start organising your life not around what inspires you, but around what feels safe. You say no to new things not because you don't want them, but because you can't guarantee how they'll end.

You learn to shrink your dreams to the size of your comfort zone, and the saddest part is that avoidance rarely feels like fear, it feels like relief.
A sigh of escape.
A temporary calm.
But relief isn't the same as peace.
It's just the pause between one avoidance and the next.

I've seen this pattern in clients, and I've lived it myself. Sometimes it looks like emotional avoidance, smiling through tension instead of naming it, because you'd rather carry the discomfort alone than risk confrontation. Other times, it's career avoidance, convincing yourself the timing isn't right for that promotion, that project, that leap. It's even spiritual avoidance the tendency to "stay positive" instead of being honest, to over-spiritualise pain instead of sitting with it. Avoidance wears many masks, but the story underneath is always the same: *a longing for freedom, trapped inside the fear of failure.*

When you finally begin to see it for what it is, something shifts. Avoidance stops being an invisible reflex and becomes a visible choice.
You can start to notice when you're dodging truth under the guise of "timing," "strategy," or "self-care."
And that awareness alone is revolutionary.

Because **real self-care isn't avoidance, it's alignment.**

It's the act of facing what scares you with gentleness and purpose, rather than pretending it isn't there.

It's learning that rest and retreat are healing, but hiding is not.

It's choosing to confront the conversation, to take the step, to send the message, even if your hands still shake.

Avoidance whispers, *"Stay safe."*
But courage answers, *"I can be safe and still move forward."*
The difference between the two isn't fear, it's honesty.
Fear wants to keep you comfortable.
Honesty wants to keep you growing.

When you start choosing honesty over avoidance, life begins to expand again. You realise that courage isn't about erasing the fear, it's about walking toward it, gently, with awareness and intention. Each time you do, the fear loses a little more of its power, until one day you look back and realise, what once felt like danger was really just your potential, waiting for permission to unfold.

Reflection Exercise: From Avoidance to Awareness

Take a few moments to reflect, not with judgment, but with curiosity.

Ask yourself:

1. What situations do I consistently avoid?

- Social events?
- Difficult conversations?
- Opportunities that require visibility or vulnerability?

2. What emotion am I protecting myself from?

- Is it shame, rejection, failure, loss of control, or exposure?

3. How does avoidance make me feel in the moment and how do I feel afterward?

- Does it bring peace, or guilt? Relief, or regret?

4. What is avoidance costing me?

- Which relationships, opportunities, or moments of growth have I traded for temporary comfort?

5. What would happen if I faced one avoided thing this week?

- Not all of them just one.
  A conversation, a call, a truth you've been postponing.
  Notice how your body reacts.
  Notice that courage doesn't erase fear, it simply moves with it.

Because avoidance is fear's favourite hiding place.
And every time you step into what you've been avoiding, you reclaim a piece of your power back.

People-Pleasing: The Fear of Disconnection

Of all the masks fear wears, few are as socially rewarded, or as quietly exhausting, as **people-pleasing**. On the surface, it looks kind, generous, empathetic. You're the reliable one, the bridge-builder, the peacemaker, the one who smooths things over and keeps everyone happy. But beneath that smile often lives a quiet ache: the fear of rejection, of disapproval, of being seen as difficult or disappointing.

I've lived that story. Early in my corporate career, I built a reputation for being the one who could "make it work."
Whatever the request, I'd say yes, I'd say yes to everything, taking on extra projects, mediating conflicts, volunteering for initiatives outside my remit.
On paper, it looked like dedication.
In reality, it was fear.
Fear of being perceived as ungrateful.
Fear of being labelled "uncooperative", especially as a young Black man in predominantly white, corporate spaces where my tone, my confidence, even my silence could be misread.

People-pleasing, for me, wasn't just about approval and acceptance, but more about survival.
It was the internalised belief that being agreeable was the safest route to belonging.
That if I was liked, I couldn't be targeted.
That if I didn't make waves, I wouldn't be seen as a threat.
That if I over-delivered, I might finally be seen as enough.

But here's what I learned the hard way: When your peace depends on everyone else's comfort, you'll spend your life negotiating your authenticity. and the cost of being liked is often being lost to yourself.

The danger with people-pleasing is that it's reinforced at every level.
Our workplaces reward it.
Our families expect it.
Our cultures romanticise it.
We're told to be team players, to be humble, to not rock the boat.
But compliance can quickly become confinement.
The more we mould ourselves to others' expectations, the more we drift from our own truth.

And the world will always take from a people-pleaser what they're willing to give.
Not because it's cruel, but because it's conditioned.
When you constantly meet others' needs first, they stop asking whether you have any left for yourself.
You teach them that your boundaries are flexible, your time is available, your "yes" is guaranteed.

I remember one particular turning point.
A senior executive asked me to lead a project that went far beyond my capacity at the time.
My calendar was already full, but I said yes, because saying no felt like disloyalty.
Weeks later, I was burnt out, behind, and resentful.
When I finally explained how much I was struggling, the executive looked genuinely surprised and said, "You should have said something sooner."
That moment hit me hard.
I realised people can't respect boundaries they don't know exist.

I wasn't being taken advantage of; I was participating in my own depletion.

That's the trap of people-pleasing, it feels generous, but it's often self-abandonment in disguise. You can't sustain connection if you have to disappear to maintain it. The truth is, saying yes to everything isn't kindness, it's fear of being unloved if you say no.

For many, this pattern runs deep. It starts early, with lessons about being "good," being "helpful," or not "causing trouble." Over time, those messages form a belief system: *If I meet everyone's expectations, I'll be safe.* However real safety doesn't come from appeasement; it comes from authenticity. And for those of us from marginalised backgrounds, the fear of disconnection carries historical weight. People-pleasing can become an unconscious inheritance, a survival tactic shaped by generations who had to adapt, code-switch/assimilate and perform respectability just to access opportunity. What begins as strategy becomes habit, and what once protected us can start to imprison us.

The work, then, is not to stop caring about others, it's to stop caring *at your own expense.*

To recognise that boundaries aren't barriers to connection; they're the framework that makes real connection possible. Because when you stop filtering your truth to keep others comfortable, you make space for relationships built on mutual respect, not silent sacrifice.

I tell my clients this often: *You don't have to be liked by everyone. You just have to be aligned with yourself.* Every time you say no to something that costs your peace, you say yes to something that protects your power.

The irony is, people often respect you more when you set boundaries.
Because clear boundaries signal self-respect, and self-respect inspires respect in others.
The more you practice it, the more you realise.
You don't lose belonging when you stop pleasing everyone.
You find it, because you finally belong to yourself.

Perfectionism: Fear Disguised as Excellence

Perfectionism is one of fear's most seductive disguises. It doesn't shout, it doesn't shake, it smiles. It sounds responsible, professional, admirable. It looks like ambition, it gets praised in interviews, rewarded in performance reviews, and admired on LinkedIn. In a world that celebrates "high standards," perfectionism thrives, because it hides in plain sight.

But beneath the polish, beneath the meticulous preparation and flawless delivery, lies something far less glamorous: fear.
Fear of being seen as inadequate.
Fear of being misunderstood.
Fear of being rejected or exposed as an imposter.

Perfectionism whispers a lie so convincing that even the most self-aware among us fall for it:
"If I do everything right, I'll finally be safe."
Safe from criticism.

Safe from judgment.

Safe from failure.

But what perfectionism really does is build an invisible cage, a beautifully designed, socially acceptable prison made of impossible expectations.

It promises protection but delivers paralysis.

It tells you that you'll rest when it's perfect, but perfection has no finish line. Every achievement becomes a new standard to maintain. Every success, instead of bringing peace, brings pressure. Because now, you have something to lose.

I've been there.

I know the taste of that pressure, the late nights, the redrafting, the second-guessing that masquerades as "care." I've spent days perfecting proposals that no one would read twice, reworking talks that were already strong, tightening sentences that didn't need tightening, not because the work demanded it, but because *fear did.*

I told myself it was about excellence. But it wasn't.

It was about control.

If I could perfect every detail, I could control how others perceived me. I could prevent disappointment, protect my reputation, avoid the sting of inadequacy.

But the price of control is connection, and the price of perfection is peace.

The truth hit me one night while preparing for a major leadership workshop. It was one of those career-defining sessions, a global organisation, senior executives, high stakes.

I knew the material. I'd delivered versions of it countless times. But this time, I couldn't stop tweaking it. I'd convinced myself that if I could get every slide *exactly right*, if every sentence flowed seamlessly, if every story landed perfectly, then I'd finally prove I belonged in those rooms.

I told myself it was diligence. But really, it was fear, fear dressed in a suit and tie, pretending to be professionalism.

I worked into the early hours, rewriting sections that didn't need rewriting, layering information until the clarity disappeared. The more I tried to protect myself from judgment, the more disconnected I became from my purpose. I was preparing to *perform*, not to *connect*.

And then, somewhere between exhaustion and self-awareness, I realised what I was doing:
I wasn't preparing to teach, I was preparing to hide.
I was perfecting not for excellence, but for acceptance.

So, I stopped.
I closed the laptop. I left the slides as they were, and I decided: I would speak from memory and from heart, not from notes.

The next day, standing in that room, something shifted. My voice wavered slightly at first, my pacing wasn't perfect, but people leaned in. They didn't want a flawless performance. They wanted truth. They wanted connection. They wanted humanity.

When the session ended, there was no round of applause, just a deep, reflective silence. That silence taught me something that perfectionism never could, **authenticity moves people more than precision ever will.**

Because perfectionism doesn't protect you from criticism, it only guarantees that you criticise yourself first.

Perfectionism doesn't drive you toward excellence; it drives you away from ease. It turns creativity into anxiety and discipline into dread. It drains joy from the process and replaces it with an endless audit of what's still not enough. It creates the illusion of progress, you're busy, productive, refining but in truth, you're circling the same fears over and over again.

At its core, perfectionism isn't the pursuit of quality, it's the avoidance of shame. It is fear masquerading as diligence.

And the saddest part is that it often works, for a while. You might achieve, impress, and ascend. But it's a lonely success. Because perfectionism doesn't allow you to celebrate, it only lets you survive. You achieve one milestone and immediately raise the bar higher. You can't rest, because rest feels like failure. You can't share the credit, because collaboration means loss of control. You can't enjoy what you've built, because your focus is already on what's missing.

Perfectionism's mantra is simple: *"Do more, do better, be flawless and maybe, just maybe then you'll be enough."* But "enough" never arrives.

I've seen this countless times in my coaching practice, high-achieving professionals who look confident on the outside but live in quiet torment. They're exhausted, hypervigilant, and relentlessly self-critical. One client, a senior executive, once told me, "I can't even enjoy my success, I'm too busy fearing the next mistake."

We unpacked that together. What emerged wasn't arrogance or insecurity, it was fear. Fear of disappointing others. Fear of being exposed as a fraud. Fear of being ordinary after being exceptional for so long.

Perfectionism had become her identity, the very thing that once earned her praise now imprisoned her. Every compliment reinforced the fear that if she ever stopped performing, she'd stop being worthy of love, respect, or belonging.

This is how perfectionism traps so many of us.

It starts as a shield, a way to stay safe in environments where mistakes were punished, or vulnerability wasn't welcomed. For some, it's rooted in childhood experiences where love and approval felt conditional. For others, it's cultural, a survival strategy shaped by identity, race, class, or gender.

As a Black man navigating corporate spaces early in my career, I understood that pressure deeply. I felt the need to be twice as good just to be seen as competent. Every sentence, every presentation, every decision felt like proof, proof that I belonged, proof that I was worthy of being in the room.

That's not perfectionism born from vanity; that's perfectionism born from survival.

But survival mode is not where we're meant to stay.

There's a point where perfectionism stops protecting and starts suffocating.
When your drive for excellence becomes a fear of visibility, when your preparation becomes paralysis, when your "standards" silence your creativity, that's not growth anymore. That's fear, disguised as discipline.

So what's the antidote?
Not lowering your standards but loosening your grip.

Reflection: Rewriting your relationship with perfectionism

Take a moment to ask yourself:

- Where in my life am I hiding behind the pursuit of perfection?
- What am I trying to protect by getting it "just right"?
- What would progress, not perfection, look like today?
- Whose approval am I chasing, and what would it mean to stop?

Try this:
Instead of asking, *"Is this perfect?"*, ask, *"Is this aligned?"*
Instead of asking, *"Is this flawless?"*, ask, *"Is this true?"*

You'll find that truth is far more magnetic than perfection ever could be.

Because people don't connect with perfection, they connect with presence.
They connect with honesty, vulnerability, and courage.

Perfectionism shrinks your humanity in pursuit of acceptance.
Courage expands it in pursuit of truth.

The moment you stop polishing and start showing up, *as you are, not as you think you should be*, is the moment you begin to lead, create, and live with freedom.

And maybe that's the ultimate act of courage:
to stand before the world, imperfect but real, and say
"This is enough.
I am enough.
Right now."

Overthinking: fear disguised as control

And then there's *overthinking*, one of fear's most persuasive performances.
It convinces us that we're being thorough, intelligent, even responsible.
We tell ourselves we're "just being careful," but often, what we're really doing is stalling, trying to think our way out of uncertainty.

We've all been there.
Hours comparing trivial details before buying something.
Revisiting old conversations in our heads.
Replaying what we *should* have said or *could* have done.

It feels like progress, but it's really paralysis in disguise.

Overthinking doesn't look like panic, it looks like preparation. It's motion, but not movement. It keeps us busy enough to feel in control, but stuck enough to avoid risk.

And that's the paradox: overthinking doesn't protect you from pain; it just delays your potential.

I've done it more times than I can count.

I've rewritten proposals, emails, even text messages, not because I didn't know what to say, but because I was afraid of how they'd be received. I told myself I was "refining," but I was really rehearsing rejection in advance.

And I learned this the hard way.

A few years ago, I was invited to speak at a major leadership event, a room full of senior executives, thought leaders, and academics. It was exactly the kind of platform I'd been working toward.
But when the invitation came through, I froze.
I told myself I needed to "prepare properly," but really, I was overthinking every detail to protect myself from rejection.

I spent days researching obscure case studies, rewriting my opening, deleting it, rewriting it again. My slides became an endless project. I even delayed confirming my attendance because I convinced myself the talk "wasn't ready yet."
What I was really afraid of was being *seen*.
Seen as not enough.
Seen as an imposter in a room full of people I admired.

And then, two days before the event, it hit me: I was about to give a talk on *courage*, while letting fear decide for me.

So, I stopped editing. I finalised what I had.
I walked into that room with a talk that wasn't perfect, but it was honest.

And it landed. Not because it was flawless, but because it was *real*. People came up to me afterward, not to praise the polish, but to say,

"That's exactly how I've felt but never said out loud."

That day changed me.
It taught me that overthinking feels like control, but it's really avoidance.
Clarity doesn't come from thinking harder; it comes from acting sooner.
Confidence isn't built in preparation, it's built in participation.

Complaining: Fear Disguised as Caution

I'll admit something else too, even *complaining* has been one of my masks.
There was a time when I could critique anything: the timing, the market, the audience, the system. It made me feel clever, even principled. But really, it was safer to critique than to create.

Because as long as I was analysing the flaws in the world, I didn't have to risk adding something of my own.
Complaining gave me the illusion of control.

It said, *If I expect disappointment, I can't be hurt when it comes.*

But all that energy went into rehearsing failure instead of daring progress.

I've seen this mask play out in teams and organisations too. Entire cultures can hide behind collective cynicism, meetings full of brilliant people who can diagnose every problem but hesitate to act on a solution. That's fear in corporate clothing: fear of blame, fear of risk, fear of standing out.

It's easier to sound wise than to sound hopeful.
But courage requires hope.
And hope is the raw material of action.

Control: Fear Disguised as Certainty

If overthinking is fear's quiet performance, *control* is its masterpiece.
It's the mask fear wears when it wants to look powerful.
Because control feels productive. It feels like leadership. It feels safe.
But underneath, it's often fear's most elegant disguise, the fear of uncertainty.

We tell ourselves that if we can just manage everything, the timing, the tone, the outcome, then nothing can go wrong.
We mistake control for competence.
But what we're really chasing is comfort.

Control begins as a form of care.

It's born from the desire to protect, a project, a reputation, a team, a dream.

But slowly, it crosses a line.

We start trying to manage people's perceptions, not just their performance.

We plan every detail to prevent disappointment.

We overwork because delegation feels dangerous.

We micromanage not because we don't trust others, but because we don't trust *ourselves* to handle what happens if they fall short.

And here's the irony: the tighter we grip, the more we lose touch with the flow that makes great work, great leadership, and great relationships possible.

When Control Masquerades as Leadership

I learned this lesson in my corporate career. I was leading a complex recruitment project for a global firm, multiple teams, tight deadlines, and high stakes. I told myself that to deliver excellence, I had to oversee everything personally. Every email, every presentation, every interaction with senior stakeholders passed through me first.

The project succeeded, on paper.
We hit the numbers, the deliverables, the deadlines.
But behind the scenes, the team was exhausted.
So was I.

One afternoon, a colleague pulled me aside and said, gently but truthfully:

"Romain, we trust you. But you don't seem to trust us."

It landed like a punch.
Because I realised she was right.
My need for control wasn't leadership, it was fear.

Fear that if I let go, things would fall apart.
Fear that if the team failed, I'd be blamed.
Fear that if I wasn't constantly seen as "on top of everything," I'd lose credibility.

But control isn't credibility, it's constraint.
When leaders operate from fear, even the best intentions can shrink possibility.
We think we're ensuring quality, but we're really limiting growth, our own and everyone else's.

That moment changed how I led.
I started handing over ownership instead of just tasks.
I began asking more questions than I answered.
I learned that trust isn't a reward, it's a risk you take first.

And what happened next surprised me.
The work got better.
Not because I stopped caring, but because I stopped controlling.
People brought ideas I never would've thought of. They took initiative, experimented, and stretched themselves.
The project wasn't just successful, it became sustainable.

That's when I realised something simple but profound:
control creates compliance; trust creates courage.

Why We Cling to Control

Control is seductive because it feels like certainty in an uncertain world.
And for many of us, especially those raised to survive rather than thrive, certainty feels like safety.

We were taught that if we just worked hard enough, planned well enough, anticipated every variable, we could avoid chaos.
But life doesn't work that way.
You can't spreadsheet your way out of vulnerability.

Control promises peace, but it delivers pressure.
Because the more we try to manage, the more fragile we become when things inevitably don't go to plan.
Every unpredicted moment feels like failure.
Every imperfect outcome feels like proof that we weren't good enough to prevent it.

And in leadership, that fragility can become contagious.
When a leader grips too tightly, a team stops taking initiative.
They wait for instruction.
They play it safe.
They learn that mistakes aren't lessons, they're liabilities.

But courage in leadership requires the opposite: it requires the ability to *let go*, to tolerate uncertainty, to empower others, and to trust that growth comes from stretch, not surveillance.

The Courage to Release Control

Releasing control isn't the same as being careless.
It's not about indifference, it's about *faith*.
Faith in your preparation.
Faith in your people.
Faith that you can handle whatever unfolds, even if it's imperfect.

True leadership is not about directing every move.
It's about creating the conditions for people, including yourself, to rise.
That means you won't always know the outcome.
But that's where real courage begins, in the willingness to move without a guarantee.

Letting go is hard because it exposes what control hides, vulnerability.
It forces you to admit, *I can't foresee everything, and that's okay.*
It asks you to redefine success not as perfection, but as progress.

That's the difference between control and courage.
Control seeks to *prevent* risk; courage seeks to *navigate* it.
Control wants predictability; courage embraces possibility.
Control says, *I'll move when it's safe.*
Courage says, *I'll move and learn to make it safe along the way.*

Reflection: Where Are You Over-Managing?

Take a moment to ask yourself:

- Where in your life are you mistaking control for competence?

- What are you afraid will happen if you let go, delegate, or allow things to unfold?
- Who could rise, if you stepped back and trusted them to try?
- And what would freedom look like if you stopped needing to manage every detail?

The truth is, courage and control can't coexist for long.
One is open-handed; the other is clenched.
And the more open-handed you become, the more life begins to flow again.

Because at its core, *control is fear's attempt to guarantee the future.*
Courage, on the other hand, is faith in your ability to meet it.

The Common Thread: Fear's Need for Certainty

When you strip them back, the overthinking, the complaining, the controlling, they all stem from the same root: a fear of uncertainty, and a longing for safety.

Each mask is fear's way of saying, *I just need to know how this will turn out before I risk being hurt.*
Overthinking says, *If I analyse enough, I can outsmart uncertainty.*
Complaining says, *If I criticise it first, I can't be disappointed by it later.*
Control says, *If I manage every detail, I can stop things from going wrong.*

They're all different expressions of the same wound, the belief that our safety depends on our ability to predict, perfect, or protect ourselves from the unknown.
But life doesn't reward perfection; it rewards participation.
The truth is, uncertainty isn't the enemy. It's the environment of growth.

When you begin to see that clearly, something shifts.
You stop trying to dominate life into obedience and start dancing with it.
You realise that the very things fear taught you to avoid, vulnerability, risk, visibility, failure, are also the gateways to connection, creativity, and courage.

I've watched this play out in myself, in my teams, and in the leaders I coach.
The moment someone stops overthinking and takes a step forward, possibility opens.
The moment they replace cynicism with contribution, progress begins.
The moment they release control and trust their people, innovation takes root.

Each time we loosen fear's grip, we create room for movement, and in that movement, courage grows.

That's the great paradox of leadership, and of life itself:
the very uncertainty we spend our lives trying to control is the soil from which everything meaningful grows.

Because courage doesn't need certainty to begin.

It needs clarity, clarity of intention, clarity of values, clarity of purpose.
The rest is built in motion.

So, when fear shows up disguised as overthinking, cynicism, or control, recognise it for what it is: a longing for safety.
Then answer it, not with avoidance, but with action.
Take the step. Start the conversation. Trust the process.
And remind yourself: *certainty is not a prerequisite for courage; it's the result of it.*

This is where the next evolution begins, the shift from managing fear to *leading through it.*
Because courage isn't just a personal practice; it's a leadership philosophy.
It's how we shape culture, build trust, and redefine what power looks like.
And that's where we go next.

Think about life, how often it mirrors that friend who's been talking for months about starting their podcast. They've bought all the right equipment, mapped out every episode idea, even designed the cover art. On the surface, it looks like progress. But when it comes time to actually hit *record*, they stall. Suddenly, there's always something else to fix: the sound quality isn't quite right, the intro music could be better, maybe the format needs more research.

They convince themselves it's about standards, but it's not the microphone that's the problem. It's the mind.

And the truth is, we've all been that friend.

We all have a "podcast", a dream we've mapped out, prepared for, even announced, but still haven't pressed *go* on. Maybe it's the business idea we keep refining but never launch. The conversation we keep planning but never have. The creative project that's always "almost ready." We stay stuck in the safety of "nearly there" because it feels like progress without the risk of exposure.

That's what fear does best, it convinces us that hesitation is preparation. That more time, more research, more tweaks will make us ready. But readiness is rarely the issue. The issue is vulnerability. The moment we act, we risk being seen. We risk falling short. We risk finding out what happens when our effort meets the world.

This is where life, and leadership, mirror each other. Whether you're an entrepreneur, a manager, or someone simply trying to take the next step, fear will always dress itself as logic. It will tell you the timing's not right, the conditions aren't perfect, that one more round of edits will make all the difference. But the truth? The perfect moment never comes. You become ready by doing. You build courage through participation, not preparation.

That's why, in coaching, I often ask clients a simple question: *"What's the podcast you haven't pressed record on?"* It's rarely about a literal podcast. It's the metaphor for the thing they've been circling, the calling, the idea, the truth, that's waiting for them on the other side of fear.

Because procrastination isn't laziness; it's a form of protection. It's fear's clever way of keeping you safe from rejection, disappointment, or failure, by keeping you busy instead. But the cost of that safety is aliveness. The world doesn't get your voice, your contribution, your brilliance, and you don't get the satisfaction of seeing what's possible when you stop waiting and start moving.

So the question becomes: *What would happen if you hit record anyway?* What might unfold if you stopped waiting for confidence and started building it through motion? Because here's the truth: the first episode won't be perfect. Neither will the first draft, the first business pitch, or the first attempt at anything that matters. But it will be *real*. It will exist. It will teach you more in a single moment of action than months of thinking ever could.

Fear loves to keep you in theory.
Courage invites you into practice.

What's really happening underneath is fear, not of the work, but of what happens *after* the work. Fear of being judged. Fear of failure. Fear that their voice won't be good enough or that no one will care. So instead of taking the risk, they stay in the safe zone of "not yet." That's what procrastination really is, fear disguised as preparation. It lets you feel busy without ever feeling exposed.

But here's the real lesson: procrastination isn't laziness, it's a self-protective strategy. The brain uses it to delay emotional risk. By staying in the planning phase, you protect yourself from potential disappointment or rejection. Yet that protection comes with a cost, it stops you from progressing, experimenting, and learning in real time.

The only way to break the cycle is to act before you feel ready. Clarity doesn't come from more thinking, it comes from *doing*. Confidence isn't built in advance, it's built through evidence. Each small step forward teaches your brain that action is survivable, even when it's imperfect. That's how courage grows. So if you find yourself in that same loop, tweaking, researching, planning, perfecting, ask yourself: *What am I really protecting myself from?* Then take one imperfect step anyway. Because while fear loves preparation, growth only happens in participation.

Leadership as a Practice of Courage

Leadership is often described as vision, influence, or strategy, but underneath all of that, leadership is courage in practice.
Not the kind of courage that roars, but the quiet kind that stays.
The kind that asks you to walk into uncertainty and make decisions without guarantees.
To carry responsibility without armour.
To keep showing up, not because it's easy, but because it matters.

In my years leading teams, from corporate boardrooms to building Diversify World, I've learned that fear doesn't disappear with success.
If anything, it evolves.
It becomes more sophisticated.
At the top, fear stops looking like doubt and starts looking like *control*.

It hides behind the language of "risk management," "timing," or "stakeholder alignment."

But beneath those polished words often sits something deeply human: the fear of losing credibility, of making the wrong call, of being seen as inadequate in front of peers who seem more certain than you feel.

I've felt that pressure.

There were times I'd sit in meetings, surrounded by senior executives, and my instincts would scream that something was off, a decision, a tone, an assumption, yet I'd hesitate to speak.

I told myself it was diplomacy.

But really, it was fear, fear of being labelled difficult, or idealistic, or out of sync with the room.

And yet, every meaningful moment of leadership I've ever had has come from the opposite choice, the decision to speak up, even when my voice shook.

Courage in leadership rarely looks like grand gestures.

It's the everyday willingness to say the thing that needs saying, even when silence would be safer.

It's holding integrity when compromise would be more convenient.

It's choosing transparency over politics, truth over polish, growth over comfort.

One moment that stands out came during my corporate career, long before I had my own company.

We were in a leadership meeting reviewing senior hires. The conversation turned, as it often did, to "fit."

It was said so casually, so reflexively, that no one seemed to notice how loaded it was.

But I did.

I'd seen too many talented people filtered out under that word.

"Fit" had become a euphemism, not for skill or potential, but for sameness.

For keeping leadership spaces familiar and comfortable.

I remember sitting there, feeling the tension rise in my chest.

Part of me wanted to let it slide, to stay invisible and keep the peace.

But another part, the part that had grown tired of watching patterns repeat, refused.

So, I asked the room:

"Can we just unpack what we mean by 'fit'? Because if we can't define it clearly, we might be gatekeeping talent without realising it."

The silence that followed was heavy.

You could feel the discomfort ripple across the table.

And yet, something shifted.

It wasn't a grand revolution, but it was a spark.

That single question planted a seed, one that, months later, led to real policy changes in how that organisation assessed potential and diversity in leadership.

That's what courage in leadership often looks like, *not dominance, but disruption.*

Not loudness, but honesty.

It's the ability to hold discomfort in service of something greater than your ego: fairness, equity, truth.

I've come to see that leadership is less about having authority and more about taking responsibility, responsibility for the tone of the room, for the stories that get told and those that don't, for the example you set even when no one's watching.
Courageous leadership is emotional labour.
It asks you to notice when fear is making your choices, and to choose integrity instead.

Because here's the truth:
People don't follow titles; they follow energy.
They follow how you handle pressure, how you respond to challenge, how you own your mistakes, and how you treat others when you could easily turn away.
When leaders model courage, not bravado, not perfection, but presence, it gives everyone else permission to do the same.

And that's how culture shifts: not through slogans, but through example.
Through leaders who choose to be human first and managerial second.

Leadership, at its highest form, isn't about being fearless.
It's about being faithful, faithful to your values, your people, and the truth of what's right, even when it costs you comfort.

The Culture of Courage: How Leaders Build Safety Through Vulnerability

The mark of courageous leadership isn't just how you perform under pressure, it's how safe people feel around you when things go wrong.
That's what culture really is: not the slogans written on walls, but the emotional climate leaders create through their daily choices.

A culture of courage begins where fear once lived.
It replaces silence with conversation, blame with learning, and pretence with presence.
It's not a culture free from mistakes or conflict, it's one where those moments become data, not danger.

But for that to happen, leaders have to go first.

Courage in leadership isn't a trickle-down concept; it's an act of modelling.
When you, as a leader, admit uncertainty, ask for feedback, or acknowledge a misstep without defensiveness, you send a quiet but radical message:

"This is a place where we can be human."

And that changes everything.

The Vulnerability Shift

Vulnerability in leadership used to be misunderstood.
It was seen as weakness, the opposite of authority.

But that's because we confused leadership with control, and control with competence.

Real leadership isn't about having all the answers; it's about creating an environment where better answers can emerge.

That requires humility.

And humility is an act of courage.

I remember working with an executive team during a major organisational restructuring.

The CEO, a highly respected but cautious leader, admitted to me in a one-to-one session:

"I feel like I'm supposed to have the plan. But half the time, I'm trying to figure it out as I go."

I told him, "So does everyone else. The difference is, they're waiting for you to say it first."

At the next all-hands meeting, instead of delivering the usual polished update, he spoke plainly. He said,

"We're in transition. Some of this will work, and some won't. But we'll learn together. My job is to keep us moving and to listen hard when we need to adjust."

You could feel the room exhale.

Not because he had all the answers, but because he was honest enough to admit he didn't.

That's the paradox of leadership vulnerability: when you stop pretending to be invulnerable, people trust you more.

Because trust doesn't grow from perfection, it grows from proximity.

People don't follow leaders who perform certainty; they follow leaders who practice sincerity.

Psychological Safety Is Built, Not Declared

We talk a lot about "psychological safety" in modern leadership, but too often it's treated like a slogan.
You can't announce safety into existence. You have to *behave* it into being.

That starts small.
It looks like how you respond when someone disagrees with you in a meeting.
It looks like whether people can bring you bad news without rehearsing their defence first.
It looks like whether your team feels seen when they share an idea that's still half-formed.

Courageous leaders create safety by *how they handle imperfection.*
Because if people see that imperfection is punished, they'll hide.
If they see it met with curiosity and respect, they'll grow.

And the more people grow, the braver they become.

The Ripple Effect of Vulnerability

A single act of vulnerability can have disproportionate impact.
I've seen it countless times in coaching sessions.

One leader apologises sincerely for overreacting in a meeting, and suddenly, the team begins communicating with more honesty. Another admits they've been struggling with workload, and a colleague finally speaks up about burnout.

It's rarely the grand gestures that change a culture.
It's the small, consistent acts of courage that accumulate until safety becomes the norm.

Vulnerability is the spark, but consistency is the oxygen.

The leader who checks in instead of checking up.
The manager who says, "I don't know yet, but I'll find out."
The CEO who shares what they learned from failure instead of only what succeeded.

These actions might seem simple, but they rewire culture at a cellular level.
They tell people: "You don't have to be perfect to belong here."
And when people feel they belong, they stop performing and start contributing.

That's the moment where teams stop fearing mistakes and start seeking mastery.
Where innovation replaces inertia.
Where courage stops being an aspiration and starts becoming an operating system.

Why Vulnerability Works

From a psychological standpoint, vulnerability activates empathy and connection, two of the strongest drivers of trust.
When leaders show up authentically, it triggers what neuroscientists call *emotional mirroring*.
Our brains attune to others' openness, lowering our own defences.
That's why one person's courage can calm an entire room.

And from a practical standpoint, it breaks the illusion that leadership means certainty.
In a complex, unpredictable world, certainty is an illusion.
Adaptability is the real strength.
Vulnerability simply opens the door to it.

The most effective leaders I've met aren't the ones who command fear or demand confidence, they're the ones who make it safe to learn, safe to speak, and safe to fail forward.
They understand that psychological safety isn't a soft skill; it's a strategic one.

When people feel safe, they perform better.
They communicate better.
They think creatively, take ownership, and act faster.
Courage in leadership, then, is not just a moral stance, it's a performance advantage.

From Safety to Significance

The ultimate goal isn't just to make people feel safe, it's to make them feel *significant*.
Safety allows people to survive; significance allows them to soar. When people feel that their ideas, voices, and stories matter, they contribute with purpose, not compliance.

That's what courageous leadership does: it transforms workplaces from systems of survival into communities of meaning. It says: "You matter here. Not because you're perfect, but because you're present."

And when leaders model that truth consistently, courage becomes contagious.
It moves from personal to cultural, from momentary to systemic. That's how organisations evolve, not through rebrands or restructures, but through the daily, human practice of courage.

Courage Cascades: How One Leader's Bravery Redefines a Whole System

Courage doesn't exist in isolation.
It's never just about the person who takes the risk, it's about what that act unlocks in others.
That's what I call the *courage cascade*: the chain reaction that begins when one person chooses to act with integrity, honesty, or vulnerability, and in doing so, gives others permission to do the same.

The beauty of leadership is that it multiplies.

Your decisions, tone, and presence don't stop at your desk, they ripple outward, shaping how people think, feel, and behave.

In every organisation I've worked with, I've seen this truth play out in real time: one brave conversation can shift an entire culture.

The Domino Effect of One Voice

I once worked with a senior leader who had been promoted into a role she quietly doubted she deserved.

She was brilliant, capable, and respected, but she spent months second-guessing herself, editing every email, overpreparing for every meeting, staying long after her team had gone home to make sure every deliverable was flawless.

In coaching sessions, she admitted she was exhausted. When I asked what she feared most, she said, *"I'm scared they'll realise I'm not as good as they think."* That sentence could have been lifted from almost any leader's internal monologue. It's astonishing how universal imposter syndrome becomes at the top.

But here's where the story turns.

After months of privately struggling, she decided to be honest, first with herself, then with her team.

In one team meeting, she said, *"I've realised I've been trying to lead by being perfect, and it's wearing me down. I want to start leading by being present instead."*

The silence that followed wasn't awkward, it was relief.

Because almost everyone in that room had been doing the same thing: overworking, overcompensating, pretending they were fine.

Her honesty gave them permission to stop performing and start connecting.

Within weeks, the tone of meetings changed. Conversations became more candid. Team members started raising issues earlier, owning mistakes faster, and asking for help without shame.

Productivity didn't fall; it improved.

Trust deepened. Energy returned.

That's the courage cascade in motion: one person goes first, and suddenly everyone else remembers they can too.

The Systemic Shift

Courage cascades don't just change behaviour, they change systems.

Every workplace system is built on human patterns: who speaks, who stays silent, who gets credit, who gets interrupted, who gets believed.

When one person disrupts that pattern courageously, even slightly, it forces the system to adapt.

I've seen this happen in boardrooms when a single director says, *"I don't think we've heard enough perspectives on this,"* and pauses the discussion until quieter voices are invited in.

That single act can permanently shift the group norm, from competition to collaboration, from dominance to inclusion.

Or when a manager challenges an offhand comment that carries bias, it interrupts the unspoken permission that allowed that language to exist.

Suddenly, others start paying attention to their own language too. That's how culture transforms: not in sweeping statements, but in everyday courage.

One conversation at a time.
One correction at a time.
One act of integrity at a time.

And as those moments accumulate, they become the new normal.

Courage as a Contagion

Neuroscience offers a fascinating explanation for this phenomenon. When we witness someone act bravely, our brains light up in a way that mirrors their courage.
It activates the same neural pathways associated with agency and empathy.
In simple terms, seeing courage awakens courage.

That's why leadership by example is so powerful, not because people copy your words, but because they unconsciously mirror your energy.
A calm leader steadies the room.
A defensive leader tightens it.
A courageous leader expands it.

Energy is contagious.
Fear contracts; courage expands.
And expansion is what drives innovation, creativity, and collective strength.

The Ripple Beyond the Workplace

The courage cascade doesn't end inside organisations.
It spills into homes, communities, and industries.
When someone learns to speak up in a meeting, they often start speaking up at home.
When a company begins having honest conversations about inclusion or wellbeing, it normalises those conversations in society.

I've seen leaders who once avoided conflict become advocates for fairness in their communities.
I've watched employees who once stayed silent about bias go on to mentor others, run initiatives, or build startups that embody the change they once only dreamed about.

That's the long arc of courageous leadership, it begins as a personal shift and ends as a social one. Every act of courage, however small, becomes part of a wider story of human progress.

Courage Multiplied: From the Individual to the Institution

When organisations embed courage into their DNA, decision-making evolves.
Risk isn't feared, it's managed.
Feedback isn't weaponised, it's welcomed.
Innovation isn't the privilege of a few, it's the expectation of everyone.

This is what separates adaptive organisations from rigid ones. Adaptive organisations don't wait for certainty; they create safety in uncertainty.
They know that sustainable success isn't built on avoiding failure, it's built on learning faster than the competition.

And that learning starts with courage.
The courage to ask better questions.
The courage to own mistakes early.
The courage to make the invisible visible, bias, exhaustion, injustice, and do something about it.

When courage becomes cultural, organisations stop managing fear and start mastering growth.

Returning to the Heart of It

At its core, this is the message I want every leader, every reader, every human being to carry:
Courage is not a heroic trait. It's a human one.
It doesn't belong to the exceptional; it belongs to the everyday.
And when one person chooses it, it multiplies.

That's the beauty of the courage cascade, you'll never know how far it travels.
You'll never know who it frees, who it inspires, or whose voice it helps rise.
But it always travels further than you think.

Because courage, once witnessed, can't be unseen.

It leaves a mark, a trace of what's possible.
And that trace becomes a map for others to follow.

So when in doubt, go first.
Go bravely.
Even if your voice shakes, even if your heart races.
Because someone, somewhere, is waiting to see that it's possible.
And when they do, they'll find their own courage, and the cascade will begin again.

The Turning Point: Seeing Fear Clearly

Every story of courage begins and ends with awareness.
You can't move through what you can't see.
And fear, clever, shapeshifting, persistent, survives best in the dark.

By now, you've seen how courage doesn't arrive as a lightning bolt. It's built slowly, through honesty, practice, and presence. It grows in conversation, in leadership, in culture. But before we can practise courage fully, we have to name the thing that keeps us from it. Because no matter how confident or accomplished we appear, fear is never far away. It changes shape, but the message stays the same: *stay small, stay safe, stay unseen.*

The truth is, fear rarely says "I'm afraid."
It prefers disguise.
It borrows the language of logic, productivity, or responsibility. It shows up in boardrooms and bedrooms alike, as perfectionism, procrastination, or people-pleasing. It hides beneath ambition

and behind exhaustion. It tells us we're being careful, sensible, or strategic, when really we're just circling the same hesitation, waiting for permission that will never come.

I've worn every one of those masks at different stages of my life. As an employee, I wore the mask of overthinking, rewriting every email to sound "professional." As a leader, I wore the mask of control, believing that if I managed every detail, nothing could fall apart. As an entrepreneur, I wore the mask of busyness, convincing myself that constant motion was the same as momentum. Each mask looked productive. Each one kept me safe. But none of them moved me forward.

That's the hidden cost of fear: not chaos, but containment.
It keeps you respectable, composed, even successful, but never free.

And that's the pivot this next chapter makes.
Because courage isn't just about moving forward; it's about seeing what's been holding you back.

Before we can change fear's influence, we have to *name it*.
To trace its outlines, understand its disguises, and meet it with compassion instead of contempt.

This is where the real work begins, the work of *unmasking*.

How Fear Shows Up in Everyday Life

Fear rarely enters our lives with grand drama.nIt doesn't always announce itself through panic attacks or crises. More often, it shows up quietly, in the small, respectable, everyday choices we make to stay safe. It lives in the tone we soften to avoid tension, the email we re-read five times before sending, the opportunity we tell ourselves we're "not quite ready for yet."

We've all lived through fear's disguises.
It doesn't crash in, it seeps in.
And the more familiar it becomes, the easier it is to mistake fear for personality.

Take procrastination. You tell yourself you're "waiting for the right time," but deep down, you're waiting to stop feeling afraid. You tidy your desk, refill your coffee, open tabs you don't need, all to avoid the discomfort of beginning. You call it organisation, but it's hesitation in a tailored suit. The irony is, that ten-second spike of discomfort you're trying to avoid often hurts less than the hours of avoidance that follow.

Or think of perfectionism, that relentless urge to get it "just right." You convince yourself it's diligence, care, professionalism. But what it really is, at its core, is the terror of being judged. You polish and polish until the work becomes a mirror of your fear instead of your message. By the time the presentation or project is finished, you're no longer striving for excellence, you're trying to outrun shame.

Fear also finds its way into the constant checking, the refreshing of inboxes, the scrolling through notifications, the quick glance at social media "just in case." On the surface, it looks like dedication or curiosity. But if we're honest, it's fear whispering, *"Don't miss anything. Don't be left behind."* For years, I thought my compulsive checking was about staying informed; it wasn't. It was about staying safe, about keeping uncertainty at bay by pretending I could control it.

And then there's busyness, perhaps fear's most socially rewarded disguise. We glorify being "booked and busy," wearing exhaustion as a badge of worth. But busyness often masks avoidance. We fill our calendars to avoid silence. We overcommit to avoid introspection. Because the stillness of slowing down means we might have to confront truths we've worked hard to ignore: Am I happy in this job? Do I even enjoy the things I'm chasing? Who am I when I'm not producing?

I've caught myself in this too, saying yes to everything, not because I wanted to, but because stopping meant listening. And the echo of that silence can be loud. It's in that quiet that you meet yourself, and sometimes, that's the most terrifying encounter of all.

People-pleasing is another quiet performance of fear. It's the art of staying agreeable, even when it costs you authenticity. You say yes when you want to say no. You overextend to keep the peace. You shrink your truth to fit the comfort of others. It feels generous, but often its survival. The underlying fear isn't rejection itself, it's the belief that your worth is conditional, that love and belonging must be earned through approval.

Avoidance, meanwhile, is fear's most direct move, the conscious sidesteps. You avoid conflict to stay "peaceful." You avoid new roles to stay "realistic." You avoid vulnerability to stay "strong." Avoidance offers short-term comfort but long-term confinement. Every time you sidestep discomfort, your world becomes a little smaller. Fear learns your patterns, your triggers, your exits, and it uses them against you.

If fear were a person, it would be a master of disguise, fluent in the dialect of discipline, charm, and composure. Some days it wears a suit and calls itself professionalism. Other days it hides behind humour, deflecting vulnerability with a joke. Sometimes it shows up as kindness that never says no, and sometimes, it sits quietly beside you, disguised as "I'm fine."

Fear speaks many dialects:

- "I'm just tired," really means "I'm afraid to say no."
- "I need more time," really means "I'm afraid to fail."
- "I'm being realistic," really means "I'm afraid to hope."
- "I don't want to bother anyone," really means "I'm afraid to be seen."

Learning to hear fear in translation is one of the most powerful forms of awareness. Once you recognise the voice, you can decide whether to listen to it.

From Mask to Mechanism

By now, we've begun to see that fear is far more intelligent than we once believed. It rarely appears as panic or paralysis; it hides in the parts of ourselves the world most applauds, the discipline, the diligence, the calm. We've peeled back the polished layers of perfectionism, busyness, control, people-pleasing, and avoidance, and seen what lies beneath: fear, dressed as safety.

Through this first chapter, we've learned that fear doesn't always shout "stop." It whispers, *"stay small."* It rewards us with temporary comfort at the cost of long-term freedom. And yet, in naming its disguises, we began to reclaim power, realising that these patterns aren't flaws but survival strategies, clever ways our minds learned to protect us when the world felt uncertain or unsafe.

We've discovered that avoidance, procrastination, and even over-preparation are not failures of willpower but languages of protection, the psyche's attempt to shield the self from rejection, loss, or exposure. Once we recognise that truth, the conversation with fear changes. It's no longer an enemy to eliminate but a message to interpret.

The unmasking has only just begun. Because seeing fear's faces is one thing; understanding how those faces form, how fear builds systems inside us, loops of thought and behaviour that repeat until they feel like personality, is another.

Core takeaways from chapter 1 summarised:

- Fear is adaptive, a clever form of protection shaped by past uncertainty.
- It's masks, perfectionism, procrastination, people-pleasing, busyness, control are learned survival strategies.

- Each mask trades short-term safety for long-term freedom.
- Courage begins with awareness; seeing the pattern is the first act of power.
- Avoidance and overthinking are just fear speaking in our own voice.
- Stillness and honesty expose fear's logic and restore our choice.
- Growth begins not by erasing fear, but by understanding its language.

In the next chapter, we move from awareness to anatomy. We'll examine the structure of fear itself, how it thinks, how it hides, and how it heals. We'll perform what I call *an autopsy of fear*: a closer look at its inner machinery, its defence mechanisms, and the stories it tells to keep us safe but small.

Because to dismantle fear, we must first understand its design. And that's where we turn next.

CHAPTER 2

The Anatomy of Fear:
How Fear Thinks, Hides, and Heals

In the first chapter, we learned to recognise fear's many disguises, perfectionism, people-pleasing, control, cynicism, busyness and to see them not as personal flaws but as protective strategies. Yet recognising fear's masks is only the beginning. To truly transform our relationship with fear, we must go deeper. We have to look beneath the surface, to trace how fear operates not just in our minds, but in our patterns, our choices, and the stories we tell ourselves about safety and worth.

This chapter is the autopsy of that invisible architecture. It asks not only *what* fear looks like, but *how* it thinks, *where* it hides, and *why* it lingers even when our rational mind knows better. Because fear isn't a single emotion that visits occasionally; it's a system, a network of loops, defences, and reflexes that quietly shape our daily lives.

Here, we begin to map that system. We'll explore how fear intertwines with habits like over-preparation and avoidance, how it masquerades as competence or kindness, and how it builds a cycle of self-protection that limits our growth. This isn't an exercise in blame or analysis for its own sake; it's an invitation to understand the machinery beneath the masks so you can begin to disarm it.

To unmask fear is to expose its logic. To dissect it is to reclaim your power.

Fear doesn't live in isolated moments. It builds systems inside us, loops of behaviour that protect and limit us at the same time. You might procrastinate in one area, over-prepare in another, and people-please in a third. Together, these form a cycle: hesitation, overcompensation, burnout, repeat.

In a single day, it can look like this:

- You start the morning anxious about a meeting (so you over-prepare).
- You get through the meeting but can't say no to a new task (so you people-please).
- You finish work feeling behind, so you skip rest (busyness).
- You end the day telling yourself tomorrow will be different (avoidance).

Each behaviour feels separate, but they're all fear playing different roles in the same performance.

At work, fear hides behind competence, the endless need to prove yourself.

In relationships, it hides behind kindness, saying yes to keep the peace.

In creativity, it hides behind procrastination, staying "in progress" so you never have to face feedback.

In leadership, it hides behind control, mistaking authority for safety.

Different contexts, same mechanism: self-protection disguised as self-discipline.

Coaching Reflection: How Fear Speaks Through You

Take a moment to consider where fear lives in your own life. Which of these voices sound most familiar?

- "I'll start when I'm ready."
- "I just want to make sure it's perfect."
- "I don't want to upset anyone."
- "I'm just too busy right now."
- "It's not the right time."

Now, look beneath each one.

What is it really protecting you from, rejection, visibility, failure, loneliness, change?

Write it down. Give fear its real name.

Because once you name it, you take back the power to choose something else.

The Truth Beneath the Disguise - Naming It: From Fog to Form

Fear's disguises may look different, but they all share the same intent: protection through limitation.
They promise safety, but the cost is freedom.
They keep you competent, but not creative.
Busy, but not brave.
Liked, but not known.

And awareness is where the shift begins.
Because once you see fear's disguises for what they are, you no longer have to play along.
You can still prepare, but without perfectionism.
You can still care, but without people-pleasing.
You can still rest, but without avoidance.
You can still work hard, but without running from yourself.

That's the real work, not eradicating fear, but recognising it in motion and choosing differently.
Moment by moment. Conversation by conversation. Choice by choice.

Because the only thing more powerful than fear disguised as safety, is truth lived as courage.

What I've learned is that fear doesn't always look the same its busyness, people-pleasing, constant checking, endless overthinking, or even complaining. The disguises are clever, but the cost is the same: fear keeps you stuck, safe, but small.

Understanding these subtle disguises is the critical first step towards unmasking your hidden fears. It requires a shift in perspective, moving away from judging these behaviors as mere flaws or bad habits, and instead recognising them as intelligent, albeit misguided, survival strategies employed by your psyche. When you catch yourself procrastinating, engaging in perfectionism, feeling excessively busy, or resorting to avoidance, pause. Instead of self-criticism, ask yourself: "What am I truly afraid of in this moment?" By learning to identify fear's many faces, you begin to dismantle its power, paving the way for genuine self-awareness and the courage to confront what truly lies beneath the surface. This recognition is the bedrock upon which all subsequent steps toward overcoming fear will be built. It's the quiet revelation that the obstacles we face are often not external, but internal constructions built by fear, and that by understanding their architecture, we can begin to deconstruct them.

For me, confronting hidden fears has never been a single dramatic moment. It's felt more like detective work, you know - slow, patient, often uncomfortable. Fear has this way of operating in the background, shaping the choices I make and the risks I avoid, without me fully realising it's even there.

I've felt it in my body, that knot in my stomach before a big meeting, the urge to cancel plans last minute, the voice that whispers I'm not good enough. For a long time, I didn't connect those feelings to something specific. It just felt like "how I am."

What I've learned is that the first step is naming it. Putting words to it. When fear stays unnamed, it feels huge, like an ominous shadow that could be anything. That vagueness makes it grow, feeding anxiety that seeps into everything. It's like being unwell but not knowing what the illness is: the uncertainty is scarier than the diagnosis.

But the moment I started naming my fears, fear of rejection, fear of failure, fear of being seen, fear of not being loved they stopped being this shapeless dread. They became something specific, something I could face. Naming didn't make the fear disappear, but it contained it. It gave it edges. Instead of a fog that filled every space, it became a challenge I could prepare for, understand, and slowly work through.

That act of naming has been the first, crucial step in breaking the spell fear holds, because once you can name it, you can start to confront it.

Learning to identify fear in my own life has taken deliberate introspection. For me, it's not about dwelling on negative emotions, but about getting curious. Whenever I catch myself procrastinating, over-preparing, or filling my time with unnecessary busyness, I try to pause and ask: why? What's really driving this behaviour? What am I afraid of underneath it all?

I've noticed it in the small moments, like before a social event. I'll feel the jitters creeping in, and suddenly I'm finding excuses: "I'm too tired, the timing isn't right, maybe I'll just stay in." But when I've stopped to ask myself what's actually going on, I've realised it isn't about being tired. It's the fear of awkward silences, of not knowing what to say, of being judged, of feeling out of place.

Naming it, "I'm scared I won't be interesting enough", takes the dread from this big foggy feeling and turns it into something specific I can work with.

Writing Your Way Through Fear

Journaling has been one of the most powerful tools for this. When I sit down and write out what I'm feeling, it often surprises me how much clearer things become. I remember once putting off updating my CV for weeks. On the surface it looked like I was just "busy." But when I journaled about it, the truth came out: "If I update this CV, I'm forced to look at my career and ask myself if I've done enough. I'm worried what I've achieved won't look impressive." Suddenly, I could see that the block wasn't about the CV at all, it was something deeper, it was about self-worth.

That's what this process has taught me: when I pause, ask questions, and actually write things down, I can often trace a behaviour back to the fear driving it. Once I've named that fear, it stops feeling like a vague, invisible weight pressing on me, and starts feeling like something I can actually face.

Take the example of updating a CV. On the surface, it might feel like "a mountain." But when you dig into that feeling, what you're really articulating is a fear of evaluation, a fear of inadequacy, and a fear of confronting the sense that you haven't progressed as far as you thought you should. If you push further and ask, "What's the worst that could happen if my CV isn't impressive enough?" the answers become more concrete: "I might realise I haven't achieved what I thought by now, and that would make me feel like a failure. Or, if I apply for jobs and get rejected, it'll confirm the suspicion that I'm not good enough."

That's the shift. Through journaling or reflection, you move from this foggy, undefined dread to a set of named fears: the fear of confronting stagnation, the fear of failure in the application process, the fear of rejection confirming inadequacy. None of these are pleasant, but once they're named, they're contained. The "mountain" is no longer endless and shapeless; it's broken down into specific challenges you can begin to address.

TRACE Method

Another tool that's helped me and could help you, is something I call **The TRACE Method**.

It's a simple, structured way to slow fear down so you can actually *see* it: how it shows up, how it moves through you, and what it's really trying to protect.

You don't need pages of journaling; a few honest lines are enough. The power lies in noticing the *pattern*, catching fear before it drives your choices unconsciously.

I created the TRACE Method after one particular moment that almost passed me by.

A few years ago, I was invited to a networking dinner hosted by a major organisation. It was one of those rooms full of people whose names carried weight, senior executives, academics, media figures. The kind of event you know could shift something if you show up with intention. And yet, on the day, I found myself hesitating.

I'd picked out my clothes, prepared my talking points, even checked the guest list twice. But as the evening approached, that quiet, familiar voice started whispering:
You don't really belong there.
You're not part of their world.
What if you run out of things to say?
What if they see through you?

By the time I was meant to leave, I was seriously considering cancelling, telling myself I was "too tired" or that "the timing wasn't right." 5But instead, I sat down and opened my notebook, and this time, instead of trying to talk myself out of the feeling, I traced it.

Here's how it works:

T – Thoughts
What was running through your mind in that moment?
Example: "I won't know anyone. I'll have to make small talk. What if I sound boring or say something stupid? What if they wonder why I'm even here?"

R – Reactions
How did your body and emotions respond?
Example: Tight chest. Butterflies in my stomach. Hands fidgeting with my phone. Emotion: anxiety mixed with mild embarrassment.

A – Actions
What did you do or avoid doing?
Example: I hovered. Checked the time repeatedly. Almost convinced me to skip it. I opened my calendar as if searching for an excuse.

C – Core Fear
What's the deeper fear underneath the surface reaction?
Example: Fear of judgment. Fear of not belonging. Fear of exposure, of being "found out" as an imposter among people who seemed effortlessly confident.

E – Environment
What was the situation or trigger?
Example: A high-profile networking dinner where I was one of the youngest people in the room.

Your Turn: Try the TRACE Method

Pick one situation from the last week that made you hesitate, something small but noticeable:

- A message you didn't send.
- A meeting where you stayed quiet.
- A conversation you kept avoiding.

Now, trace it using the five steps:

T – Thoughts: What story was your mind telling?
R – Reactions: What did your body do? What emotions surfaced?
A – Actions: How did you respond, or retreat?
C – Core Fear: What was the deeper fear driving the behaviour?
E – Environment: What was happening around you?

Once you've traced it, look for patterns.

You'll start to see that the fears repeating themselves aren't random. They form a map, showing you where your growth, your boundaries, and your healing are waiting.

The more you practise TRACE, the quicker you'll catch fear in real time.

And each time you catch it, name it, and still choose to act, you reclaim a little more of your freedom.

Because self-awareness isn't the end of courage; it's the beginning of mastery.

TRACE in Leadership: From Personal Insight to Collective Courage

Fear doesn't just live in individuals, it lives in organisations too. It hides in systems, meetings, and decision-making processes. It shapes who speaks and who stays silent, which ideas get approved, and which risks never get taken.

And just like in our personal lives, fear in leadership rarely looks like fear.

It looks like "caution," "due diligence," "alignment," or "managing expectations."
It sounds like:

"Let's wait until we have more data."
"The timing isn't quite right."
"Let's not rock the boat."

Of course, sometimes those are sensible strategic calls. But other times, they're fear wearing a tie, fear of failure, fear of blame, fear of visibility.

This is where **TRACE** becomes a powerful tool for leaders and teams.

It's not just about identifying fear in yourself, it's about recognising how fear shapes culture, strategy, and collective behaviour.

Using TRACE in Leadership Decisions

Let's take a common example.

Imagine a leadership team debating whether to launch a new product or make a bold shift in strategy. The market is uncertain, the competition fierce. Some people advocate for innovation; others want to play it safe. The conversation sounds practical, but underneath, something else is happening, fear.

Here's how the TRACE Method can help leaders unearth what's really driving the conversation:

T – Thoughts (The Story We're Telling)

What narratives are shaping our thinking right now?

"If this fails, it will damage our reputation."
"We've tried before and it didn't work."
"We can't afford another risk this quarter."

Ask the team:

"What assumptions are we making? And are they based on data, or on past fear?"

This question alone often shifts the tone from defensiveness to curiosity.

R – Reactions (The Emotion in the Room)

How is fear showing up physically or emotionally, even if unspoken?

Tension in posture.
Hesitation before speaking.
Quick agreement to avoid conflict.
Defensive language like "I just think we should be realistic."

As a leader, learn to read not just the words, but the *energy* in the room.
Are people leaning forward with engagement, or shrinking back with self-protection?
Sometimes, leadership begins with noticing silence.

A – Actions (The Behaviours That Follow)

What do we do, or avoid doing, as a result?

We delay decisions.
We create endless review processes.
We water down bold ideas to make them "safer."

Ask:

"What actions are we avoiding, and why? What would we do if fear wasn't running this conversation?"

Courage in leadership often begins with that one uncomfortable question.

C – Core Fear (What's Really at Stake?)

What deeper fear is influencing our behaviour?

Fear of failure.
Fear of reputational damage.
Fear of stakeholder backlash.
Fear of losing control.

Naming this out loud shifts power. Once you identify the core fear, it stops controlling the decision subconsciously and becomes something you can address collectively.

When a leader says,

"I realise part of my hesitation here is fear of getting it wrong," it doesn't make them weak. It makes them human, and it creates permission for others to be honest too.

E – Environment (The Context and Culture)

What conditions in our environment are reinforcing this fear?

A culture that punishes mistakes.
A history of micromanagement.
Lack of psychological safety.
Unrealistic performance metrics.

If fear is a recurring theme, the environment needs redesigning, not the people.

Ask:

"What systems are rewarding caution instead of courage?"

Because no amount of mindset work can thrive in an environment that punishes risk and authenticity.

When leaders start applying TRACE collectively, something profound happens. Fear moves from being a hidden undercurrent to a shared language. People begin to recognise it, name it, and work through it together.

A manager might say:

"I'm noticing I'm in the R stage right now, my body feels tense, and I'm playing out worst-case scenarios."

Or a team member might add:

"Before we dismiss this idea, maybe we should check if our hesitation is data-driven or fear-driven."

Over time, this language normalises vulnerability and reflection.

Fear stops being a taboo and becomes a signal, information the team can work with instead of work around.

And that's the shift that changes everything.
Because when leaders and teams learn to name fear, they stop being controlled by it.
Decision-making becomes clearer. Communication becomes braver. Innovation becomes safer.

A Practical Application

Try using TRACE in your next team debrief or strategy meeting. Ask everyone to reflect quietly for two minutes before sharing:

1. **T:** What story am I telling myself about this situation?
2. **R:** What emotions or physical cues am I noticing?
3. **A:** What actions am I leaning toward, and which ones am I avoiding?
4. **C:** What fear might be sitting underneath this?
5. **E:** What in our culture or context is influencing this?

Then, invite honest conversation without judgment.
You'll find that beneath every cautious decision or delayed action is a story waiting to be rewritten.

Because courageous leadership isn't about having no fear, it's about *leading through it*.
It's about turning fear from an unspoken force into a conscious teacher.

Closing Reflection

The TRACE Method started as a personal journaling tool.
But over time, it's become a mirror for leaders, a way to see where fear hides in plain sight.
And once you can see it, you can reshape it.

Because leadership isn't just about driving performance.
It's about creating spaces where people feel safe enough to bring their full selves, fears included and still move forward together.

Fear thrives in silence; courage grows in dialogue.
The more we trace it, the more we transform it.

The key here is honesty, especially in the "Core fear" section. That's where the real naming happens. At first you might write something broad, like "I'm afraid of the retreat." But when you question it further, you may discover it's not the retreat itself, but the fear of awkward social interactions, the fear of not fitting in, the fear of not being accepted.

This little practice of slowing down and recording helps you strip fear of its disguise. Instead of being run by invisible forces, you can start to see clearly what's at play and once you can see it, you can do something about it. By filling out a log like this consistently, you're doing more than just noticing your reactions, you're digging beneath them, looking for the root.

Naming the Pattern: When Fear Masquerades as "Losing Interest"

Naming fear doesn't just help in one-off moments of anxiety; it also shines light on the long shadows it casts across our habits, choices, and self-perception.

Because fear doesn't always stop you from *starting*, sometimes it stops you from *staying*.

Maybe you've noticed it too.

You start new projects, ideas, or hobbies with excitement. You feel the spark, that initial rush of energy and possibility. For a few weeks, you're fully in it. You're researching, planning, maybe even sharing updates with others. Then, quietly, something shifts. The spark fades. The enthusiasm feels forced. Suddenly, it's easier to move on to something else.

On the surface, it looks like inconsistency. You tell yourself, *Maybe I just lose interest easily. Maybe I'm not disciplined enough.* But if you pause and if you apply the same curiosity you would with the TRACE Method, you might discover something more honest beneath the pattern.

Ask yourself:

- What happens emotionally right before I start to pull away?
- When does the excitement turn into avoidance?
- What story do I tell myself at that point?

Because often, what we label as "laziness" or "lack of commitment" is really fear wearing another disguise.

The Fear of Mastery

At the beginning of anything new, we get to stay in the safe zone of potential.

We can imagine being brilliant without yet having to prove it.

But once you start to improve, once you get close to competence, fear changes shape.

It whispers, *What if you give this your all and still fall short? What if you're exposed as not being as good as people think? What if, after all that effort, you're still just average?*

And so, without realising it, we pull back. We drift. We convince ourselves we've "lost interest", but really, it's the fear of what happens *after* interest: accountability, visibility, judgment.

Because once you get good at something, it becomes real.

And once it's real, it can fail.

That's the paradox of mastery, the closer you get to it, the more it demands vulnerability.

My Own Version of This Pattern

I've lived this pattern myself more times than I'd like to admit.

When I first started writing publicly, I'd have bursts of creative energy, drafting essays, outlines, ideas for talks. I'd share a few posts, get some engagement, feel inspired, then suddenly, I'd stop. Weeks would go by. I'd tell myself I was "waiting for inspiration."

But what I was really doing was hiding.

The closer my writing got to being seen by more people, the more exposed I felt.

I worried: *What if the next post doesn't land as well?*

What if people realise I'm not as insightful as they think?

That wasn't a lack of discipline it was a fear of being fully visible, of putting something meaningful out there and having it fall flat.

And once I named it for what it was, fear of not being *enough*, disguised as "I need a break", I could finally see the pattern for what it was: protection. My mind was trying to shield me from disappointment by sabotaging progress.

The Comfort of Potential

Potential is seductive because it's safe.

You can't fail at potential.

You can't be judged for an idea that's still in your head.

But mastery demands exposure. It invites feedback. It asks you to keep showing up long after the novelty has worn off, to move from performance to perseverance.

That's where fear likes to intervene.

It says, *Quit now, while you can still say you could have been great.* And so, we become brilliant at beginnings but inconsistent with follow-through.

But here's the truth:

Mastery doesn't require constant motivation, it requires tolerance for discomfort.

You don't need to love the process every day; you just need to stay through the resistance long enough to see what's on the other side of it.

That's where confidence is built, not in the spark of starting, but in the quiet repetition of continuing.

Reframing the Pattern

Next time you catch yourself losing steam or abandoning something halfway through, try this small reframing exercise:

1. Name the shift.
When did enthusiasm become avoidance? Was there a specific trigger, a moment of feedback, comparison, or self-judgment?

2. Identify the emotion.
What's really underneath? Is it boredom, or is it fear of inadequacy, visibility, or failure?

3. Ask what this fear is protecting.
Maybe it's protecting your sense of competence, your self-image, your identity as "the one who always delivers."

4. Thank it, then act anyway.
Acknowledging the fear disarms it. The goal isn't to banish it, but to move through it consciously.

Because once you see the pattern, you can choose differently. You can replace self-criticism with self-understanding, and self-understanding with consistency.

The Deeper Truth

When you name your patterns, you reclaim your power.
You stop interpreting every pause as failure and start seeing it as data.
You realise that behind every "I lost motivation" moment, there's usually a story of self-protection.

Fear doesn't just stop us from trying, it can also stop us from *continuing*.
But naming that truth, gently, without shame, is how you break the loop.

Because fear might build the walls, but awareness is what opens the door.
And every time you choose to keep going, to show up one more time, you tell fear:
You can ride with me, but you don't get to steer.

Meditation or visualisation can also help bring hidden fears to the surface. I've found it useful to sit quietly, close my eyes, and picture a situation that unsettles me. Then I ask myself, "What's the strongest fear here?" At first, the answer might sound vague, "I'm afraid of messing up." But if you sit with it, you can dig deeper: does "messing up" mean failing publicly? Losing respect? Being seen as incompetent?

Each of those is a named fear you can work with.

Take job interviews. You might say to yourself, "I'm just nervous." But nervous is only the emotion. Underneath are usually specific fears: "What if they ask me something I don't know? What if I freeze? What if they don't like me?" Once you name them, you can prepare for them. For not knowing an answer, you can practise responding with honesty and composure. For freezing up, you can learn grounding techniques. For rejection, you can remind yourself that interviews go both ways, not every job is meant for you.

When Naming Changes Everything

The shift happens the moment you name a fear. When it's left vague, it feels like an external force pressing down on you. Once it's named, you can see it as part of your inner world. You don't have to deny it or fight it; you can acknowledge it and plan around it.

For example, I realised once that I was procrastinating on a creative project, one I deeply cared about, because of the fear of creative blocks.

On the surface, I told myself I was "waiting for inspiration." I convinced myself that I needed more clarity, more research, a better concept.
But underneath all that logic was fear.
Not fear of failure exactly, but fear of *stuckness*, that horrible moment when you sit in front of a blank page, or a silent microphone, or an unresponsive idea, and nothing flows.

The irony was that the very thing I feared, the block, had already arrived, just wearing a different outfit: procrastination.

So I paused and used the TRACE method. I traced what was really happening.

- My **Thoughts** were all about readiness: *"I don't want to start and get stuck."*
- My **Reactions** were subtle tension in my jaw, that quiet hum of anxiety behind my ribs.
- My **Actions** were disguised avoidance reorganising my workspace, revising notes, convincing myself I was "preparing."
- The **Core Fear** was exposure, the possibility that maybe, when I finally did create, it wouldn't be good enough.
- And the **Environment** was simple: an open laptop and a deadline approaching.

Once I named it, something shifted.

I realised that creative blocks weren't proof I shouldn't start, they were proof that I'd started something meaningful.
Blocks aren't the enemy; they're part of the terrain. They show up precisely because you care.

That reframing changed my entire relationship with creativity.
Instead of treating fear as a stop sign, I started treating it as information.
It told me where my growth was hiding.
It pointed me to the edge of what mattered most.

So, I stopped waiting for perfect clarity and began experimenting instead.

Some days that meant writing one messy paragraph.
Other days it meant stepping away, walking, letting the idea breathe.
The pressure to "get it right" gave way to curiosity: *"What happens if I just begin?"*

The Ripple Effect of Reframing

That small act, naming fear and reframing it, had consequences far beyond that one project.
It changed how I approached every act of creation, from designing workshops to writing this very book.

Because once you understand that fear of "the block" is really fear of imperfection, you free yourself to create anyway.
You start to measure progress not by polish, but by honesty.
You stop waiting for the muse, and start trusting the process.

And the impact doesn't stop there.
When I began sharing this mindset with clients and teams, I noticed something powerful: it spread.
Leaders stopped apologising for not having all the answers.
Writers stopped deleting their first drafts.
Teams stopped postponing meetings because "we're not ready."

Naming the fear behind the behaviour gave everyone permission to move.
It shifted energy from *avoidance* to *engagement*, from *perfectionism* to *progress*.

That's the quiet revolution of self-awareness, it doesn't just change how you feel; it changes how you *act*.

From Paralysis to Play

I started approaching creative blocks like puzzles rather than verdicts.
Instead of asking, "What's wrong with me?" I began asking, "What's fear trying to protect right now?"
Usually, the answer was simple: *my ego*.
Fear wanted to protect my image, to make sure what I produced was impressive, validated, safe from criticism.

But once you see that clearly, you can smile at it. You can say, *"Thank you, but I don't need protection right now, I need movement."*

From that point on, I began to see creativity not as an act of perfection, but as an act of courage, a willingness to engage with uncertainty in public.

And that's the gift of naming.
When you name the fear, you loosen its grip.
You turn paralysis into play.
You reclaim energy that was once trapped in rumination and redirect it toward creation.

Reflection: Spot the Fear Beneath the Pause

If you notice yourself avoiding something important, a project, a decision, a conversation, try this:

1. **Name the Surface Story.**
   What excuse are you telling yourself? ("I'm waiting for the right time." "I'm not ready yet.")
2. **Ask What Fear Might Be Protecting.**
   Is it fear of failure? Of judgment? Of being seen?
3. **Reframe It as Information.**
   What might this fear be trying to tell you about what matters most?
4. **Act Small but Honest.**
   Take one step forward, not a perfect one, just an intentional one.

You'll notice something subtle but profound:
fear shrinks in proportion to movement.

Because once you move, even a little, fear loses the argument that you can't.

A Closing Thought

That creative project I almost abandoned?
It became one of the most meaningful pieces of work I've ever completed.
Not because it was perfect, but because it was *true*.
And it reminded me that the purpose of creation, and of life itself, isn't to avoid uncertainty, but to dance with it.

When you name fear, you reclaim authorship.
When you act through it, you reclaim freedom.

That's the real art of courage: not waiting until the fear is gone, but creating something beautiful in its presence.

That's the empowerment that comes with naming. Fear no longer controls you from the shadows; you start to meet it head-on, not as a vague enemy, but as something you can understand, work with, and overcome.

It's important to remember that identifying and naming your fears isn't something you do once and tick off the list. It's an ongoing practice. As you grow, new challenges will bring new anxieties, and old fears can resurface in different forms. That's why cultivating a habit of self-reflection matters. Regularly check in with yourself: *"What anxieties are present in my life right now? What fears might be steering my choices without me realising it?"*

When you build that kind of inner dialogue, you become more resilient. Instead of being blindsided by hidden fears, you develop the awareness to catch them early, And the more you practise naming them, the less hold they have.

What once felt like a paralysing weight starts to look more like a stepping stone, an invitation to grow, rather than something to run from.

Exercise: Spot Your Disappearing Act

Tracing the Fear Behind Abandonment

We've all had moments where we start something with excitement, only to fade before the finish line. The goal of this exercise isn't to criticise yourself, it's to understand the hidden fears that cause the fade. Because when you name the fear beneath the pattern, you take back control of it.

Find a quiet space and reflect on one or two projects, habits, or goals you've started but didn't finish. Then move through these prompts slowly, honesty is more important than speed.

1. Identify the Scene
What was the last thing you started with genuine enthusiasm but didn't complete?
It could be a hobby, a course, a piece of writing, a business idea, a relationship, or a personal goal.
Write it down. Name it clearly.

Example: "I started building a personal website but stopped halfway through."

2. Track the Turning Point
When did the energy shift?
What moment, event, or emotion marked the change from enthusiasm to avoidance?
Describe it in detail, what was happening around you, and what thoughts appeared?

Example: "I showed a draft to a friend, and they said it looked 'okay', I felt deflated and stopped working on it."

3. Unmask the Fear

What fear was hiding beneath that turning point?
Was it fear of being judged, fear of mediocrity, fear of visibility, fear of losing control, or fear of commitment?
Be specific, precision weakens fear's power.

Example: "I was afraid the final result wouldn't live up to the version I imagined. I'd rather quit than confirm I'm not as capable as I thought."

4. Reframe the Story

How can you reinterpret that fear as protection, something that was trying, in its own way, to keep you safe?
Then, decide how you can move forward differently next time.

Example: "My fear of failure was trying to protect me from embarrassment. Next time, I'll share early drafts sooner, to normalise imperfection."

5. Create a Micro-Commitment

Now, choose one small, low-pressure way to re-engage with something you've paused.
Not to complete it overnight, just to *reopen the door*.

Example: "Spend 20 minutes revisiting my old draft, with no expectation of posting it. Just curiosity."

6. Anchor the Insight

End with one sentence that reframes the old story into a new truth.

Something like:

"I don't lose interest easily, I retreat when I'm afraid of being seen."

"My inconsistency isn't weakness; it's an invitation to practise courage."

"Finishing isn't about perfection, it's about presence."

By revisiting your "disappearing acts" with compassion and clarity, you begin to dissolve their power. You'll start to notice that what once felt like a pattern of failure was really a pattern of self-protection, and that's something you can now meet with awareness rather than avoidance.

Each time you return to something you once abandoned, you reclaim a piece of your self-trust.

That's how courage grows, not in sudden transformations, but in the quiet act of coming back.

The Mind's Defence Team

Of course, the human mind doesn't always make this easy.

We've evolved sophisticated defence mechanisms to shield us from pain, and *denial* is one of the strongest. Denial isn't usually an outright lie we tell ourselves; it's an unconscious avoidance. When a fear feels too heavy, too shameful, or too destabilising to confront, we quietly close the door on it. On the surface, this gives us a sense of control. But beneath the surface, it's like holding back water behind a dam, it takes constant effort, and eventually, the cracks show. The fear still leaks out, shaping our behaviours and limiting our potential in ways we don't always notice.

At the root of denial is an aversion to vulnerability. Many of us grew up being told to be "brave," to "toughen up," or to "not be afraid." While these messages are well-intentioned, they can teach us that admitting fear equals weakness.

So instead, we find ways to mask it

- to intellectualise it
- rationalise it,
- or bury it entirely.

Rationalisation is one of the most common, I've done it myself, rather than admitting, *"I'm scared of public speaking, and that's why I don't want to do this presentation,"* I'd say things like, *"I'm just too busy right now,"* or *"This isn't really my area of expertise."* These excuses sounded logical even professional. But deep down, it wasn't about time or relevance. It was fear: fear of judgement, fear of embarrassment, fear of not being good enough in front of an audience. And the more I leaned on rationalisations, the safer I felt, but the smaller I played.

Another subtle disguise is *intellectualisation*. Instead of facing fear directly, we bury ourselves in facts, theories, and endless analysis. Imagine you're thinking about a big career change. The truth is, you're scared, scared of leaving your comfort zone, scared of failing, scared of being found out. But rather than naming those fears, you dive into research. You read every article, build complex spreadsheets, map out every possible outcome. On the surface, it feels like preparation. But really, it's protection, like an armour of information to keep you from admitting the vulnerability underneath.

I've caught myself here too, convincing myself that if I just knew enough, I'd stop being afraid.

It's such a convincing illusion: that certainty can cure fear. So I'd research endlessly, analyse every angle, and gather data like armour. If I could prepare enough, plan enough, anticipate every possible outcome, then maybe I'd never have to feel the sting of being unprepared, embarrassed, or wrong.

But no amount of knowledge can protect you from what only experience can teach you. No amount of theory substitutes for the vulnerability of doing.

I remember one particular moment that brought this lesson home. I was preparing for a major workshop with a global organisation, one of those big opportunities that could shape future partnerships. It was a topic I knew inside out. I'd delivered versions of it countless times before. And yet, the closer the day came, the more my preparation turned into obsession.

I wasn't just rehearsing, I was hiding behind the preparation. I read every article I could find, redrafted the slides at least ten times, adjusted the exercises until they lost their simplicity. I told myself it was diligence. But really, it was fear, dressed as professionalism.

I was terrified of not being seen as "the expert." Of someone in the audience catching a flaw, questioning a statistic, challenging a perspective. The fear wasn't about the content, it was about my feeling of not being enough.

The night before the session, surrounded by notes and coffee cups, I realised what I was doing. I wasn't preparing to connect I was preparing to protect. And the more I tried to protect myself, the more disconnected I became from the very reason I do this work: to move people, not to impress them.

So, I stopped. I shut the laptop, walked away from the desk, and told myself: *You know this because you've lived this. That's enough.* The next day, I spoke from memory and from heart, not from notes. I forgot a few statistics, but I remembered the stories. And something shifted in the room, people didn't just learn, they leaned in.

The session ended not with applause, but with silence, the kind that comes when people are genuinely reflecting. And that's when I learned a truth I still return to: fear doesn't disappear when you collect more information; it dissolves when you tell the truth about what it's protecting.

The Fear Behind the Data

For me, the data was a defence mechanism, a way to intellectualise fear instead of feel it. It looked responsible, even admirable: *"I'm just being thorough."* But thoroughness had become a shield. Because if I stayed in research mode, I could delay vulnerability. And as long as I was still "preparing," I never had to risk being seen.

That's the trap of all fear-based defences, they look clever, they sound reasonable, but they keep you at arm's length from the very thing you need to face. Fear will let you stay busy, productive, even successful as long as you stay safe.

But growth doesn't happen in safety; it happens in exposure.

The Real Work Begins Here

The real growth begins when you notice the disguise, name what's hiding underneath, and give yourself permission to feel it. Not to fix it. Not to reason it away. Just to feel it, fully, honestly, without apology.

The moment you do that, the fear loses some of its power. You stop wrestling with shadows and start engaging with something real.

That's what happened for me that day. Once I said out loud, *"I'm scared I won't be good enough,"* the fear stopped running the show. It was still there, I still felt the flutter in my chest, the sweat on my palms but it no longer dictated my behaviour. I could move with it instead of against it.

And that's the quiet miracle of self-awareness: once fear is named, it becomes navigable. You can make choices again. You can return to purpose instead of perfection. You can be human and still deliver something extraordinary.

Reflection: So where are you hiding behind preparation?

If you often find yourself endlessly researching, editing, or refining before taking action, pause and ask:

- **What am I really trying to avoid by preparing more?**
  Is it embarrassment? Judgment? The risk of being seen as not enough?
- **What's the smallest step I can take without another round of research or reassurance?**
  Remember, clarity comes *after* movement, not before.
- **What would happen if I showed up as prepared, but not perfect?**
  Sometimes, that's where the magic happens in the small cracks where authenticity breathes through.

Preparation has its place, but perfectionism disguised as preparation is fear in a business suit. And the cost of that disguise is *aliveness*.

So, when you catch yourself saying, *"I just need to know a little more,* "pause, take a breath and remind yourself that you don't need to know more, you just need to begin.

The cultural story we grow up with around success and emotions plays a huge part in why denial takes root. We're constantly shown images of people who seem effortlessly capable leaders, celebrities, even colleagues who appear to move through life without a crack in their armour. The message is subtle but powerful: fear is weakness, and if you feel it, you're somehow failing. Over time, many of us internalise that message. To admit fear feels like admitting defeat.

Think of someone with a fear of heights. Instead of saying, *"I'm scared of falling,"* they laugh it off with bravado: *"I'm not afraid of heights, I just don't like the view up there,"* or *"It's the wind that bothers me."* These sound convincing, but what's really happening is rationalisation, finding a more acceptable story that hides the real vulnerability. The true fear of falling, of losing control, of the dizzying sensation of being far from the ground, of death remains buried. The cost of denial is that they never get to face or work through the fear itself.

Much of this starts in childhood. If your fears were dismissed with, *"Don't be a baby,"* or, *"There's nothing to be afraid of,"* you learned quickly that showing fear invited shame. So you suppressed it.

Imagine a child ridiculed for being afraid of dogs. Maybe they were forced to pet the family dog while being told, *"See? Nothing to be scared of."* The fear doesn't disappear it doubles. First, the fear of the dog, and second, the fear of feeling humiliated again for being afraid. As an adult, that person might avoid parks or social situations with dogs, but when asked, they'll insist, *"I just find them unpredictable,"* or *"I prefer to keep my distance."* The denial protects them from old wounds, but it also keeps them stuck.

Denial is never just about avoiding an emotion; it's about avoiding what might come if you admitted it. If you tell your boss, *"I'm scared I'll fail at this project,"* you risk them questioning your ability. If you admit, even to yourself, that you fear conflict, you may have to face difficult conversations or risk rejection. So instead, you cloak it. You say things like, *"I just value harmony,"* or *"Arguing isn't productive."* They sound reasonable, but often they're disguises for something deeper: the fear of confrontation, of anger, of alienation. And while the denial keeps you safe from those risks in the short term, it costs you authenticity and the chance to build genuine connection.

Sometimes denial is driven by the image we want to hold of ourselves. We like to see ourselves as confident, capable, in control. Acknowledging fear threatens that picture, so instead we overcompensate. You've probably seen it: the person who acts overly confident, always agreeable, desperate to keep everyone happy. On the surface, they seem warm and cooperative. But often, underneath, there's a gnawing fear: *"If I'm not liked, I won't be loved. If I'm not perfect, I'll be abandoned."* When confronted, they'll brush it off as being a "people person," when really it's fear dressed as friendliness. The trouble with denial is that it works temporarily. It pushes the discomfort away just enough to carry on. But it creates a loop: the more you deny, the less practice you have in facing fear, and the more overwhelming it becomes when it inevitably resurfaces.

Intellectualisation can be just as deceptive because it *looks* productive.

It makes us feel like we're doing the work, when really, we're circling around it.

Take relationships, for example. Someone afraid of commitment might bury themselves in research, reading every book on attachment theory, analysing compatibility tests, or debating the psychology of love. On the surface, they appear thoughtful, careful, even wise. But underneath, the fear of vulnerability, of losing independence, of being rejected, of being *seen*, remains untouched.

They'll say, *"I just want to be informed before I commit,"* but the truth is, the knowledge-seeking is a shield. It keeps us safe in the world of ideas, so we don't have to step into the "messiness" of real intimacy.

I've been there, too, convincing myself I was "processing" when I was really protecting myself from being exposed. It's easier to intellectualise emotions than to feel them. Easier to study connection than to risk heartbreak. It's way easier to *know about* vulnerability or think we know about it than to actually allow ourselves to *be* vulnerable.

But you can't think your way into intimacy, you can only feel your way there. Love, trust, and connection live in the unpredictable, unscripted moments that can't be reasoned into safety.

I've seen this same pattern in leadership, too. Some bury themselves in theories of motivation, frameworks of culture, or endless diagnostics on "employee engagement." It all looks sophisticated, but sometimes it's a way of avoiding the harder, human work, sitting with discomfort, owning mistakes, asking someone, *"How are you really?"* and waiting long enough to hear the truth.

Data can tell you many things, but it can't teach you courage. Whether in love or leadership, intellectualisation offers the illusion of control. It lets us believe that if we just know enough, we can prevent pain, avoid rejection, or manage uncertainty.

But knowledge doesn't protect us from vulnerability; it only distances us from it. At some point, we have to put the book down, close the tabs, and step into the living, breathing world, where people might misunderstand us, where things might not go as planned, but where connection, growth and joy happen.

Knowing is comfortable.
But *experiencing*, that's where life begins.

Because wisdom isn't built from what you know, it's built from what you live.

That's the insidiousness of denial and its cousins, rationalisation and intellectualisation: they all give us the illusion of control, the temporary relief of not having to face our fear head-on. But the cost is high. What's pushed down doesn't disappear it festers, it shapes our choices, it limits our lives. The work of naming fear isn't easy, but it's the only way to stop running from shadows and start living with honesty, courage, and freedom.

The real work of overcoming fear often starts with dismantling the defences we've built to hide it. Denial, rationalisation, intellectualisation they're clever coping strategies, but ultimately, they're just sticking plasters on a deeper wound. They protect us in the short term but never get to the root. By recognising *why* we deny our fears whether it's the shame of vulnerability, the cultural pressure to appear strong, or the habits we picked up in childhood we can begin to loosen their grip. The move from denial to acceptance is a turning point: it's where fear stops being an unseen enemy and becomes something we can face honestly. That shift requires effort noticing the masks we wear, naming the fears beneath them, and choosing compassion instead of shame.

Why are you hiding behind understanding?

If you tend to overthink, overanalyse, or overprepare, ask yourself:

- **Where am I using knowledge to delay experience?**
  Is it reading another book instead of having the conversation? Taking another course instead of pitching the idea?
- **What am I trying to control by knowing more?**
  Is it the fear of failure, rejection, or simply being seen as imperfect?
- **What's one area of my life that needs less research and more presence?**
  Maybe it's finally sending the message, showing up to the meeting, or saying how you actually feel.

You don't need another book, quote, or strategy. You need to *step in*.

Because wisdom isn't built from what you know, it's built from what you live.

Two Big Shadows: Failure & Success

And here's where the paradox shows up: many of us aren't just afraid of failure we're also afraid of success. On the surface they look like opposites. One keeps you from trying; the other stops you from enjoying the outcome. But often, they come from the same root: doubts about our worthiness and our ability to handle what comes next.

The fear of failure is the more familiar voice. It's the one that whispers: "What if I'm not good enough? What if I mess this up? What if everyone sees me fall?" That voice can paralyse you. It convinces the artist to keep their paintings hidden because "they're not ready yet." It tells the aspiring entrepreneur to polish their business plan endlessly but never share it. It's not that you lack talent or drive; it's that the sting of criticism or the shame of getting it wrong feels unbearable. You play small, you set safe goals, you aim low enough that you can't miss. It feels protective, but it also robs you of growth.

I've seen this play out with people I've coached, and I've lived it myself. Take someone like Alex highly skilled, consistently praised, ready on paper for the next big step. Alex is offered a promotion: more responsibility, more visibility, more influence.

But instead of excitement, anxiety floods in. Suddenly the mind is full of imagined disasters mishandling a project, failing their team, stumbling in front of senior leaders, and so the rationalisations begin: "I still have more to learn," "Someone else is better suited," "I prefer staying hands-on." On the surface, those reasons sound reasonable. But underneath, they're fuelled by fear: fear of being exposed, of disappointing others, of falling short when the stakes are high.

You might recognise yourself in Alex. You get the chance to step up, but the comfort of the familiar feels safer than the risk of failure. You tell yourself you're "not ready," when what you really mean is, "I'm scared."

Here's the thing: the fear of failure isn't really about ability. It's about magnifying the possible pain until it feels bigger than the possible reward. The challenge is learning to reframe it, to accept that failure is part of growth, not proof of inadequacy. That shift doesn't silence fear completely, but it does stop it from running your life.

However, the psychology of fear becomes even more intriguing when we turn our attention to the *fear of success*. This is often a more subtle and less acknowledged anxiety, yet it can be equally, if not more, debilitating. The fear of success isn't about the absence of desire for achievement; it's about the apprehension of what success brings. Success often means increased visibility, higher expectations, greater responsibility, and sometimes, a shift in relationships with peers.

For some, the prospect of achieving their goals can feel as daunting as the prospect of failing to do so. This fear can manifest as self-sabotage, a tendency to perform just below one's potential, or an unconscious effort to remain in the background, even when opportunities for advancement are present.

And yes, that's exactly what Alex was doing.

When we began working together, he'd just been offered a leadership role, one that perfectly aligned with his skill set and ambition, yet he was hesitating. He told me he wanted to "think it through," but beneath that surface of logic was fear: *What if I can't handle the pressure? What if they realise, I'm not as capable as they think?*

So we started small.

The first step was **naming the fear**, saying it out loud. It sounds simple, but the act of naming transforms fear from something amorphous into something manageable. "I'm afraid of being seen as a fraud," he said one session, "because if I succeed, people will expect even more."

Next, we worked on **reframing success**, not as exposure, but as expansion. Together, we explored what success *meant* to him, beyond the title. We discussed how visibility could be a platform for impact, not a spotlight of scrutiny. We revisited his past achievements, times he'd thrived under pressure, solved complex problems, and supported others, to rebuild evidence that he could, in fact, rise to meet new challenges.

Then came **gradual exposure.** Rather than leaping straight into every responsibility at once, we designed small, controlled "tests", leading a meeting he'd usually observe, pitching one bold idea per week, seeking feedback instead of avoiding it. Each small win built momentum and rewired the association between success and threat.

We also integrated **reflection rituals.** After each success, no matter how small, he'd write down what he did well and how it *felt*. This shifted the focus from external validation ("Did they like it?") to internal ownership ("I did that. I handled it."). Over time, this built a quieter, sturdier confidence, one rooted not in performance, but in progress.

And finally, we addressed the **fear of change** that often shadows success. For Alex, part of the hesitation was emotional, the worry that stepping up would distance him from his peers, that leadership meant isolation. We reframed leadership not as separation, but as service, a way of amplifying the good he already brought to the team.

By the time he accepted the promotion, the fear hadn't vanished, but it had softened. It no longer dictated his decisions. He'd built new evidence that courage isn't the absence of fear, but the willingness to move forward with it.

Alex didn't just step into a new role, he stepped into a new story. One where fear was no longer the author, but simply a character he'd learned to work alongside.

Why are you holding back from success?

Alex's story isn't unique. Many of us have our own version of that moment, the opportunity that scares us because it confirms what we secretly hoped for. Success asks for expansion, and expansion always brings exposure. If you've ever found yourself hesitating when things start going *right*, this reflection is for you. Take a few quiet minutes to answer honestly, not from logic, but from your gut.

1. What opportunity am I currently downplaying or delaying and why?
Be specific. Maybe it's applying for a promotion, launching a project, or sharing your work publicly. What's the story you're telling yourself about why it's "not the right time"?

2. What am I afraid success will *change*?
Sometimes, it's not failure we fear, but transformation, how others might see us, how our relationships might shift, or how new responsibilities might expose our limits. What feels at risk if you succeed?

3. What would it look like if success didn't threaten you but expanded you?
Reframe it. Instead of, "I'll lose balance," try, "I'll learn new rhythms." Instead of, "People will expect more," try, "I'll grow into those expectations."

4. What small, courageous step can I take this week toward that success?
Don't wait for readiness, create evidence. Send the email. Make the call. Share the idea. Take one concrete action that signals: *I'm no longer letting fear drive.*

5. What proof do I already have that I can handle growth?
List past moments when you rose to challenges. The goal isn't to erase fear, but to remind yourself that you've done this before, just in different forms.

Let's take another example. Sarah, one of my coaching clients, was, by every measure, accomplished. She'd built a successful career in communications, earned awards for her writing, and was known among colleagues for her insight and creativity. On the surface, she had it all together, articulate, disciplined, quietly confident. The kind of person others came to for advice.

But privately, Sarah carried a secret project close to her heart: her first novel. She'd been working on it for years, in the quiet hours before work and long after midnight. The story was deeply personal, a tapestry of her heritage, loss, and hope. When she finally finished the manuscript, it wasn't just good, it was extraordinary. Her early readers were moved to tears. A few publishers expressed interest almost immediately. She was, by all accounts, standing on the edge of her next big breakthrough.

And that's when she froze.

Instead of sending her manuscript out, she slipped into a cycle of delay. One more round of edits. One more "structural review."

Another week to polish the language. She created colour-coded submission trackers and rewrote her author bio five times but never pressed send.

When we began working together, I asked her what was really happening beneath the surface. She smiled, almost embarrassed, and said, "I thought I'd be excited. But I'm not. I'm scared."

At first, she thought it was fear of rejection. But as we dug deeper, it became clear: Sarah wasn't afraid of failure, she was afraid of *success*.

Her thoughts tumbled out:
"What if my next book isn't as good?"
"What if people expect too much from me?"
"What if success changes me, or changes how people see me?"
"What if my friends start treating me differently?"

Like so many high-achievers, Sarah was used to working toward something. She knew how to strive. She didn't yet know how to *arrive*. Success, for her, meant visibility, and visibility meant vulnerability.

We unpacked that slowly. She realised that she'd built safety around striving. Striving gave her control, purpose, and a clear identity: *the hardworking writer chasing the dream*. But success threatened that narrative. If she actually reached the goal, the story she'd been living by would have to change. And that's what she feared most, not failure, but transformation.

So we worked on reframing that fear.

Instead of asking, *What if success changes me?*, she began asking, *What if it grows me?*

Instead of worrying, *What if success makes me different?*, she began exploring, *What if success helps me become more of who I already am?*

I gave her an exercise: **Name the story your fear is telling, then write a new one.**

Her fear's story said:
"Success will isolate me."

Her new story became:
"Success will connect me with people who are moved by my work."

Her fear's story said:
"If this book does well, I'll never top it."

Her new story became:
"Every story I tell will reach a new part of me and that evolution is the point."

Sarah didn't conquer her fear overnight. But she learned to move with it. She sent one query letter. Then another. Then she accepted a call with a publisher. Each small act built evidence, proof that she could stand inside her visibility without losing herself.

When her publishing deal finally came through, she cried. Not out of shock, but relief. "It's not that the fear went away," she told me, "it's that I finally understood it. I wasn't scared of failing. I was scared of expanding."

And that's what I see in so many of the people I coach, leaders, creatives, professionals. They're not afraid of being incapable. They're afraid of what happens when they finally become everything they're capable of being. Because success doesn't just ask you to perform, it asks you to *be seen* and being seen, in all your fullness, is one of the most courageous things you'll ever do.

This is the fear of success. Not fear of failure, but fear of what happens if things go right. Fear of the spotlight. Fear of higher expectations. Fear that achieving the dream might change her or her relationships in ways she isn't ready for. For Sarah, the possibility of success feels as threatening as the risk of failure. The fear of success often hides beneath questions of worthiness. If you grew up internalising the message that you weren't good enough, or that ambition should be kept in check, success can trigger deep anxiety. It can feel like stepping into a role you haven't earned, not because you lack the skill, but because you doubt your right to occupy that space.

For many, the fear of success overlaps with **imposter syndrome**, that quiet, constant hum of "What if I don't actually deserve this?" But for others, especially those navigating life at the intersections of race, gender, class, or culture, that voice isn't just personal, it's historical.
It's inherited.
It's systemic.

Because imposter syndrome doesn't emerge in a vacuum.

It grows in the spaces where brilliance is questioned, where belonging is conditional, and where people are applauded for their resilience but rarely protected from the reason they need it.

When I coach leaders from underrepresented backgrounds, I see the same pattern in different forms. They've earned their place, every qualification, every promotion, every win, but something inside them still whispers, *"Don't slip up."*
It's not arrogance that holds them back; it's hyper-vigilance.
The learned instinct to prove, perform, and perfect, not to impress, but to stay safe.

I know this firsthand.
Early in my career, walking into boardrooms where no one looked or sounded like me, I would straighten my posture, adjust my tone, carefully weigh every word before speaking.
It wasn't about insecurity; it was about survival.
Because when you're "the only one" in the room, the stakes of authenticity feel higher.
One misstep doesn't feel like a mistake, it feels like a headline.

Even when success came, it carried a strange heaviness.
Because with every new opportunity came the unspoken fear: *Will this be the moment they realise I'm not what they think I am?*
That's what imposter syndrome looks like when filtered through identity.
It's not just the fear of being exposed as inadequate, it's the fear of confirming someone else's bias.
The fear that your failure won't just be yours; it will be read as collective.

I've seen this so many times in my coaching work.
Brilliant, accomplished individuals, CEOs, founders, creatives, public servants, quietly battling the same silent tension: wanting to grow, but afraid that visibility will come with scrutiny.
Afraid that their authenticity will make others uncomfortable.
Afraid that in order to stay accepted, they'll have to keep dimming their light just enough to blend in.

One of my clients, a senior executive, said to me during a session, *"It's not that I'm afraid to lead, I'm afraid of what leading as myself will cost me."*
That sentence stayed with me.
Because it captured the truth of what so many people of colour, women, and those from marginalised backgrounds experience in leadership.
It's not the fear of success that's paralysing, it's the fear that success might demand erasure.

That's why, when I coach through this, we don't just talk about strategy or mindset.
We talk about *belonging*.
We explore how systemic structures shape self-perception.
We work on building what I call *internal belonging* a deep-rooted confidence that doesn't rely on external approval to feel real.

Because belonging isn't just being invited into the room; it's being able to bring your full self into it.
And courage, in that context, isn't about being loud it's about being *whole*.

To lead as yourself, not as who the world has trained you to be.

Over time, I've come to believe that dismantling imposter syndrome isn't just personal development it's social transformation.
Every time someone from an underrepresented background steps into visibility without shrinking, they challenge centuries of conditioning about who gets to lead, create, and belong.
That's not just courage; that's reclamation.

So, if you've ever found yourself hesitating to step forward because you fear being "too much," "not enough," or simply "different," I want you to know this:
Your difference is not a deficit. It's your distinction.
And the moment you stop performing for acceptance and start leading from authenticity, fear begins to lose its power.
Because you're no longer waiting to belong, you're defining belonging on your own terms.

Coaching Reflection: Identity, Fear, and Belonging

Take a few quiet minutes for this reflection.
These prompts are designed to help you uncover how your *background, culture, or lived experience* might be shaping your relationship with success, visibility, and self-belief.
Write freely, without editing. The goal isn't perfection, it's honesty.

1. **When I think about success, what emotions come up for me, excitement, pressure, guilt, fear?**

What do those emotions remind me of from earlier in life, family expectations, cultural lessons, past experiences of being "different"?

2. **Whose standards of success have I been trying to live up to?**

Are they mine, or were they inherited from my upbringing, community, or workplace culture?

3. **What messages did I receive about visibility and humility growing up?**

Was I taught to stay modest, to avoid standing out, to "keep my head down"? How might that shape the way I approach opportunity today?

4. **Where in my life do I still feel like I need permission to be fully myself?**

What would it look like to give myself that permission instead of waiting for it?

5. **If I could redefine success in a way that aligns with my identity, my values, and my truth, what would it look like?**

Who would I be if I stopped performing and started leading as my whole self?

6. **What support or community do I need to sustain this version of success?**

Who reminds me I belong, even when I doubt myself?

The work of unlearning fear and imposter syndrome isn't about becoming fearless.

It's about remembering that you were never an imposter in the first place, you were simply walking through systems that weren't designed with you in mind.

Your presence is not the proof of an exception; it's the evidence of expansion.

And every time you choose to show up fully, accent, story, identity, truth, you make more space for others to do the same.

That's the kind of leadership this world needs more of.
Not performative confidence but embodied courage.
The courage to belong to yourself first, and to lead from that place of grounded truth.

The fear of success can also stir fears of alienation. Imagine someone who spent much of their life overlooked or undervalued. When they finally achieve recognition a promotion, an award, a platform, the achievement itself isn't what unsettles them. It's the implications. "Will people expect more of me than I can give? Will colleagues or friends resent me? Will I lose the closeness I once had?" Instead of celebrating the win, they shrink from it, downplay it, or even sabotage it. Better to stay where things feel familiar, they tell themselves, than to risk success becoming the thing that cuts them off from others.

The fear of success can also be rooted in responsibility. To succeed is often to carry more weight decisions, risks, accountability. For someone uneasy with pressure, or who doubts their resilience, success can feel like a trap rather than a triumph. I've seen people turn down leadership roles, not because they lacked the ability, but because they were afraid of the burden. They told themselves, "I just prefer to stay hands-on," or "I value work-life balance," when underneath was a fear of being responsible if things went wrong.

The paradox is clear: the fear of failure stops you from starting, while the fear of success can stop you once you've started. Both pull from the same root the stories you tell yourself about your worth and your capacity to handle the weight of life. Together, they create a prison of hesitation. You never climb the ladder for fear of falling, or you stop halfway up for fear of what's at the top. Either way, potential is left untouched.

The architecture of this fear is often built in the past. A child praised for their talent but isolated by it may learn that success equals loneliness. An adult who once achieved something only to face envy, pressure, or burnout may carry a subconscious equation: success = pain. So when opportunity arises again, resistance kicks in. It doesn't always look like fear it might look like "reasonable" excuses about balance, timing, or priorities. But beneath those reasons is often the same unease: a belief that success will cost too much.

Here's the truth: fear of success isn't weakness it's human. But unless you name it, it will quietly hold you back. The work is to ask yourself: "What am I really afraid success will take from me? What story am I telling myself about who I'll become if I achieve this?" Once you can answer honestly, you can begin to unpick the knot. Success doesn't have to equal pressure, isolation, or loss. It can mean growth, expansion, and opportunity if you're willing to confront the fear that says otherwise.

Another side to the fear of success is the way it can make us feel like we're losing who we are. If you've spent years seeing yourself as the underdog, the hard worker still climbing, or the quiet one in the corner, then stepping into success can feel disorientating. You're no longer the person fighting to get noticed now you are noticed. That shift can be unsettling.

Sarah and I worked together through a series of **executive coaching sessions**, not to "fix" her fear, but to understand its language. Fear always has a logic; you just have to learn how to listen to it.

In those sessions, I guided Sarah through a process of slowing down, naming, and reframing, the same core approach I use with many of my clients who are standing on the edge of growth. We explored what her fear of success was really protecting. For her, it wasn't the fear of being unprepared or incapable, it was the fear of losing her sense of belonging.

As her visibility grew, she worried she'd outgrow her circles, that the intimacy and familiarity she valued would be replaced by distance, envy, or misunderstanding. These are not unusual fears, they're deeply human ones. For many high-performing professionals, success feels like stepping out onto a stage you never auditioned for. You're proud but exposed. Seen, but scrutinised.

In coaching, we used practical reflection tools to help Sarah ground herself in her values, rather than her anxieties. Together, we reframed success not as *a departure* from who she was, but *a continuation* of who she'd always been.

We explored questions like:

- What parts of you are afraid of being seen, and what parts are ready to be known?
- What relationships do you fear success might test, and what if they evolve instead of end?
- How can you build internal safety so that external recognition doesn't shake your foundation?

Over time, Sarah built what I call *emotional infrastructure for growth* the mindset, boundaries, and inner steadiness that allow you to expand without losing yourself. By the time her book launched, she wasn't chasing validation anymore; she was standing in alignment. She wasn't trying to prove her worth — she was expressing it.

That's what **coaching** can do when it's done well. It helps you see what's driving your hesitation, reframe fear into information, and move forward with clarity and confidence. Whether it's launching a project, stepping into leadership, or navigating change, the goal isn't to silence fear, but to help you lead with it, rather than from it.

Fear of Success Reflection: Are you holding yourself back from your own growth?

Take a few moments to reflect on the following prompts. Write your answers honestly, without judgment. You might be surprised by what surfaces.

1. **Where in your life are you hesitating, even though part of you knows you're ready?**
2. **What do you imagine might change if you succeed and which of those changes do you secretly fear?**
3. **What story does your fear tell you about success?** (e.g., *"It will make me isolated," "It will make me arrogant," "It will make me lose balance."*)
4. **Now, rewrite that story through the lens of truth.** (e.g., *"Success will connect me to my purpose," "Success will expand what's possible," "Success will allow me to help others grow."*)
5. **Finally, ask yourself:** What's one small step I could take this week to move towards the thing I've been delaying?

Remember, courage doesn't come from ignoring fear, it comes from understanding it.

And that's the essence of this work: moving from hesitation to harmony, from fear-driven avoidance to purpose-driven action.

If you recognise yourself in Sarah's story, successful on the surface, but quietly stuck at the edge of your next chapter, you're not alone.

I've coached countless leaders, entrepreneurs, and creatives through this exact crossroads.

The truth is, fear doesn't mean you're unready, it means you're standing in front of something that matters.

And the work we do together in coaching is about helping you *step into that space with courage, clarity, and conviction.*

Adaptive Pathways for Neurodivergent Bravery
(A Special Note on Fear, Courage, and the Neurodivergent Mind)

Courage is universal in essence, but deeply individual in expression. Whilst the framework in this book, unmasking fear, tracing its anatomy, acting through discomfort, and building courageous habits speaks to human patterns we all share, it's crucial to recognise that the experience of fear is not uniform.

For many neurodivergent individuals, including those who are autistic, ADHD, dyslexic, dyspraxic, or have other forms of non-typical cognitive or sensory processing fear may represent only *one aspect* of a much broader lived experience. In such cases, the sensations of fear can intertwine with sensory overload, executive-function challenges, working-memory strain, or emotional dysregulation, physiological and neurological realities that shape how fear feels, when it arises, and how it's best supported.

As researcher and occupational therapist Winnie Dunn observes, sensory systems play a direct role in emotional regulation; when environments are unpredictable or overstimulating, the body's stress response can activate long before conscious thought (Dunn, 1997, *American Journal of Occupational Therapy*). Similarly, studies on executive functioning in ADHD and ASD populations, such as those by Kofler et al. (2019) and Barkley (2014) reveal that short-term memory limitations, time blindness, and processing delays can heighten the sense of threat or self-doubt. Fear, in these cases, is often the *visible symptom* of a much deeper physiological imbalance.

This understanding reframes fear not as a flaw of willpower, but as a *signal* within a complex neurobiological system. As such, while overcoming fear is possible, the **journey varies greatly from person to person**. It is important to note that for some, courage means confrontation and exposure; for others, it begins with *stabilising the nervous system* and *reducing environmental load* so bravery becomes accessible at all. This distinction matters deeply: it transforms courage from a moral performance into a physiological partnership with the self.

Fear and Anxiety: The Statistical Landscape

Fear behaves differently in neurodivergent minds, not because it is weaker or stronger, but because it moves through different pathways. Research consistently shows that neurodivergent individuals experience significantly higher rates of anxiety and fear-based responses than the general population.

A systematic review by van Steensel, Bögels, and Perrin (2011) found that approximately 40% of children with Autism Spectrum Disorder (ASD) meet diagnostic criteria for at least one anxiety disorder, nearly three times the rate among neurotypical children (*Clinical Child and Family Psychology Review*, PMC5764108). Similarly, Hollocks et al. (2019) reported that among autistic adults, prevalence rates of anxiety range between **27–42%**, over twice that of non-autistic peers (*Psychological Medicine*, PMC6946757). In ADHD populations, Kessler et al. (2006)

identified anxiety comorbidity rates between **30–50%** in adults (*American Journal of Psychiatry*). The CDC (2023) also notes that nearly **4 in 10 children with ADHD** experience diagnosable anxiety.

These figures reveal something vital: for neurodivergent individuals, fear rarely travels alone. It often arrives entwined with sensory overload, executive dysfunction, or chronic vigilance, a physiological readiness that has nothing to do with choice and everything to do with neurology. When we talk about *fear's disguises* in this book perfectionism, avoidance, overthinking, for neurodivergent people, those masks may reach deeper. They can reflect not only learned psychological patterns but the embodied vigilance of navigating a world built for different nervous systems.

Sensory Overload, Uncertainty, and the Body's Fear Circuit

Traditional models of courage often centre on reframing thought, changing the story we tell ourselves about fear. For many neurodivergent individuals, fear is not simply cognitive; it is *somatic*. It lives in the body in the heartbeat that accelerates before words can form, in the muscles that tighten without command, in the brain's circuitry firing signals of danger long before logic catches up.

In neurotypical models, fear is typically seen as a misfiring of perception, a story exaggerated by the mind. But for neurodivergent people, especially autistic and ADHD individuals, the story often begins *in the sensory system itself*. The world can arrive louder, brighter, faster, and more chaotic than the nervous system is designed to process. Studies by **Cardon et al.** (2023) found a strong link between **sensory hyperreactivity**, **intolerance of uncertainty**, and **anticipatory anxiety** in autistic adults (*Frontiers in Psychology*, PMC10361392).

Similarly, Green and Ben-Sasson (2010) discovered that more than 80% of autistic individuals experience sensory hyperreactivity that triggers physiological fear responses indistinguishable from the classic fight-or-flight state (*Research in Autism Spectrum Disorders*). Neuroscientifically, this is the body's amygdala-hypothalamic-adrenal (HPA) axis in action. This is a feedback loop designed to keep us alive by signalling danger. But when sensory input becomes overwhelming, that system remains active longer than it should. The brain floods with cortisol. The vagus nerve, which helps the body return to calm, struggles to regulate. The body remains "on," even when there is no visible threat, a condition described by Stephen Porges (2011) in the *Polyvagal Theory* as "neuroception of danger." For many neurodivergent individuals, this heightened state of arousal isn't episodic, it's *daily life*. A flickering light in an office, the hum of an air conditioner, a perfume in a crowded train, each can provoke a cascade of reactions invisible to others but deeply consuming to the body. Over time, that physiological vigilance becomes an emotional one: an expectation that the world will overwhelm.

This is why courage cannot always begin in the mind. You cannot *reframe* a sensory overload any more than you can meditate away a fire alarm. You must first quiet the environment before you can quiet the brain. For some, bravery looks like adjusting the lighting, muting the noise, or introducing routine, not as a means of control, but of safety, psychological safety, something that is often overlooked in society but also in the workplace. Predictability becomes the scaffolding that allows exploration. A calm nervous system becomes the soil from which authentic courage grows.

In this sense, *self-regulation is the first act of bravery*. To listen to your body, to modify your surroundings, to design your world to fit your neurology these are not accommodations, they are expressions of agency. They are how you teach your body that the world can be safe enough to try again. Stephen Porges notes that safety is not the absence of threat but the presence of cues that tell the nervous system it can rest. For neurodivergent individuals, courage begins precisely there, in the quiet work of teaching the body how to rest.

This notion of psychological safety brings me back to early 2025 when the **Group Head of Diversity and Inclusion** at a global company specialising in **airport experiences, travel loyalty, and customer engagement** reached out to me to deliver a series of workshops on *psychological safety* as part of their *Mental Health at Work* campaign.

From the very beginning, I approached the work the way I always do, with listening first. Before a single slide was written, I spent time understanding their company culture, the pressures of their industry, and the lived realities of their people. The D&I lead shared details about their internal wellbeing policies and employee networks, and I wove those into the content so that the sessions wouldn't feel abstract or theoretical, but grounded and familiar.

My aim was simple: to make psychological safety tangible, something leaders and employees could feel, practise, and replicate, not just talk about. Over the course of a month, I delivered multiple sessions across global teams. Some were small and intimate; others had over a hundred participants. Regardless of size, I treated each space as an experiment in safety. I began every session with a short grounding reflection, an invitation for people to pause, breathe, and check in with themselves. Then I asked a question: *What does safety feel like here?*

That one question opened the room. People began sharing stories, about belonging, about burnout, about moments they'd felt unseen. Senior leaders, often the most guarded in these conversations, started speaking with humility and honesty. You could feel the temperature of the space shift, from performance to permission. Even in virtual sessions with hundreds of faces on-screen, there was stillness, presence. A collective exhale, that's when I realised that safety isn't a luxury, it's infrastructure. It's what makes learning, creativity, and courage possible.

After the final session, the D&I Head shared this feedback with me:

"Romain delivered multiple sessions for us during a month-long Mental Health at Work campaign. Collaboration in the run-up to the sessions was great. Romain took time to understand the needs of our company, and allowed me to share specific details (such as policies and employee networks) that he incorporated into his content. Delivery was great, Romain created open spaces for people to reflect, providing opportunities for engagement throughout, despite some group sizes being over 100 people. Feedback has been really positive."

That reflection stayed with me, because what this experience reinforced is that psychological safety isn't just about kindness, it's about courage. The courage to lead without armour. The courage to tell the truth, even when the truth is uncomfortable. And the courage to design systems that make vulnerability possible. Fear thrives in silence, but when safety is present, courage becomes contagious.

So if courage is a practice, then for neurodivergent individuals, it must be a *supported* practice, one structured not around conformity, but around *rhythm, regulation, and recovery*. For years, society has praised the idea of "facing your fears" as a solitary act of willpower, but courage without context can easily become cruelty. For those whose nervous systems process the world differently, the challenge is not simply *doing more* or *pushing harder*. It's about creating conditions where bravery is *possible*, where the mind and body can safely collaborate rather than collide. True courage, in this sense, is *adaptive*. It meets you where you are and grows with you, not against you.

Adaptation Strategies Supported by Research

The practice of courage, for neurodivergent minds, must be both evidence-informed and compassion-driven. Research across psychology, occupational therapy, and neuroscience consistently demonstrates that bravery grows not from grand gestures, but from *small, structured acts repeated in safety*.

1. Short, Repeatable Exposures: The Science of Micro-Bravery

Psychologists have long emphasised that fear extinction, the gradual reduction of anxiety through exposure works best when paired with predictability, safety, and repetition. **Craske et al. (2014)** found that *graded exposure* facing manageable doses of discomfort rewires the brain's fear circuitry far more effectively than "flooding" or forced confrontation (*Behaviour Research and Therapy*). For neurodivergent individuals, this means *micro-bravery* is not a compromise, it's the optimal path.

- Speaking once in a meeting
- Attending an event for ten minutes.
- Sending the email draft instead of perfecting it endlessly.

Each small step trains the nervous system to tolerate uncertainty, teaching the body: *"I survived this — I can try again."* Courage, then, is not built in leaps; it's built in layers.

2. Environmental Design: Building Courage from the Outside In

Occupational therapist **Winnie Dunn's (1997)** *Sensory Processing Framework* demonstrated that the environment is never neutral, it either soothes or overstimulates the nervous system. For neurodivergent individuals, courage often begins outside the body: in the lighting of a room, the noise level of an office, or the predictability of transitions.

Changing harsh fluorescent bulbs to warm light, reducing background chatter, or creating quiet zones aren't indulgences; they're neurobiological supports. Dunn's research showed that environmental modification can dramatically alter anxiety and engagement, because only when the sensory world feels safe, the nervous system can finally exhale and relax.

In practice, this means courage isn't always an internal breakthrough; it's often an *external redesign*.

Using noise-cancelling headphones, scheduling breaks between meetings, or arranging seating to reduce visual clutter are not signs of weakness, they're strategies of self-preservation. If the brain perceives constant threat through sensory input, no amount of positive thinking can override the alarm. When we build sensory safety into our environments, we stop demanding heroism just to function.

For neurodivergent minds, adjusting the environment is not avoidance, it's wisdom. Courage, in this sense, sometimes begins with a single question: **What does my body need to feel safe enough to try?**

3. Cognitive Scaffolding: The Architecture of Courage

Executive dysfunction is one of the most under-acknowledged barriers to courage. When the mind struggles to sequence, plan, or transition, even the simplest task can activate a fear response. It's not laziness or avoidance, it's cognitive overload. Beardon and Edmonds (2007) found that consistent external supports visual prompts, written checklists, structured routines, significantly reduce anxiety and decision fatigue in autistic adults. Their research revealed something profound: when we externalise organisation, we internalise calm.

Cognitive scaffolding transforms *overwhelm* into *order*. In courage terms, it's not hand-holding, it's architecture. Each scaffold frees mental space for emotional presence, allowing bravery to feel less like chaos and more like choreography.

True courage, then, can be designed. It's not about independence at all costs, but about creating interdependence, systems that hold us steady while we stretch.

In practical terms, this might look like:

- Using scripts or sentence starters for difficult conversations.
- Preparing agenda notes before meetings to minimise processing overload.
- Chunking goals into smaller steps to turn ambition into achievable rhythm.

Neurodivergent courage is rarely spontaneous — it's engineered through thoughtful design.

And in that design lies its genius: when structure supports the mind, the heart finally has room to be brave.

4. Rest as Resistance: The Physiology of Recovery

In neurotypical culture, rest is often framed as a pause from productivity, a reward granted after exertion. But for neurodivergent people, especially those masking daily to navigate environments that weren't built for their neurology, rest is not a pause; it's *repair*.

Mazurek et al. (2012) documented high rates of chronic fatigue and emotional burnout among autistic adults, not from laziness, but from *constant adaptation* (Journal of Autism and Developmental Disorders). The ongoing demand to "keep up" in neurotypical spaces depletes energy faster than it can be restored. Every conversation, sensory adjustment, or self-editing act becomes micro-exertion. Over time, this doesn't just tire the body, it fractures the self. Recovery, then, is not optional, it is the maintenance of identity, the process by which the nervous system reclaims coherence. To rest intentionally, to switch off the demand to perform, is not withdrawal from courage; it is courage in action.

As **Tricia Hersey (2022)** writes in her book Rest is Resistance:

"Rest is a form of justice. It is a reclaiming of our bodies from systems that have taught us to view exhaustion as a virtue."

For neurodivergent individuals, rest is precisely that *reclamation* and resistance. It's an act of defiance against a culture that equates constant activity with worth and silence with strength. Rest says: *My nervous system needs peace, not performance.* To rest is to resist the mythology of endless resilience. It's to honour the cycles of energy, overstimulation, and recovery that shape neurodivergent experience and it's to remember that courage cannot thrive in depletion.

In this light, bravery looks different.
It looks like scheduling downtime without guilt.
Leaving overstimulating environments early.
Unapologetically declining commitments that compromise recovery.
Protecting your rest becomes protecting your truth.

Because real courage doesn't demand burnout as proof of effort, it demands compassion as proof of understanding. when rest becomes part of the practice, not a pause from it, we stop measuring strength by endurance and start defining it by awareness.

That is not weakness, its wisdom and it is, perhaps, the most radical act of all.

5. Body-Based Regulation: Courage That Starts in the Nervous System

Fear lives in the body and so does healing. When we treat courage as purely cognitive, we overlook its most essential foundation: the nervous system. As Stephen Porges explains in *The Polyvagal Theory*, the body's sense of safety is governed by the vagus nerve, which constantly scans the environment for signs of threat or security a process he calls *neuroception*. When we regulate the vagus nerve through rhythm, breath, or movement, we send a message to the body, *You are safe enough now*. This simple shift, from vigilance to regulation is where bravery truly begins.

For neurodivergent individuals, this regulation might not look like meditation or stillness.

It might look like deep pressure, stimming, rocking, pacing, or rhythmic motion, small, intuitive acts that recalibrate the body's internal alarm. These aren't distractions or quirks, they're *technologies of survival*, nervous system strategies refined through lived experience.

Courage cannot be sustained in a dysregulated body. A mind that feels unsafe cannot innovate, connect, or take healthy risks. That's why *body-based regulation*, sometimes called *"bottom-up"* processing, is the foundation of psychological safety. In therapeutic and coaching contexts, this approach emphasises calming the body first so that the mind can follow. Only then can executive functions like reflection, problem-solving, and communication return online.

Breathwork, rhythmic movement, grounding exercises, or even sensory tools (weighted blankets, fidget devices, music) activate the **ventral vagal state**, the body's physiological signal of connection and calm.

When the body feels anchored, the mind stops scanning for danger and when the mind feels safe, courage stops being an act of force and starts being an act of flow.

Sometimes courage begins not with the question, *"What should I do?"* but with a gentler one:
"How does safety feel in my body right now?"

A trembling hand doesn't need motivation, it needs grounding and grounding is not retreat. Grounding is the rehearsal space where bravery learns its rhythm.

Leadership and Systemic Courage

Fear doesn't just live in individuals, it lives in *institutions*. In workplaces, neurodivergent employees often face a quiet hierarchy of acceptable difference: be creative, but not too unconventional; speak up, but not too often; disclose, but only if it's convenient. In 2023 study by Birkbeck, University of London found that **65% of neurodivergent employees fear discrimination** at work even within organisations that publicly advocate inclusion. Clearly this is not an individual failure of confidence but a a systemic and institutional failure of safety.

So when leaders model vulnerability by acknowledging difference, allowing flexibility, or admitting uncertainty, they *redistribute safety*. They replace conformity with connection. This is what psychologist **Amy Edmondson (1999)** defined as *psychological safety*: an environment where individuals feel free to take interpersonal risks without fear of punishment or ridicule. Courage in leadership, is not about charisma, it's about *culture*. It's creating conditions where people don't have to be brave just to belong and where speaking truth isn't rebellion, but routine.

Reframing Courage Through a Neurodivergent Lens

What emerges from both research and lived experience is that for neurodivergent individuals, fear is not simply psychological; it is *physiological, environmental, and cultural.*

Traditional courage asks:

"How do I overcome my fear?"
Neurodivergent courage asks:
"How do I work with my fear while protecting my nervous system?"

The difference is profound. One demands denial; the other invites dialogue.

As **Dr. Devon Price** writes in *Unmasking Autism* (2022):

"The goal is not to make the world less frightening by changing yourself, it's to make your life more yours."

That, ultimately, is the essence of bravery, not erasing difference, but embracing it as the site of power. Because courage is not about pushing harder through systems that harm; it's about *building systems that heal.* When we design courage around regulation instead of repression, inclusion instead of imitation, we don't just create safer people, we create safer worlds.

If your nervous system speaks a different language, courage will have a different accent.
It might not roar; it might whisper.
It might not stand tall; it might rest deeply.

But wherever it lives in you, in the boundary you hold, the truth you tell, the mask you set down know this:

That, too, is courage.

Because bravery was never about volume, it was about honesty. The courage that honours your nervous system - your pace, your rhythm, your truth, is not a smaller version of bravery. It is the most authentic form of it.

Fear as an Identity

I've seen people cling to their old identity, even when it holds them back. They downplay their wins, stay deferential when assertiveness is needed, or avoid leadership opportunities altogether because the role of "leader" feels alien. The fear here isn't about failing at success but about losing the self you've grown used to.

Fear, over time, can become a kind of identity. It doesn't just sit in your chest or whisper in your ear, it seeps into your habits, your tone, your posture, your choices. You begin to confuse it with personality. You start to think that playing small is just who you are. You call it "being realistic," "staying humble," or "not wanting to cause a fuss." But what you're really saying is, *I've learned to live with fear so long, I no longer know who I'd be without it.*

When you've spent years in environments that reward compliance and punish boldness, fear becomes a form of self-preservation. You learn to read the room before you speak, to soften your ideas, to shrink your brilliance so it doesn't threaten anyone else's comfort. You learn that invisibility can be safer than being seen. And so fear takes root, not just as a feeling, but as a framework for being.

It becomes woven into your sense of self. You stop saying *I'm afraid* and start saying *I'm just not that type of person*. You start believing that leadership, confidence, or courage belong to other people, the louder ones, the chosen ones, the ones who seem built for visibility. But the truth is, fear has trained you to forget the fullness of who you are.

Many of us were taught to wear fear like a uniform. Especially if you grew up in a world that told you to "stay in your lane," to "know your place," or to "be grateful for what you have." You start to internalise limitation as identity. You become fluent in self-censorship. You tell yourself, *I'm just cautious,* but what you really mean is, *I've learned that safety matters more than self-expression.* Fear starts to shape your choices, your voice, your very rhythm in the world.

And because it's familiar, you begin to find comfort in it. Predictability feels like peace, even when it's quietly suffocating you. You know how to navigate fear it's the unknown that terrifies you. Success demands expansion, but expansion means exposure. It means new rooms, new responsibilities, new risks, and so, you cling to what you know, even if it hurts.

But identity built on fear is brittle. It cracks under the weight of growth. It keeps you safe from rejection, but also from recognition. It protects you from embarrassment, but also from evolution. It convinces you that control is freedom, when in truth, it's a cage with your name carved into the walls.

There's a point where you realise: the version of yourself that once protected you can't take you any further. You can honour that version, the one who learned to stay quiet, to survive, to observe, but you cannot let them lead your future. Fear might have built your foundation, but courage is what finishes the house.

The moment you begin to separate *who you are* from *what you fear*, something begins to shift. You start to see fear not as a reflection of identity, but as a residue of experience something you can wash off, heal through, rise beyond, and in that moment of awareness, power returns to you.

Because the truth is, most people aren't afraid of failure they're afraid of transformation. They're afraid that success will demand they shed too much the relationships, the personas, the protective shells. But growth always involves a kind of grief. You must mourn who you were before you can become who you're meant to be.

That's why stepping into leadership, visibility, or authenticity can feel so disorienting. It's not just that you're moving toward something new, you're also moving away from something familiar. The silence that once kept you safe now feels suffocating. The modesty that once felt noble now feels like self-erasure.

To outgrow fear as an identity is to rewrite the narrative of yourself. It's to say: *I am not my hesitation. I am not my self-doubt. I am the one who learned to survive it, and now, I'm learning to live beyond it.*

And that's the work. Not to eliminate fear, but to stop worshipping it. To see it for what it is a shadow cast by old experiences, and to choose, every day, to walk toward the light that reveals who you really are.

And it's not just personal identity at play society feeds into this too. We're told to strive, to push, to aim high, but the moment someone achieves something big, there can be suspicion, envy, or even backlash. Think of "tall poppy syndrome" the idea that anyone who stands out will be cut down. Many of us absorb that message early on: don't shine too brightly, or you'll become a target. That fear of drawing attention, of attracting criticism, can lead us to shrink ourselves tempering our achievements, deflecting praise, keeping a low profile even when our work deserves recognition. In this way, success itself becomes threatening, not because of what it is, but because of what we imagine it will draw towards us.

This tug of war between fearing failure and fearing success really shows how much we crave safety. The fear of failure shields us from the sting of "not good enough." The fear of success shields us from the upheaval and pressure that achievement might bring. Both are protective in their own way, but both are also limiting. One stops us starting, the other stops us stepping fully into what we've earned. To move forward, we need to confront both: the fear of falling and the fear of soaring. That means building resilience not just for setbacks, but also for growth because both come with their own challenges.

The fear of success is really the fear of the unknown. We fear what we don't know, and for a lot of us, success feels more foreign than failure. Failure we can handle, we've all been there, we know what it looks like. But success? That's different. It asks you to step outside your comfort zone, to carry new responsibilities, to make sacrifices, to change routines you've clung to for years. And you fear all of it, the pressure, the loneliness, the disruption, the possibility that success could cost you more than you're ready to give. But if we're honest, the real fear isn't just about the demands of success. It's about you. Deep down, you don't really believe in yourself, do you? That's why you fear it. Because if you did succeed, you'd have to face the truth you've been running from: that you were always capable. And if you fail after all that? That thought feels heavier than never trying at all.

The Inheritance of Fear: Childhood Trauma, Cognitive Dissonance, and the Architecture of Safety

Fear is not only emotional; it is architectural. It lives in the structures of the mind, the wiring of the body, and the blueprints passed down through generations. Before it becomes thought, fear is chemistry, cortisol in the bloodstream, adrenaline in the gut, the nervous system deciding whether the world is safe or not.

The Biology of Fear and Trauma: The Body as Archive

When a child grows up in an environment marked by unpredictability where love comes and goes, or safety is conditional, the nervous system reorganises itself to survive. This is not metaphor; it's neuroplasticity. The **Adverse Childhood Experiences (ACE) Study** (Felitti et al., 1998) revealed how early adversity is not merely psychological but physiological. Children exposed to chronic stress develop an overactive **amygdala** (the brain's fear centre) and a weakened **prefrontal cortex** (responsible for executive regulation). In plain terms: their brains learn to detect danger faster than they can reason through it. Repeated activation of the **HPA axis**, the hypothalamic-pituitary-adrenal system floods the body with stress hormones. Over time, this leads to what neuroendocrinologist **Bruce McEwen (2007)** calls *allostatic load*: the price the body pays for constant adaptation. It shows up as anxiety, hypervigilance, difficulty sleeping, even autoimmune disorders.

As **Bessel van der Kolk** wrote in *The Body Keeps the Score* (2014):

"Trauma results in a fundamental reorganization of the way mind and brain manage perceptions. It changes not only how we think and what we think about, but also our very capacity to think."

Trauma literally teaches the body to anticipate threat, even in safety.
For some, it manifests as fight - irritability, control, perfectionism. For others, it's flight - overworking, pleasing, escaping into busyness.

For others still, it's freeze or fawn - silence, compliance, self-erasure.

These aren't character flaws. They are the body's long-term strategies for staying alive.

The Polyvagal Lens: The Science of Safety

As we saw earlier on in this chapter, the polyvagal theory first introduced by **Dr. Stephen Porges (2011)**, deepens our understanding of this dynamic. It teaches that the vagus nerve, a vast, branching network connecting brain to body, which regulates how we respond to stress. When we feel safe, the *ventral vagal system* engages heart rate slows, digestion resumes, we connect, speak, create. When threatened, the *sympathetic system* activates heart races, muscles tense, focus narrows. If the threat persists, we drop into *dorsal vagal shutdown*: numbness, fatigue, disconnection.

In trauma, this ladder of safety gets stuck.
The body can no longer climb back up.

Psychologist **Deb Dana (2018)** calls this *"the science of feeling safe."* Without safety, courage is impossible and so the work of healing fear is not simply mental reprogramming, it's *nervous system retraining*. To teach the body, slowly and consistently, that the present is not the past.

Safety, in this sense, is not a concept.
It's a practice.

It's the breath you take before speaking truth, the unclenched jaw in a hard conversation, the heartbeat that steadies when you remember you're no longer in danger.

The Psychology of Dissonance: When two opposites like Love and Fear Coexist

If the body stores trauma, the mind must make sense of it, often through distortion. This is where **cognitive dissonance** enters: the mental conflict that arises when two opposing truths collide. **Leon Festinger (1957)** first defined it as the tension between belief and behaviour, but in trauma, dissonance lives deeper. For a child who depends on a caregiver who is also a source of fear, two realities coexist:

"The person who loves me also hurts me."

That's too painful to hold, so the child's psyche resolves the

contradiction by internalising blame:

"It must be my fault."
"If I am quieter, better, more pleasing, I'll be safe."

This psychic bargain preserves attachment but installs a lifelong undercurrent of self-doubt, the foundation of perfectionism, people-pleasing, and self-criticism. As psychoanalyst **Donald Winnicott (1965)** described in his theory of the *False Self*, when authenticity feels dangerous, the child constructs a version of self that prioritises approval over truth.

Later, psychologist **Alice Miller (1981)** in *The Drama of the Gifted Child* called this adaptation "a survival of love."

She wrote:

"When we are children, we cannot bear to know that our parents do not love us as we need. So we learn to adapt, to anticipate, to please. In that adaptation, we lose contact with the authentic self."

Fear, in this sense, becomes not only a reaction, but an identity. We don't just *feel* afraid; we *become* the strategies that kept us safe.

Trauma in the Blood: Epigenetics and Fear as Social Inheritance

Fear is one of the oldest languages we speak, and like all languages, we learn it from those who came before us. But who teaches us its vocabulary, and how fluently we speak it, depends on where we stand in the world. We inherit not just fear itself, but the rules that come with it, the silent codes passed down through generations, written in glances, warnings, and what goes unsaid.

A mother tells her Black son how to keep his hands visible when stopped by police. A working class parent warns their child to "keep your head down at work, don't draw attention." Each lesson is love disguised as caution. Each one says: *this is how we stay alive here.*

For those living at the intersections of identity, fear is not only emotional, it's instructional.

It becomes a manual for survival, but a kind of ancestral technology also designed to anticipate harm before it arrives.

Over time, those lessons become muscle memory. They live in posture, in silence, in the subtle restraint of a laugh that doesn't feel safe to be too loud.

In some families, fear travels like folklore, stories told to keep the next generation safe. In others, it travels through silence the things never spoken but always felt. Either way, it leaves fingerprints on how we show up in the world.

We inherit more than memories, we inherit the biological echoes of survival. Nowhere is that inheritance more profound than in the experience of **childhood trauma** the first teacher of fear, and often, the last one we learn to unlearn.

In the last two decades, the field of **epigenetics** has transformed how we understand inheritance. It reveals that trauma doesn't rewrite DNA, but it changes how genes *express themselves*.

In a groundbreaking 2016 study, **Rachel Yehuda** and colleagues found that children of Holocaust survivors carried **altered methylation** in the *FKBP5* gene, which governs the stress response (*Biological Psychiatry*, 2016). Similarly, **Tobi et al. (2009)** discovered comparable changes among descendants of the Dutch Famine. This means the body can inherit *biological memories of fear*. Sociologist and therapist **Resmaa Menakem** writes in *My Grandmother's Hands* (2017):

"The body remembers what the mind cannot. Trauma decontextualised in a person looks like personality. Trauma decontextualised in a people looks like culture."

Our families don't just pass down stories, they pass down stress responses. A grandmother's silence becomes a mother's worry becomes a child's perfectionism. Each generation refines the mask, calling it responsibility, discipline, or composure when, in truth, it's inheritance disguised as personality.

Not every fear you carry belongs to you. Whilst some of it may born from your own failures, heartbreaks, and disappointments, some of it isn't yours at all. It's inherited, handed down like an heirloom, stitched into the fabric of your upbringing, reinforced by culture, whispered in family sayings, and rooted in history.

We don't always see it at first because it hides in plain sight. It sounds like wisdom, like caution, like love:

- Keep your head down.
- Don't give them a reason to notice you.
- Be twice as good if you want half the chance.
- Don't aim too high disappointment will crush you.

I've heard every single one of those in my own life. Maybe you have too. They sound like protection, and at one time, they were.

But underneath each one sits a deeper message: *fear*. The kind of fear that once kept our parents, grandparents, and communities safe but which, unexamined, now keeps us small.

I've heard every single one of those in my own life. Maybe you have too.
They sound like protection and at one time, they were.
But underneath each one sits a deeper message: fear.

The kind of fear that once kept our parents, grandparents, and communities safe, but which, unexamined, now keeps us small.

I think of my grandmother, her mornings beginning before the sun, starching blouses until they stood stiff as armour. She never left the house without her hair pressed, her shoes shined, her back straight. Not because she wanted to impress anyone, but because she knew that to be seen as neat was to be seen as worthy. Respectability was her shield, she carried it like scripture just as she carried her Holy Bible. To her, dignity was survival, not luxury. Her generation learned that the slightest crack in composure could be misread as threat, laziness, or defiance. So, she became fluent in composure. It was the language that kept her safe even if it cost her the comfort of being fully herself. But *every generation translates fear differently.* My grandmother's fear was quiet, polished and polite, dressed in Sunday best and measured speech. It taught her children that to survive in Britain was to blend, to be impeccable, to never give anyone reason to doubt your worth. But her children, my mother, uncles, and aunts inherited that fear and reshaped it into something else. They were born in a new Britain, one rebuilt by their parents' hands yet still reluctant to claim them. Theirs was a generation raised on endurance but hungry for change, the bridge between survival and self-definition.

I think about my mother, my uncle, and my aunt, all from the same generation. The descendants of the Windrush pioneers. The first to be born in Britain, the first to be called Black British. They were the children of citizens Britain once invited but never fully embraced. They grew up straddling two worlds, raised in a Jamaican household with British accents and British passports, but constantly reminded they didn't quite belong to either. Too British for their parents' islands, too foreign and 'othered' for the country of their birth.

I call them the generation of resilience and protest.

They were less passive than their parents who some of they criticised and saw as willing to bow to the quiet dignity of endurance. Their resistance looked different: sharper, louder, more visible. They were the ones who marched, organised, studied, and challenged. They built the infrastructure of Black Britain, from the supplementary Saturday schools that taught children their history, to the community centres that fed and protected families when institutions refused to.

They created poetry that spoke of pride, music that roared of belonging, movements that demanded justice. The Mangrove Nine, the Brixton and Broadwater Farm (Tottenham) Uprising, the Notting Hill Carnival, these weren't just moments of defiance, they were manifestations of resistance and declarations of identity and belonging. They refused invisibility. They learned to turn rage into rhythm and protest into power.

Yet, even as they pushed back against injustice, they still carried the residue of fear, that generational whisper of caution that came from watching their parents navigate a country that smiled at their labour but frowned at their presence.

They were raised by survivors, and survival leaves marks.

They inherited both the courage to fight and the caution to endure.
They were taught to speak up, but only so far. To dream, but not too loud.

That's where my mother stood, between her mother's silence and her own simmering voice.

I think of my mother, who stayed in jobs where she was overworked and underpaid, telling me she didn't want to "cause trouble." What she really meant was: I've seen what happens when we speak up. Her generation learned that survival sometimes meant swallowing words that burned your throat. It's why so many of us inherited that carefulness, that quiet calculation before we say what we really think.

I think of my uncle, who turned down a promotion because he said, "I don't want the stress."
But the truth was, he didn't want the scrutiny. He didn't want to be the only one in the room, again, explaining himself, proving himself, carrying the weight of representation. His fear was never about incompetence, it was about exhaustion, and when exhaustion lasts long enough, it starts to disguise itself as contentment.

And then there's me, and maybe you.
Sitting in a meeting with an idea burning at the back of your throat, but you hesitate.
You tell yourself it's strategy, "I'm waiting for the right time."

But really, it's inheritance. You can still hear the echoes of the generations before you whispering, *be careful, don't stand out, don't make them uncomfortable.*

We carry these voices like heirlooms, passed down in tone, in caution, in instinct. They live in how we walk into a room, how we introduce ourselves, how we apologise for simply existing too boldly. We inherit fear not because our ancestors were weak, but because they were wise enough to survive a world that demanded their restraint.
They taught us how to endure.
But endurance is not the same as freedom.

Their fear was love in disguise, a language of protection spoken through warnings.
"Don't speak too loud."
"Be grateful for what you have."
"Keep your head down and work twice as hard."
Those were survival codes, not life goals.
And yet, somewhere along the way, we began to mistake them for identity.

Because when fear gets passed down often enough, it becomes culture.
And culture, if left unexamined becomes truth.
We begin to build our lives around old rules, old anxieties, old ghosts.
We limit ourselves not because we lack courage, but because we've been trained to prioritise safety over self-expression.

Maybe your version looks different.

Maybe you've stayed in a job that no longer fits because stability feels safer than uncertainty.

Maybe you've downplayed your achievements because confidence was called arrogance in your household.

Maybe you've hidden parts of your identity because you were taught that visibility invites danger.

Maybe you've apologised for being ambitious because you feared being labelled "too much."

Whatever your version, the root is the same: fear that started as love.

Fear that once protected us but now confines us.

And here's the tragedy, that inherited fear can look noble. It can even win applause.

We praise ourselves for being humble, for not "making waves," for being the dependable one. But sometimes what we call humility is really hesitation.

Sometimes what we call modesty is really learned invisibility.

And sometimes what we call wisdom is really trauma dressed in grown-up language.

These stories, our grandmother's starch, our mother's silence, our father's restraint, they're not just individual anecdotes. They're cultural artefacts, evidence of a collective strategy for survival in a world that didn't see our full humanity.

But we don't live in their world anymore.

And yet, we still live by their rules.

That's the quiet violence of inherited fear, it outlives its purpose. It builds walls long after the danger has passed.

So the question becomes: how long will we keep obeying fear that isn't even ours?
How long will we let inherited caution dictate the size of our dreams?

There's a moment in every life when you realise you've been loyal to a version of safety that no longer serves you. That the fear that once kept your grandmother alive is now keeping you stuck.
That the voice in your head saying "be careful" is not your intuition, it's your inheritance.

And when that moment comes, you face a choice.
You can keep carrying the old protection like a relic, or you can lay it down and build something new not out of fear, but out of faith.
Because fear may have built our foundations, but it's courage that must finish the house.
We are the generation that gets to do what they couldn't, not because we are braver, but because they made it possible.
Their survival gave us space to dream.
Our responsibility is to use it.
It's time to stop carrying what they needed to survive and start building what we need to thrive.
To speak where they had to whisper.
To rise where they had to bow.
To dream without apology.

That's how we honour them, not by repeating their fear, but by redeeming it.

By turning their survival into our freedom.

History Living in Us

Inherited fear doesn't start with us. It is history living through us.

For some communities, fear is not merely familial, it's structural. It's written into history, policy, and everyday life. Colonialism, slavery, displacement, and systemic racism have conditioned entire populations and communities to live in chronic vigilance. As **Frantz** wrote in *Black Skin, White Masks* (1952), colonial domination produced not only physical subjugation, but psychological dissonance divided self forever negotiating between belonging and survival. Similarly, **Dr. Joy DeGruy (2005)** coined *Post-Traumatic Slave Syndrome* to describe how generational trauma shapes behavioural adaptations, hyper-achievement, distrust, and suppression of emotion patterns that mirror trauma's biological markers. This context is vital, what looks like "fear of visibility" for one person might be **ancestral memory** for another. Centuries of knowing that standing out could cost everything. The courage to speak, to lead, to be seen, therefore carries not only personal but historical weight. To heal fear within such lineages is not self-help; it is resistance. It's the reclamation of humanity from systems that once demanded our silence.

My grandmother was part of the Windrush generation. She boarded a plane in 1961 from Jamaica believing she was coming to the "Mother Country," a citizen among citizens, ready to help rebuild Britain after the war. But when she arrived, the welcome wasn't warmth, it was hostility. It was No Blacks, No Dogs, No Irish signs in shop windows. It was being underpaid, overlooked, and treated as if she didn't belong in the very country she'd been invited to help rebuild.

Survival required caution. Don't make a fuss. Don't challenge authority. Work hard, say little, keep your head down. That wasn't just her way of living; it became the script she passed down. To her children. To me. To all of us in ways we don't even notice.

And of course, it didn't begin with Windrush. Across the Caribbean, Africa, and South Asia, colonial rule drilled fear into entire peoples through violence. Speaking your language, resisting injustice, even dreaming too boldly could get you punished. Generations absorbed the lesson: safety lies in silence. Silence became inheritance.

In the United States, the same cycle repeated. From slavery to Jim Crow, from redlining to police brutality, Black families taught their children codes of survival: Don't run in the wrong neighbourhood. Don't talk back to the police. Don't ever forget the system isn't built for you. Those weren't just warnings; they were armour. And they were necessary. But armour, when carried too long, weighs you down.

James Baldwin once said, "People are trapped in history and history is trapped in them." That's what inherited fear feels like: history breathing through us, shaping choices we don't even realise we're making.

For some communities, fear is not merely familial, it's structural. It's written into history, policy, and everyday life. Colonialism, slavery, displacement, and systemic racism have conditioned entire populations and communities to live in chronic vigilance. As **Frantz** wrote in *Black Skin, White Masks* (1952), colonial domination produced not only physical subjugation, but psychological dissonance divided self forever negotiating between belonging and survival. Similarly, **Dr. Joy DeGruy (2005)** coined *Post-Traumatic Slave Syndrome* to describe how generational trauma shapes behavioural adaptations, hyper-achievement, distrust, and suppression of emotion patterns that mirror trauma's biological markers. This context is vital, what looks like "fear of visibility" for one person might be **ancestral memory** for another. Centuries of knowing that standing out could cost everything. The courage to speak, to lead, to be seen, therefore carries not only personal but historical weight. To heal fear within such lineages is not self-help; it is resistance. It's the reclamation of humanity from systems that once demanded our silence.

Personal Echoes

I've felt this inheritance of fear in my own life.

When I first started pitching for big contracts, I carried more than nerves.
I carried voices.
Not just my own inner critic, but echoes of generations.
Voices whispering: *Who do you think you are?*
They'll laugh you out of the room.

Stay small. Play safe.

Those weren't really my words. They were the echoes of a culture that taught us to be grateful just to have a seat at the table.
Don't expect too much. Don't push too far. Don't forget who you are.

I pitched anyway. And some I lost.

Not because I wasn't capable, but because I was still learning how to show up as myself, not as the version I thought would be accepted.

I remember leaving one boardroom, my suit sharp but my confidence in shambles, replaying every word I'd said as if confidence itself had been a test I'd failed.

But even in that defeat, I realised something: every "no" wasn't rejection it was resistance, resistance to the version of myself that fear had built.

I've felt that inheritance in subtler ways too.

Before every speaking engagement, before signing contracts, before walking into certain rooms, that flutter in my stomach wasn't just adrenaline. It was memory.

It was my grandmother's voice telling me, *be impeccable.*

My mother's voice reminding me, *be careful.*

My father's sigh of exhaustion saying, *it's not worth the stress.*

Generational advice, dressed as caution.

Love wrapped in fear.

And even when I succeeded, I often made myself smaller to make others comfortable.

I learned early that confidence could be mistaken for arrogance.
That clarity could be read as aggression.
That excellence could invite envy instead of respect.
So I perfected the art of self-editing, trimming edges, softening truths, calibrating my tone until authenticity became negotiation.

There were moments I'd sit in high-level meetings, contracts worth millions being discussed and still feel like I was trespassing. Not because I lacked skill, but because some part of me still believed I was lucky to be there. That quiet conditioning, that reflex to "earn" belonging is one of fear's oldest disguises.

And then there were moments when that fear turned into fire. When I'd look around a room, see no one who looked like me, and think of my grandmother in her pressed blouse, my mother swallowing her words, my father declining promotions to keep his peace, and I'd feel something rise in me. A defiance that said, *I'm here because they couldn't be. I'm speaking because they stayed silent. I'm building because they built me.*

That's when courage stopped feeling like rebellion and started feeling like responsibility.

Still, the echo of fear is clever it doesn't disappear when you succeed.
Sometimes it hides inside your ambition, whispering that you have to overdeliver to deserve rest.
Sometimes it hides inside humility, telling you to shrink when it's your time to shine.

Sometimes it hides in your voice, urging you to be palatable instead of powerful.

But these days, I know how to recognise it.
I know how to sit with it, thank it for trying to protect me, and then walk past it.
Because the truth is, the voices that warned me were never trying to stop me, they were trying to save me from a world that once punished boldness.
Their warnings were love in translation.

And now, it's my turn to translate that love into something new.
To turn fear into faith.
Caution into clarity.
Survival into purpose.

So yes, I've felt this inheritance in every boardroom, every negotiation, every decision where I've had to choose between safety and authenticity.
But each time I choose authenticity, the echo fades.
Each time I speak without softening, or walk into a room without apology, I quiet that old voice a little more. Until all that remains is gratitude, for the ones who endured so I could expand.

Because that's what healing generational fear really looks like:
Not silence, but sound.
Not perfection, but presence.
Not armour, but authenticity.

The echoes of fear don't disappear overnight.

They fade as courage finds its voice one act of self-belief at a time.

But here's the truth: the win was in the showing up. The win was refusing to let inherited fear make the decision for me. Sometimes courage isn't about triumph. Sometimes it's about breaking the chain proving to yourself, and to those watching you, that we don't have to keep repeating the old script.

Fear as protection, Fear as prison

The paradox of inherited fear is this: what once kept people alive can keep their descendants stuck.

- A grandmother who lived through scarcity teaches her grandchildren not to dream too big better to expect little than to be crushed.
- A father who faced racist policing teaches his children never to challenge authority better to comply than to risk violence.
- A community scarred by exclusion teaches it's young to blend in, to work harder than everyone else even if it means erasing themselves in the process.

These were strategies for survival. But when repeated in a different world, they become prisons. They turn into ceilings that cap our ambition, chains that bind our imagination.

The fears that protected our elders from danger don't always protect us from irrelevance, invisibility, or self-betrayal.

Scarcity and Silence

One of the strongest inherited fears I've seen and lived, is scarcity.

My grandmother would keep things. Tins stacked high in the cupboard, clothes carefully folded away even if they no longer fit. It was never just about possessions. It was a mindset: you never know when the rug will be pulled out from under you.

That mindset trickles down. Even when you're financially stable, even when you've built success, you might still find yourself restless, anxious, overworking, unable to enjoy what you've earned. Scarcity whispers: You're one mistake away from losing it all.

It shows up in perfectionism terrified one slip will cost you everything. It shows up in control unwilling to delegate in case things fall apart. It shows up in the way we hoard energy, knowledge, even opportunities, because deep down we believe there's never enough to go around.

And then there's vulnerability.

Many of us were taught that emotions were dangerous.
To cry, to ask for help, to show weakness all of that risked shame or rejection.
So we bottled it up. Guarded ourselves. Handled things alone.

And what started as protection slowly turned into distance into loneliness, into walls we didn't even mean to build.

I learned that lesson early.

Growing up, I don't remember seeing many men cry. The ones who did were spoken about in hushed tones, as if tears were contagious. I learned to translate emotion into action to fix, not feel. To stay composed, because composure was how you kept control. Even when life was heavy, funerals, heartbreak, failure, I stayed stoic. I'd smile through the weight, call it resilience, and move on.

But what I really was, was *numb*.

Years later, I realised how costly that conditioning was.

During one of my lowest points, burnt out, juggling business, family, and expectations, I remember sitting alone in my car outside a client meeting, completely still. Not broken, just… empty.

I had built an identity on being dependable, on being the one people called for answers. But that day, I didn't have any, and I didn't know how to say, *I'm not okay.*

It took time and a lot of unlearning to realise that the strength I'd been taught to perform was actually a shield against feeling. The version of strength I'd inherited was quiet, polished, and proud. But it was also lonely. It kept me from asking for help, from admitting fear, from being seen in the moments I needed connection the most.

That's when I started to understand vulnerability differently, not as weakness, but as truth without disguise.

I remember coaching Kate, a Chief People Officer for a fast-growing fintech scale-up. She was brilliant, sharp-minded, respected, relentlessly composed. Her calendar was a battlefield of back-to-back meetings, her tone measured, her posture impeccable, but behind that control was exhaustion. During one session, I asked, "When was the last time someone asked how you're really doing?" She laughed, that polite, practiced laugh of someone who hasn't been asked that question in years, and then, for the first time in months, she paused. Her voice cracked slightly as she said, "I can't afford to fall apart."

A moment later, a single tear fell, and in that small act, something enormous shifted.

She didn't collapse; she *came alive*.

We spent weeks after that unpacking what strength really meant to her. She realised that by hiding her emotions, she wasn't protecting her team she was depriving them of permission to be human. When she started to lead with vulnerability sharing moments of uncertainty, asking for input, admitting when she was tired her team didn't lose respect. They trusted her more, because people don't connect to perfection. They connect to presence.

That's the paradox of vulnerability: the thing we fear will break us is often what frees us.

It's the moment our armour falls and our humanity steps forward.

I've seen this same truth in my own journey.

When I finally started sharing the full story not just the polished version of success, but the anxiety, the doubt, the nights I questioned everything, people didn't turn away. They leaned in, because authenticity invites authenticity, when we let others see our cracks, we give them permission to stop hiding theirs.

And that's what leadership really is, not managing perception, but modelling permission.

These days, I teach this to every client I work with, especially to leaders who've been taught that strength and vulnerability are opposites.
I tell them: *vulnerability is not weakness; it's clarity.*
It's the bridge between credibility and connection.
It's how we build cultures where people don't just perform, they belong.

I still feel the old instinct to guard myself sometimes. To retreat behind composure.
But I've learned that the courage to be seen fully joy, fear, mess and all is what transforms strength into impact.

Because the truth is, vulnerability isn't the opposite of strength, it's what gives strength its depth.
It's the difference between looking strong and *being* strong. One performs; the other transforms.

And in a world that still rewards stoicism over softness, choosing vulnerability is rebellion. It's how we remind ourselves and those watching us that strength isn't about how well you hide, but how truthfully you live. The echoes of fear don't disappear overnight. They fade as courage finds its voice one act of self-belief, one moment of honesty, one tear of truth at a time.

Our grandparents-built walls to survive; we're learning to open doors. Vulnerability is the bridge between their resilience and our liberation.

Whose Voice Is It?

This is where the work begins. The question isn't just What am I afraid of? It's whose voice is this?

When fear rises, ask yourself:

- Is this my fear, or my grandmother's?
- Is this my caution, or my parent's survival strategy?
- Is this fear reflecting my reality or their past reality?

I've coached people who refused to apply for jobs because they believed "people like us don't get those roles." When we traced it back, the belief wasn't theirs. It was their parents', echoing from a time when those doors really were closed.

The tragedy is that sometimes we're standing outside doors that are already open, still convinced they're locked.

Turning inheritance into fuel

Here's the hope: inherited fear doesn't have to be baggage. It can be fuel.

- The fear of poverty can drive us to build financial independence.
- The fear of exclusion can push us to create spaces where others feel they belong.

- The fear of being silenced can inspire us to raise our voices louder, unapologetically.

When we stop carrying fear unconsciously and start using it consciously, its power shifts. It ceases to be a chain and becomes a catalyst.

This isn't just about us. It's about what we pass forward.

Our parents and grandparents gave us survival. That was their gift. But survival is not enough anymore.

Our responsibility is to pass on freedom.

Every time we walk into a room our grandparents were excluded from... every time we speak truths, they had to swallow... every time we choose courage over silence... we're breaking the chain.

The greatest inheritance we can leave is not fear, but courage. Not silence, but voice. Not shrinking but standing tall.

That is how we honour the past not by carrying its fears unexamined, but by transforming them into fuel for a freer future.

From Shadow to Strategy

In the end, recognising and understanding inherited fears is one of the most powerful acts of self-empowerment. It reminds us that not every limitation we feel is of our own making. Some of the doubts, anxieties, and restrictions we carry were never ours to begin with, they were handed down, absorbed through family stories, cultural expectations, or unspoken rules.

By shining a light on these echoes, we give ourselves a choice. We can honour the lessons of the past where they still serve us, but we don't have to carry the anxieties that keep us small. We can decide to thank those who came before us for their caution, it kept them alive and then choose a different way for ourselves.

This isn't about rejecting or forgetting the past. It's about integrating its wisdom with compassion and then stepping forward in alignment with who we truly are. It's about saying: "I see the fears I've inherited, but they don't get to define me."

The Physiology of Healing: Teaching the Body Safety Again

If trauma teaches the body to fear, then healing must teach it to trust. This process, what neuroscientists call **memory reconsolidation** is the re-writing of old emotional memories through new, corrective experiences.

As trauma therapist **Peter Levine (1997)** describes in *Waking the Tiger*,

"Trauma is not in the event, but in the nervous system. Healing is not about remembering differently but about experiencing safety in the body that was once unsafe."

In practice, this involves building *somatic literacy*, the ability to recognise and regulate physical sensations of fear. Therapists like **Pat Ogden** (*Sensorimotor Psychotherapy*) and **Janina Fisher** (*Healing the Fragmented Selves of Trauma Survivors*, 2017) teach that awareness of posture, breath, and muscle tension becomes a map for healing. Each time we pause before reacting, breathe before apologising, or rest before overworking, we're retraining the nervous system to choose safety over survival. This is the foundation of courage, not heroic leaps, but incremental restoration of trust between body and self.

Psychologist **Lisa Feldman Barrett** (2017) reframes emotion as *construction*: the brain's ongoing attempt to make meaning of bodily sensations. When we reinterpret racing heartbeats as readiness, not danger, fear begins to transform from *signal of threat* to *invitation to presence*.

The Courage to Be: Fear, Freedom, and Meaning

Beyond biology and psychology lies the existential dimension of fear, the part that connects us to all who have ever trembled before us.

Philosopher **Paul Tillich** wrote in *The Courage to Be* (1952) that *"Courage is the affirmation of one's being in spite of non-being."*

To live fully, we must continually choose presence over paralysis, faith over withdrawal. Similarly, **Viktor Frankl** who survived the Holocaust, wrote in *Man's Search for Meaning* (1946):

"Between stimulus and response there is a space. In that space is our power to choose our response. In our response lies our growth and our freedom."

That "space" is where trauma transforms and where the body's instinct to retreat meets the soul's desire to rise. Fear, when understood through this lens, becomes sacred, not a barrier but a compass pointing toward meaning. To integrate trauma, then, is to reclaim authorship of that space. To say: *Fear will still speak, but I decide the meaning.*

Reclaiming Safety: The Practice of Integration

True healing requires integration across three dimensions:

1. **Biological**: calming the body's stress systems.
2. **Psychological**: resolving cognitive dissonance and shame.
3. **Existential**: rediscovering purpose beyond pain.

In applied terms, this looks like:

- **Co-regulation:** surrounding yourself with people whose calm steadies your own.
- **Boundaries:** understanding that "no" is not rejection but self-respect.
- **Embodiment:** noticing where fear lives in the body jaw, stomach, chest and softening gently.
- **Meaning making:** transforming fear into data, information about what matters most.

These practices, repeated daily, become what neuroscientists call *experience-dependent plasticity*, tthe process by which consistent, safe experiences reshape the brain's fear networks. And over time, the impossible happens: the body learns safety as fluently as it once learned fear.

Reflection: The Story the Body Still Believes

"The body remembers what the mind denies."
— Resmaa Menakem

Take a quiet moment to ask yourself:

- What story does my body still believe about safety?
- When did I first learn that fear meant survival?
- What does safety feel like and do I allow myself to feel it?
- Which patterns are not my personality, but my protection?

Then write down one act however small that signals to your nervous system: *You're safe now.*

Maybe it's taking a deep breath before replying.
Maybe it's saying no without over-explaining.
Maybe it's letting your shoulders drop when someone praises you.
Each one is a micro-act of rebellion against inherited fear.

Fear born of trauma is not a flaw to fix, it's proof that you survived what others could not.
But survival is not the same as safety.
The work now is to teach your body that it no longer needs to live in the posture of defence.

To turn vigilance into vision.
To let courage become your new nervous system.
And to realise that healing is not the absence of fear, it's the integration of it.

You do not have to erase fear to be free.

You only have to stop letting it speak louder than your truth.

From Understanding to Embodiment

In Chapter 1, we learned to recognise fear's disguises the perfectionism we praise, the control we defend, we mistake for wisdom. We saw how fear doesn't just live in our emotions, but in our habits, our histories, and our inherited caution. Naming those masks was the first act of liberation. Awareness turned the unseen into something we could finally work with.

In Chapter 2, we took that awareness deeper. We stepped inside fear itself into its anatomy, its psychology, its rhythm. We learned that fear isn't just an intruder; it's information. A messenger with something to say about what we value most. Fear thinks in patterns, hides in logic, and heals through understanding. When we stopped running from it and began studying it, we discovered its intelligence.

We saw that fear isn't just mental. It's physiological, a full-body event designed for survival. The trembling hands, racing pulse, and quickened breath we once saw as weakness are, in truth, signs of readiness. The body's way of saying, *this matters*. Once we reframed those sensations not as panic but as preparation, fear stopped feeling like a wall and began to move like a wave.

We also explored the paradox of fear as both protector and prison. It shields us from danger, but when left unexamined, it also shields us from growth. The task, then, is not to silence fear, but to translate it, to listen for the value it's trying to defend. Behind every fear lies something sacred: belonging, excellence, authenticity, love. When we name the fear, we rediscover the value beneath it and reclaim the power to move toward it rather than away.

Through frameworks like the TRACE Method, we turned understanding into practice. We learned to *tune in, recognise, accept, choose,* and *engage* to move from reaction to response, from paralysis to presence. Fear became not the signal to retreat, but the compass pointing toward what matters most.

If Chapter 1 taught us how to see fear clearly, and Chapter 2 taught us how to understand it deeply, then what comes next is about *living* that understanding.

Because knowing the anatomy of fear is one thing; embodying courage is another.

Awareness gives us clarity, but only action creates change.

Core takeaways from Chapter 2 summarised:

- Fear is intelligent, often disguising protection as perfection.
- Naming fear reduces its power and returns you to control.
- Your patterns are protection, not flaws but they limit freedom.
- Awareness creates choice and ends automatic reaction.
- Avoidance feeds anxiety; small action breaks its hold.
- Both failure and success can trigger fear in different ways.
- You are not your fear; awareness begins transformation.

Where We Go Next

In the next chapter, we'll widen the frame. In chapter 3 examines the systems that teach those fears to us in the first place.

We'll trace how fear moves through history, culture, and power, how it becomes gendered, racialised, and institutionalised. We'll see how belonging, safety, and visibility are not evenly distributed, and how identity shapes the kind of courage the world requires from us.

Because fear doesn't only whisper in our thoughts; it is built into the architecture of society, into who is believed, who is protected, who is punished for speaking too loudly or loving too freely.

This next chapter asks us to look beyond the self and into the systems, to understand how fear is inherited, learned, and reinforced through the intersections of race, gender, class, and culture.

Only then can we begin to unlearn it not just personally, but collectively.

CHAPTER 3

Fear and Intersectionality
- The Masks and Architectures of Survival

Just as we explored earlier on in the boom in the section on Neurodiversity, fear does not express itself the same way in every mind or body. Its shape shifts with context, neurological, cultural, historical, and social. What looks like avoidance in one person may be sensory overwhelm in another. What registers as hesitation for one may be survival for someone else. Fear does not live equally in all bodies. It moves differently through race, gender, class, and culture, tracing the outlines of history across our nervous systems, whispering inherited lessons about who can speak, who must shrink, and who is safe to be seen.

And its important that we as human working in an interconnected society, particularly in our workplaces and communities to really have a solid understanding of intersectionality. Really important it is

We often talk about fear as a private emotion, something to "manage" or "master."

But fear is never just psychological, it's also sociological.

It's not only what happens inside us, but what happens to us and around us.

It has a postcode, a passport, and a history.

To truly understand fear, we have to look beyond the individual and into the collective. Beyond diagnosis into design, because how we experience fear is shaped by how the world experiences us.

The same trembling that one person calls "stage fright" may, for another, carry the memory of being silenced. The same pause before speaking may come not from doubt, but from decades or generations, of social consequence. Fear may live in the body, but it's raised by the world around it and the histories that have influenced it.

And so, just as we acknowledged that neurodivergent minds experience fear through unique neurological pathways, we must also recognise that marginalised identities experience fear through *social* pathways, through histories of exclusion, bias, and erasure that live on in policy, in culture, and in everyday interactions.

Understanding fear through this intersectional lens allows us to see it not simply as emotion, but as evidence, evidence of what society rewards, what it punishes, and who has had to learn caution to survive.

This is where psychology meets history. Where emotion meets power. Where the story of fear becomes the story of us and his is where our understanding must evolve. If fear adapts to the body it lives in, then intersectionality is the map that helps us trace its movement. Because fear doesn't exist in isolation, it converges, multiplies, and compounds at the crossroads of identity. Gender, race, class, sexuality, and ability don't just shape how we are seen, they shape what we must survive. At those intersections, fear becomes layered: personal and political, emotional and ancestral, internal and environmental. To explore it fully, we have to look at the systems that teach it, the cultures that sustain it, and the courage required to live beyond it.

Intersectionality: When Identity Meets Power

When **Kimberlé Crenshaw** introduced *intersectionality* in 1989, she wasn't simply mapping identity; she was mapping danger. Her work revealed that discrimination doesn't occur in neat categories, it compounds. The experiences of a Black woman, for example, cannot be separated into just "racism" or "sexism" because they exist simultaneously, producing unique forms of vulnerability.

Fear behaves the same way. It doesn't arise in a vacuum. It gathers at intersections. A neurodivergent Black man in a corporate space might not fear failure, but misinterpretation. The question is not only *what are you afraid of?* but *what do you risk by being fully yourself?*

As Crenshaw said in her 2016 TED Talk,

"If you're standing in the path of multiple forms of exclusion, you're likely to get hit by all of them."

Intersectionality gives us the language to see fear not just as emotion, but as exposure, a measure of how much safety the world extends to us. But intersectionality is more than a framework of identity, it's a map of consequence. It shows how power decides whose fear is believed, whose pain is minimised, whose safety is optional.

For some, fear is temporary, a challenge to overcome.
For others, it is structural, a constant negotiation with systems that were never built for them.

This is why two people can stand in the same room, hear the same words, and feel entirely different kinds of danger. One may feel nervous about speaking up whilst another may feel unsafe doing so. One fears embarrassment, the other fears erasure. So, intersectional fear is not only emotional, but also spatial. It shapes how freely you move, how loudly you speak, and how much of yourself you bring into the room. In that sense, intersectionality isn't simply about identity, it's about *access to ease*.

To understand fear in its truest form, we must stop asking only what people are afraid of, and start asking what conditions make that fear rational.

History's Echo: The Fear That Built Resilience

History offers no shortage of examples where fear became a collective inheritance. In post-emancipation America, formerly enslaved Black families taught their children not to look white people in the eye, not to speak too loudly, not to challenge authority, habits born from a time when defiance could mean death. Generations later, those behaviours evolved into cultural codes of respectability: dress sharply, speak carefully, overperform, all subtle negotiations with power to remain safe.

Sociologist **E. Franklin Frazier** observed this transformation in *The Black Bourgeoisie* (1957), noting how middle-class Black families internalised restraint as both armour and aspiration. These patterns weren't pathology; they were strategy, proof of how social trauma can transform into cultural adaptation.

Across the world, similar inheritances exist. Descendants of colonised peoples, Indigenous communities, migrants, and refugees all carry echoes of the survival tactics their ancestors once needed. Fear, in these contexts, was never irrational, it was rational within the logic of danger. But what kept our ancestors safe in oppressive systems can quietly restrict us in freer ones. The whisper that once said "stay quiet and live" can later evolve into "don't risk and thrive." Fear changes costume, but not intent, its mission is always protection, even when it overprotects.

Coaching in Context: When Fear Becomes a Legacy

In a recent coaching session with a senior Black woman executive, she spoke about her frustration at being overlooked for promotion. On paper, she was exceptional: performance scores, mentoring, leadership impact. But every time she was invited to advocate for herself, she hesitated. *"I don't want to come across as entitled," she said softly. "My mum always told me to let my work speak for itself."*

As we explored this, Denise realised that her hesitation wasn't rooted in doubt, but in inheritance. Her mother had grown up in a Britain where speaking up as a Black woman could cost you your job, or your dignity. Silence had once been a form of strength, a way of surviving environments that punished confidence.

But now, in a corporate world that rewarded self-advocacy, that same inherited caution was quietly sabotaging her visibility. Once she reframed that behaviour, seeing it not as a flaw, but as a learned protection, she could begin to thank her mother's wisdom *and* outgrow its limits.

We worked together on separating the old context from the new reality:
"What kept your mother safe isn't what will keep you stuck," I said.
That shift was everything.

Within months, Denise began speaking up differently, not louder, just freer. And when her promotion finally came, she told me, "It wasn't about learning to be confident. It was about unlearning fear that wasn't mine to carry anymore."

bell hooks captured this truth in *Teaching Community: A Pedagogy of Hope* (2003), where she wrote,

"Dominator culture has tried to keep us all afraid, to make us choose safety instead of risk, sameness instead of diversity."

At its root, intersectional fear is not about fragility or personal weakness, it's about *constrained choice*.

Some of us fear failure. Others fear punishment for simply existing.

Some fear rejection; others fear recognition.

And many live in the quiet, lifelong negotiation between both.

Across generations, this inheritance shapes not just our decisions but our very sense of possibility.

It decides how loud we speak, how long we wait before asserting ourselves, how much we believe we are allowed to want. Yet, within this transmission of fear, there is also evidence of something powerful endurance. The fact that these lessons exist means survival was achieved.

Fear may have been our first teacher, but it doesn't have to be our last.

Our task now is to learn how to listen to its wisdom without obeying its limitations, to hold gratitude for the ancestors who kept us safe, while choosing new definitions of safety for ourselves.

Because the moment we recognise fear as inheritance, we gain the ability to change what the next generation will inherit from *us*.

The Mirror of Double Consciousness

To live at the intersections of identity is to live with multiple mirrors.
You see yourself not only through your own eyes, but through the eyes of power, through the distorted reflections society projects back at you.

This is what W. E. B. Du Bois called *double consciousness*

"The sense of always looking at one's self through the eyes of others, of measuring one's soul by the tape of a world that looks on in amused contempt and pity."
(*The Souls of Black Folk*, 1903)

Du Bois was describing more than a feeling; he was naming a condition, a fracture produced by racism and colonial modernity. For Black people in America (and by extension across the African diaspora), he argued, identity was never singular. It was split between two warring ideals. One was the desire to belong to the wider nation, and the second was the knowledge that this nation refuses to see you fully. To be both African and American, yet never wholly either.

That *twoness*, as Du Bois called it, becomes an inner negotiation: a constant translation between authenticity and acceptability. It is the psychological cost of navigating worlds that misrecognise you, where your existence is politicised and racialized before it is even humanised.

Avtar Brah later expanded on this idea through her concept of *diaspora space*, the lived reality of those who "live between cultures." In *Cartographies of Diaspora* (1996), she describes this space as one where identity is continuously made and remade through the meeting of histories, memories, and geographies. For Brah, diasporic identity is not about being "from two places," but about *belonging in tension*, existing in the in-between, where multiple cultural logics coexist and sometimes collide.

Where Du Bois's double consciousness focused on racialised psychological division, Brah's diasporic consciousness attends to the fluid, intersectional nature of modern identity: race, gender, class, migration, religion, sexuality which all moving parts of the self, shaped by history and displacement.

Living between cultures, then, is not simply about hybridity; but about negotiation about reconciling competing expectations and learning to breathe between worlds that each demand fragments of you.

In contemporary psychology, this tension is mirrored in research on *identity threat*, the strain that arises when one's social identity is stigmatised or devalued. Claude Steele and Joshua Aronson's (1995) landmark studies on *stereotype threat* showed that when individuals fear confirming negative stereotypes about their group, their performance and confidence suffer. What this reveals is that vigilance, the constant awareness of how you're perceived, consumes cognitive and emotional energy. It narrows freedom.

Fear, in this context, isn't irrational. It's socialised. It's learned. It's survival.

For many of us, the mirror of double consciousness becomes both armour and burden:

- Armour, because awareness keeps us alert, strategic, prepared.
- Burden, because constant self-monitoring erodes ease, authenticity, and joy.

To exist in this space is to live with a constant hum beneath the skin, the hum of self-editing, the pressures of code switching and assimilation to the point where authenticity is eroded and were one can be longer recognise themselves and of translation, of anticipation. It's to know that your body, your voice, your name, your tone may all be misread before they are truly heard.

Yet within this tension lies a paradoxical power. Those who live between worlds often develop what cultural theorists like Paul Gilroy namely in in *The Black Atlantic and* Patricia Hill Collins in *Black Feminist Thought* (1990) call *double vision*. This is the ability to see systems of power from both inside and outside. It can become a form of wisdom, a heightened social literacy, a consciousness that allows one to critique, adapt, and imagine differently.

To heal from double consciousness does not mean to erase one side of yourself, but to integrate the fragments into wholeness and to refuse to see yourself only through the world's eyes. It is the journey from being defined to defining, from surviving through vigilance to living through truth. Perhaps, as Avtar Brah reminds us, the beauty of diaspora lies not in choosing one world over another, but in the courage to inhabit the space *between*, and call that space home.

Reflection: Living Between Worlds

Take a quiet moment and ask yourself:

- Where in my life do I still measure myself through someone else's eyes?
- What parts of me have I muted to feel accepted or understood?
- When have I felt the strain of living between cultures, languages, or expectations, and what has that taught me about adaptability and courage?
- What would it look like to live from my *own* definition of safety, rather than the one I inherited or internalised?

Write freely, not for grammar or perfection, but for truth.
Let your reflection become your reconciliation.
Because integration begins the moment you stop trying to belong in halves and start recognising that you were never incomplete.

A British Inheritance and the Ambivalence of Belonging

For me, this double consciousness was not born in the Jim Crow South that Du Bois wrote about, but in post-industrial Britain, in the paradox of being British-born yet perpetually foreign.

WHAT ARE YOU SO AFRAID OF?

I grew up in the 1990s, in the so-called *Cool Britannia* era, Tony Blair's vision of a modern, multicultural nation draped in Britpop confidence and political correctness. On the surface, Britain was reinventing itself: cosmopolitan, diverse, forward-looking. Yet beneath that optimism lived a quieter dissonance, the hum of a country that wanted the image of inclusion without the discomfort of introspection.

It was the decade of Stephen Lawrence, whose murder in 1993 and the Macpherson Report (1999) that followed forced Britain to confront a truth long known in Black and brown communities, that racism was not a malfunction of the system but one of its features. The report's conclusion that the Metropolitan Police were "institutionally racist" was a watershed moment, but it also revealed the limits of recognition. Awareness does not equal transformation. The language of equality became more polished, yet the structures remained largely intact.

This is where Avtar Brah's idea of *diaspora space* and her notion of *ambivalence* began to make sense to me. In *Cartographies of Diaspora* (1996), Brah describes belonging as a **negotiation**, not a destination, a continual movement between attachment and alienation. For those of us born in Britain to parents or grandparents who came from elsewhere, identity is never static; it is a practice of ongoing translation. You are forever crossing cultural borders that no one else can see, forever negotiating who you are against who the world believes you to be.

There is an ambivalence in this existence, sitting between two cultures, two histories, two languages of selfhood. You learn to code-switch with precision, to read the room before you enter it, to translate your identity into palatable fragments that fit the space you're in. You learn that "professionalism" often means assimilation, that "confidence" can be recoded as "threat," and that "diversity" doesn't always mean belonging.

Frantz Fanon captured this fracture in *Black Skin, White Masks* (1952) when he wrote,
"Consciousness of the body is solely a negating activity."

To be seen through the lens of stereotype is to experience the self as divided, to become hyper-aware of your body, your tone, your presence. For many, that vigilance becomes second nature, the woman who lowers her voice to avoid being called emotional, the Black professional who over-prepares to avoid being called unqualified, the neurodivergent person who masks exhaustion with humour.

That negotiation takes its toll. What psychologists might now call *identity fatigue*, the exhaustion that comes from constantly editing, performing, and recalibrating yourself, is something I've lived with for as long as I can remember. You learn to shape-shift: to code-switch in meetings, to read tone before speaking, to carry your belonging like paperwork that might be checked at any moment. It's the quiet labour of making others comfortable enough to see you as you truly are.

Honestly though London has always felt like home, well my London, my version of it. A city of rhythm, refuge, and reinvention, yet step outside its postcodes and the illusion of inclusion faltered. The further you travelled from the city's pulse, the more your difference became a conversation. Accents softened. Names shortened. You learned which version of yourself was safest to present. Brah calls this the *ambivalence of belonging*, the simultaneous pull of home and homelessness. The feeling of being "in" but never "of." To exist between cultures is to live with a constant awareness of edges, knowing that one misstep, one misunderstanding, one moment of unfiltered honesty could remind you how conditional your belonging really is.

Then came the *War on Terror*, an era that redefined suspicion. Brownness, Blackness, and Muslimness were recoded as potential threat. Fear was securitised; identity became evidence. You learned to anticipate the gaze before it landed, to pre-empt misunderstanding, to manage your visibility as though your safety depended on it because sometimes, it did.

I experienced this firsthand when I was twenty-one. I had planned a trip to America, my ESTA was approved, my bags were packed. But on the morning of my flight, I received an unexpected email: *"There has been a change to your visa status."* When I checked, it said "rejected." I assumed it was a glitch and decided to travel anyway.

Upon arrival, my friend and I were detained under **Section 7 of the Terrorism Act** by border force officers. We were held for hours and interrogated, questioned about my travels, my studies, my faith.

Why did I study Arabic?
Who did I know there?
What did I think of British foreign policy?
What did I pray about?
What do I think of other religions ?

I had never been arrested. Never been questioned by police. Never been charged with anything. And yet, in that moment, I was treated as though my existence itself required explanation.

When I asked why I was being detained, they told me I had a "suspicious profile."
Was it my name? My religion? The Arabic I'd studied two summers earlier?
Or was it simply that, in that political moment, all three together made me a symbol of fear?

At that time, under Section 7, I could have been held for up to two weeks without charge. I remember sitting in that sterile room under the hum of fluorescent lights, watching hours pass. I remember feeling small, not as a citizen, but as a question mark. For the first time in my life, I realised how thin the line is between being *British* and being *suspect*.

Even now, writing this is difficult.
This is the first time I've ever put it into words, because for years, I feared the repercussions of even naming the experience.
In that moment, I feared not being released and forgotten.
Afterwards, I feared being remembered.

That was fear, not just emotional, but sociological. Fear manufactured by systems, reinforced by policy, normalised through culture. It taught me that fear doesn't just live in the mind but it's embedded in institutions. That belonging, for people like me, is never neutral, it is monitored, measured, and, at times, revoked.

That day, I understood something Du Bois and Avtar Brah had both written about in different languages, that double consciousness is not only psychological, but political. It is the awareness of being seen through a lens you did not choose, a gaze that has already made up its mind.

That day was when I also realised I was being *racialized*, not just seen as different, but as dangerous. I was being criminalised not for what I had done, because I had done nothing, not even close but for who I was. Islamophobia was not abstract or invisible; it was state-sanctioned, woven into policy, legitimised by fear.

You see that's where fear enters the picture. Not the loud, obvious kind, but the quiet, cumulative fear that comes from always being aware of how you're perceived. The fear that the ground you stand on is never fully yours. The fear that belonging, no matter how hard-won, can be revoked at a moment's notice.

I've carried that fear for years, through boardrooms, airports, and classrooms.

It's the background noise of double consciousness, the echo of a country that tells you to be proud of who you are while still asking, *but where are you really from?*

That's the cruel paradox of conditional belonging: it teaches you to celebrate visibility while bracing for its cost. You learn to succeed with one hand on the door, just in case you're asked to prove you deserve to be inside.

Fear, in this context, isn't irrational.
It's learned. It's historical. It's survival.

And even now, after all the progress, all the representation, all the "inclusion". I still feel it sometimes, the tension in the shoulders, the rehearsed smile, the mental checklist before I speak. That is what it means to live with cultural negotiation and identity fatigue, to love a country that never fully loves you back, to belong to a home that still makes you prove it.

The Conditional Belonging of the British-Born

Even with English as my mother tongue, a British passport in my pocket, and a life built entirely on this soil, I was and still am reminded again and again that citizenship, for some, is conditional. I remember the summer of the 2020 Euros, when England lost on penalties and the three Black players who missed, Saka, Sancho, and Rashford, were flooded with racist abuse. Not just the players but even random black people on the streets of the UK were racially abused and some even attacked. But to me this was a familiar ritual: celebration when we win, vilification when we lose. In that moment, every Black Briton felt the cold breath of conditional belonging.

It was a reminder that to be both Black and British is to live in a house that sometimes forgets you built it.

It is to carry the legacy of **Windrush**, the weight of **colonial memory**, and the ghost of **empire**, all while being told to "go back where you came from." The phrase that I hear ever so often on social media.

This is not metaphorical fear, it is political, social, and embodied. It is the fear of being misread, misunderstood, or misplaced. It is what Du Bois foresaw, "two souls, two thoughts, two unreconciled strivings", not as some abstract theory, but as the lived reality of those navigating the cultural contradictions of postcolonial Britain.

The Coaching Lens: Reclaiming the Mirror

In my coaching work, I've met countless professionals who carry this psychic weight.
One client, a British Pakistani manager, described it as *"being fluent in two selves."*
Another, a Black teacher in a predominantly white school, said, *"I'm never sure if I'm being evaluated or interpreted."* Their fear was not of failure, but of misrepresentation.

The work, then, is not to erase the double consciousness, that would mean denying history, but to *reconcile* it. To help people see themselves through their own eyes again, not only through the mirrors power holds up.

Courage, in this context, is the act of *self-definition*.
It's reclaiming the right to speak, to take up space, to belong without permission.

And perhaps that's what the journey of this book has been all along, not just to understand fear, but to understand the world that taught us to fear ourselves.

This section reminds us that fear is never just personal, it is relational, historical, and cultural.
It teaches that double consciousness is not a flaw of identity but a *response* to imbalance, a creative, adaptive intelligence that helps people survive in systems that misrecognise them.

It shows that vigilance has a cost: the exhaustion of always performing safety. But it also reveals a truth, that the ability to read multiple worlds, to navigate tension, to translate between cultures, is itself a form of *cognitive and emotional brilliance*.

To unlearn the limits of double consciousness is not to discard it; it's to integrate it. To see both mirrors, how you see yourself and how the world sees you, and then choose which reflection to honour.

The work, then, is threefold:

1. **Recognition**: naming how fear and identity intertwine, and how systemic forces shape what feels personal.
2. **Reclamation**: reclaiming the right to define yourself beyond the gaze of others.
3. **Reimagining**: using that awareness as fuel for authenticity, leadership, and empathy.

Because when you understand that your fear was never purely your own, that it is the residue of history, policy, and power, you can finally stop carrying it as shame and start holding it as knowledge. And knowledge, when turned inward, becomes liberation.

Gendered Fear: The Politeness of Survival

This tension lives in gender too. From childhood, girls are taught to fear being too visible, while boys are taught to fear being too vulnerable. One is punished for taking up space, the other for yielding it.

The result is a choreography of constraint, women softening language to avoid labels, men armouring tenderness to maintain approval. Gender theorist Judith Butler (1990) called this *gender performativity*. This is the idea that gender is not something we are, but something we do: a script rehearsed under social surveillance.

Fear directs the performance.
It tells the woman to smile through discomfort.
It tells the man to suppress empathy in exchange for power.
It tells the nonbinary person that to exist authentically is to risk erasure.

As Audre Lorde wrote,
"For women, the fear of being visible and the fear of being invisible are one and the same." Fear becomes the quiet regulator of identity, the invisible script that decides what version of ourselves we present to the world.

Sociologist Raewyn Connell (1995) described how patriarchy constructs masculinity and femininity as opposing currencies of power. Boys are rewarded for stoicism, independence, and control, qualities that align with dominance. Meanwhile, girls are socialised toward empathy, modesty, and care, traits that ensure likeability but often at the expense of authority.

Psychologist Carol Gilligan (1982), in *In a Different Voice*, found that young girls begin speaking in what she called an "ethic of care", a moral language centred on connection and relationship. But as they grow, that voice becomes muted. They learn that too much honesty risks rejection, too much ambition risks alienation. They learn to edit themselves.

This is not just socialisation; it's self-preservation.
The price of social belonging is self-limitation.

In the workplace, these early lessons evolve into professional habits:

- Women using hedging language ("I might be wrong, but…").
- Men avoiding vulnerability for fear of being perceived as weak.

These are not individual flaws, they are collective instructions. They are how power maintains itself through politeness.

Gender Beyond the Binary: Other Ways of Seeing

The Western binary of gender, with its oppositional hierarchies of strength versus softness, dominance versus care is not universal. In many pre-colonial African, Indigenous, and Asian societies, masculinity and femininity were understood not as rivals but as **reciprocal forces** complementary, interdependent, and cyclical.

In Yoruba cosmology, for example, *Aṣẹ* (spiritual power) is not gendered but balanced. The orishas embody both masculine and feminine energies in fluid proportion, Shango's fire coexists with Oshun's sweetness, Ogun's force with Yemaya's nurturing. Power is measured not by domination but by harmony. As Oyèrónkẹ́ Oyěwùmí (1997) writes in *The Invention of Women*, "*The category of 'woman' is a Western social invention ... in the Òyó-Yorùbá world-sense, age and seniority, not sexual difference, determined social ranking.*" Her argument reveals that gender, as we know it, is not a universal organising principle but a colonial imposition that reordered societies which once prized relationality over hierarchy.

Among the Akan of Ghana, the concepts of *ntoro* (spirit) and *mogya* (blood) represent a union of paternal and maternal lineages, each essential, neither superior. Social equilibrium depends on cooperation between the two, not competition (Gyekye, 1996).

Similarly, many Native American nations, such as the Navajo (Diné), speak of *hozho*, a philosophy of balance, beauty, and harmony where masculine and feminine energies are seen as parts of a single whole. The Diné recognise *nádleehi*, individuals embodying both masculine and feminine spirits as sacred, not deviant. Anthropologist Will Roscoe (1991) wrote that "the man-woman [among the Zuni] embodied the tribe's deepest values of balance and wholeness, uniting qualities Western culture keeps apart."

In classical Chinese philosophy, *yin* and *yang* are not fixed genders but relational principles. Each carries a seed of the other; neither can exist without its counterpart. To live in harmony is to let these energies flow, not to suppress one in favour of the other (Ames & Hall, 2003).

Even within South Asian traditions, from the Hindu *Ardhanarishvara*, the deity depicted as half-Shiva, half-Parvati, to the *Hijra* communities that have long existed beyond binary frameworks, the coexistence of masculine and feminine has been acknowledged as both natural and divine. As Serena Nanda (1990) observed, "Hijras challenge the very idea of a binary sex/gender system: in India they demonstrate that masculinity and femininity are not always opposed, but often interwoven in culturally meaningful ways."

Across these cosmologies, gender is not a battlefield but a balance. Fear does not govern expression, harmony does.

Colonialism, Christianity, and the Gendering of Power

Colonial modernity fractured this equilibrium. Where balance once signified power, the Western gaze recoded difference into deficiency, fluidity into deviance, and interdependence into hierarchy.

When colonial and Western systems expanded across the world, they didn't just conquer land they conquered meaning. The harmony between masculine and feminine that had once anchored Indigenous, African, and Asian cosmologies was recoded through the binary lens of European patriarchy. Where complementarity once existed, hierarchy took its place.

European missionaries and administrators exported Victorian ideals of patriarchy, rigid, heteronormative, and hierarchical into colonised societies. They recast complementarity as opposition and equilibrium as control. The imposition of Christian moral codes and capitalist divisions of labour turned gender from a relational identity into a tool of governance. As sociologist Oyèrónkẹ́ Oyěwùmí (1997) argues in *The Invention of Women*, Western colonisation **gendered African societies** that had once organised themselves by seniority and kinship, not by male-female hierarchy. What had been systems of social balance became systems of dominance. Similarly, anthropologist Ifi Amadiume (1987) called this transformation deliberate, not accidental: "Colonialism invented African patriarchy." In societies such as the Igbo of Nigeria, gender roles had once been flexible, with authority and status accessible to women as well as men. But European missionaries and administrators, interpreting African structures through their own patriarchal worldview, redefined power as inherently male and recast spiritual and social balance as disorder.

This pattern repeated globally. Missionaries in Polynesia banned gender-fluid ceremonies. British colonial codes in India criminalised *Hijra* communities that had existed for centuries. In North America, boarding schools suppressed Two-Spirit identities, replacing Indigenous teachings of balance with Western doctrines of shame.

Across continents, the message was the same: equilibrium was replaced with control. Colonialism not only imposed race as a category of power; it imposed gender as hierarchy, tethering worth to control, reason, and dominance. Traits coded as masculine, while subordinating emotion, intuition, and care traits coded as feminine.

Fear became the enforcer of these imported binaries. It taught women to internalise subservience as virtue and men to equate gentleness with shame. It created a world where empathy was feminised and power masculinized, where the two could no longer coexist in one body without suspicion. Under colonial modernity, the masculine was elevated as logic, strength, and reason; the feminine was demoted to emotion, care, and weakness.

In that shift, gender ceased to be a spiritual equilibrium and became a site of surveillance, a system for policing who could lead, nurture, or belong. Where Indigenous societies once taught that power flows through harmony, colonial modernity taught that power demands control.

The result is the gendered fear we inherit today, the learned instinct to police our softness, to doubt our tenderness, to equate vulnerability with danger. Fear, then, is not simply personal or psychological; it is historical and structural. t is the residue of centuries spent learning that to survive, one must conform.

In patriarchal modernity, fear polices the borders of gender expression.
It keeps men from softness, women from self-assertion, and everyone from wholeness.
It tells us that balance is weakness, that duality is confusion, that harmony is naïve.

In older cosmologies, African, Indigenous, and Asian alike, wholeness was wisdom. The task was not to choose between masculine and feminine, but to integrate them. To lead with courage and compassion. To know that the strength to protect and the strength to nurture come from the same root.

Perhaps that is the quiet truth we have lost, that fear fractured what culture once held together and that courage, in its truest form, is not the assertion of one over the other, but the reunion of both within ourselves.

The Echo of Gendered Fear Today

Centuries later, the residue of that colonial script still shapes how we move through the world.

You can see it in boardrooms where women soften their expertise to sound "approachable," in performance reviews where assertiveness reads as aggression, and in offices where men are rewarded for control but rarely for compassion. You can hear it in the silence that follows a woman of colour speaking her truth, the quiet discomfort that tells her she's crossed an invisible line. Gendered fear no longer needs chains or laws to function; it survives through subtler architectures, tone policing, *microaggressions*, professional codes of "fit." It asks: *How safe is it to be fully yourself here?*

But not all women experience fear the same way, as Kimberlé Crenshaw (1989) taught us through the framework of intersectionality, gender never operates in isolation. It intersects with race, class, sexuality, and ability, shaping who is protected by the rules of femininity and who is punished by them.

For white women, fear might mean the pressure to be perfect, poised, and polite. For Black women, it often means the burden of being strong. The "Strong Black Woman" archetype, celebrated by some, weaponised by others, denies vulnerability, demanding endurance in place of empathy.

It's why Black women in Britain and the US face disproportionate rates of stress-related illness, are less likely to be believed when reporting pain, and are four times more likely to die in childbirth than white women (Knight et al., 2023; MBRRACE-UK, 2022). These are not biological disparities, they are the outcomes of racialised fear, cultural biases and neglect. They reveal how systems respond differently to bodies based on the stories society attaches to them. When medicine assumes stoicism, when workplaces mistake assertiveness for aggression, when society confuses resilience with invincibility, fear shifts from emotion to infrastructure.

It becomes systemic.

It's what sociologist Leith Mullings (2005) called *the Sojourner Syndrome*, the compounded toll of race, gender, and class on Black women's health and longevity. Intersectionality, as Crenshaw reminds us, is not merely a theory of identity; it's a map of survival.

It names the invisible weight carried by those whose lives sit at the intersections of power and prejudice.

A white woman's experience of sexism cannot be equated to a Black woman's, nor can a cis man's understanding of vulnerability mirror that of a trans man navigating survival within structures that deny his existence.

This is the modern choreography of fear, where power still scripts performance and belonging is still conditional. But beneath it, another truth endures: the memory of balance, the ancestral knowledge that power was never meant to divide us.

Maybe courage today is a kind of remembering, a return to the wholeness our ancestors already knew and a refusal to let fear define the limits of our becoming.

Because when we remember that gender, like power, was once shared we begin to unlearn the fear that taught us to play small. And in that remembering, we start to rebuild the harmony that history tried to erase.

Misogynoir and the Burden of Visibility

For women of colour, visibility itself becomes a double bind.
To be unseen is to be erased; to be seen is to risk scrutiny.
Each step toward confidence is shadowed by the fear of being misread, "angry," "difficult," "intimidating," "unfeminine."
It's a fear born not of insecurity, but of experience.

Research by psychologist Valerie Purdie-Vaughns and Richard Eibach (2008) on *intersectional invisibility* describes how Black women often fall outside the prototypical images of both "woman" and "Black," rendering them hyper-visible in moments of bias yet invisible in moments of recognition. The world alternates between overexposure and erasure.

That oscillation, being both hyper-visible and unseen, breeds a unique exhaustion. It's what scholars like Moya Bailey (2010) term *misogynoir*: the specific hatred directed at Black women, where racism and sexism intertwine to form a distinct system of fear. This is not abstract theory, it's lived, daily negotiation.
It's the teacher correcting her tone so she isn't called aggressive.

The doctor raising her pain threshold to be believed.
The corporate leader who smiles while being mistaken for the assistant.

This is not abstract theory, it is lived, daily negotiation.
It's the teacher correcting her tone so she isn't called aggressive.
The doctor raising her pain threshold to be believed.
The corporate leader who smiles while being mistaken for the assistant.
The journalist who moderates her truth to remain employable.

These are not individual acts of politeness; they are strategies of survival, ways to exist in spaces that celebrate diversity in language but punish it in practice.

In March 2024, it was revealed that Conservative Party donor **Frank Hester** told colleagues that looking at **Diane Abbott** "makes you want to hate all Black women" and added that she "should be shot."

Meanwhile, Abbott, the UK's first and longest-serving Black woman MP, has long spoken about receiving a disproportionate volume of abuse online; one study found that she received **nearly half of all abusive tweets** directed at women MPs.

Despite the severity of these remarks, some argued that the broader system of accountability remained weak or inconsistent, illustrating how fear and surveillance around Black women's bodies and voices persist, even when the abuse is explicit and public. The Hester comment is not an anomaly; it is a mirror. It exposes how *misogynoir* operates in plain sight, tolerated, rationalised, and quietly excused.

Additionally, it is a striking example of misogynoir in action, the collision of racism and sexism that marks Black women as both *too visible* and *not fully seen*.

Abbott's visibility as one of the few Black women in British politics renders her symbolic scrutinised, contested, dissected. Her humanity, however, remains negotiable. The fact that a man could publicly say "you just want to hate all Black women" with limited consequence shows how fear becomes structural: a system where Black women learn that their safety, credibility, and belonging are never guaranteed.

It ties directly into the theme of gendered fear, that fear is not only about what happens to us, but how we must *live* under the possibility of it happening. For Abbott, that tension is magnified by her role: required to represent millions yet rarely protected by the institutions she serves.

For Black women in particular, misogynoir transforms visibility into risk. It teaches that recognition can arrive hand-in-hand with hostility, and that public presence requires private armour.

Diane Abbott's experience is not isolated, it is part of a wider pattern of historical and structural forces that police who gets to belong safely. It is the modern echo of what bell hooks once described as *"choosing safety instead of risk, sameness instead of diversity."*

To exist at the intersection of race and gender is to live in constant negotiation:
to love a country that doubts your belonging,
to speak truth knowing it may invite threat,
to carry the burden of visibility and the pain of invisibility all at once.

That, too, is *fear* not irrational, but inherited.

Not imagined, but institutional.

And yet, in surviving it, there is also *courage*, the quiet, daily defiance of being visible anyway.

Fear lives differently in everybody, but its architecture is collective.

It teaches women to apologise for confidence, men to repress tenderness, and those in between to camouflage truth.

It rewards compliance and punishes authenticity. But when we begin to name it, not just as emotion but as inheritance, not just as socialisation but as survival, we begin to unlearn its hold.

Because fear, when seen clearly, loses its power to disguise itself as discipline.

And courage, when practised collectively, becomes more than resistance, it becomes redesign. The redesign of what power, leadership, and care can look like when they're no longer built on fear.

Misogyny, Masculinity, and the Fear of Softness

Misogyny is not only the hatred of women, but also the policing of softness wherever it appears.
It punishes men for tenderness and women for power.
It tells boys to fight and girls to forgive.
It rewards dominance, not depth; detachment, not intimacy.

Toxic masculinity thrives on the fear of emasculation, the dread of being perceived as "less than." That fear drives silence, aggression, and emotional isolation.
It is not strength that men are taught to pursue, but invulnerability.
And invulnerability is not resilience, it is repression dressed as control.

Meanwhile, women internalise a mirrored version of the same fear, the fear of being "too much."
Too loud, too ambitious, too emotional, too assertive.
They are taught that survival depends on shrinking strategically.
On smiling while being interrupted, on being pleasant even when provoked, on apologising for the space they've rightfully earned.

This is what philosopher Kate Manne (2017) calls *the moral economy of misogyny*, a system that enforces patriarchal order not only through violence, but through reward and withdrawal of approval.
Women who conform to expectation are praised for their grace.
Those who resist are labelled "difficult," "angry," or "ungrateful."
Fear, once again, becomes the currency of compliance.

What unites misogyny and toxic masculinity is a shared terror of deviation from gender roles, from emotional norms, from the illusion of control. Patriarchy survives by teaching everyone to fear the traits that make us whole: empathy, softness, uncertainty, interdependence. In men, fear manifests as dominance; in women, as deference; in others, as disappearance. But at its root, all gendered fear is a negotiation with safety, a calculation of what must be hidden to remain unharmed.

And that is what makes gendered fear so insidious: it hides beneath civility.
It masquerades as etiquette, professionalism, politeness.
It tells us we are being reasonable when, in truth, we are being erased.

Fear as the Quiet Architect of Gender

Fear is the quiet architect of gender performance.
It builds invisible walls around who we are allowed to be, scripting our gestures before we can even name them.

For some, it whispers: *Don't take up too much space.*
For others, it commands: *Don't ever appear weak.*
But in both, the message is the same: *Your safety depends on your silence.*

From early on, we learn that gender is not simply something we are, it is something we do under surveillance. We perform composure, charm, confidence, or submission in exchange for approval, protection, or belonging.

And fear is the director of that performance, shaping our tone, posture, and presence long before we are aware of the script.

For many women, fear is not dramatic; it is disciplined.
It's the smile held too long in a meeting, the nod of agreement when silence would be more honest, the apology before expertise. It is a choreography of self-containment, learned to keep peace, preserve perception, and protect opportunity.

Sociologist Arlie Hochschild's (*The Managed Heart*, 1983) concept of *emotional labour* captures this perfectly, the internal regulation of feeling, to meet the emotional expectations of others. Fear fuels that labour - the fear of being seen as difficult, aggressive, or ungrateful. It teaches women to manage not only their own emotions but the comfort of everyone around them.

This emotional management is not merely personal, it is political. What begins as self-regulation becomes social regulation. The pressure to appear calm, kind, and accommodating doesn't emerge in isolation; it reflects a wider moral framework that rewards compliance and punishes resistance. In other words, the labour women perform to maintain harmony is also the mechanism through which patriarchy maintains itself. The emotional costs borne in private uphold hierarchies that remain invisible in public. And as philosopher Kate Manne (2017) argues, these dynamic forms part of what she calls the *moral economy of misogyny*, a system that maintains patriarchal order not just through punishment, but through reward and withdrawal. It grants belonging to those who comply and withdraws it from those who don't.

Women who smile, soothe, or self-silence are rewarded with approval; those who resist are disciplined through exclusion, discredit, or ridicule.

This is not hatred, but control. Fear becomes the internal currency that keeps the system running.

For men, fear hides behind control.

The moral economy of misogyny extends even into the storylines we consume. Take Netflix's *Adolescence*, for example: a 13-year-old boy accused of murdering a female classmate, a storyline inspired by real incidents of youth violence, the "manosphere," and the policing of girls' bodies.

In this narrative, the boy's violence becomes a symptom of a culture where fear, invisibility, and hyper-visibility collide. The series asks: what happens when boyhood is shaped by messages that kindness is weakness, vulnerability is suspicion and power must be asserted by force?

For men, fear hides behind control. As bell hooks argued in *The Will to Change* (2004), patriarchy doesn't free men; it imprisons them cutting them off from tenderness, empathy, and vulnerability. They learn that emotion threatens authority, that to cry or comfort is to lose their claim to manhood. And so fear masquerades as composure, anger replaces sadness, humour masks hurt, detachment passes for strength. In performing power, many men become estranged from themselves.

That Netflix example doesn't just dramatise an extreme event. It mirrors the everyday gender script: risk demands suppression, visibility demands performance, and safety demands silence. Fear becomes currency. It is a quiet architect, shaping who gets to speak, who gets to lead, who gets to live.

Across these performances, the woman's politeness, the man's stoicism fear is the hidden choreographer. It sustains the illusion that gender order is natural when, in truth, it is maintained by anxiety: the fear of rejection, the fear of disapproval, the fear of exile from the social script.

To unlearn this fear is not to reject masculinity or femininity, but it is to release the fear that governs them. It is to build new definitions of power that make room for care, new models of courage that include vulnerability, and new languages of strength that sound like truth.

Because until we dismantle the fear that underpins gender itself, equality will always feel like risk
and safety will always come at the cost of authenticity.

A Case Study: Leadership and Gendered Fear

A senior leader I once coached called Nadia came to me exhausted. She was highly respected, but she confessed: "I feel like I'm performing a version of myself all day long." When we unpacked that, she realised how much of her leadership was shaped by fear, fear of being labelled "too direct," fear of appearing "cold" when she was simply decisive.

She would preface ideas with disclaimers, smile through interruptions, and over-apologise for asserting boundaries.

When I asked her where she learned that behaviour, she paused and said quietly,

"My Aunt used to tell me, 'you have to make people comfortable, even when you're not.'"

It was love disguised as training.

A survival strategy that helped her navigate the world as a woman, but one that was now holding her back as a leader.

As we worked together, Nadia began to unlearn politeness as protection.

She started naming discomfort, setting boundaries, and speaking without softening her truth.

Her authenticity didn't make her less liked, it made her more respected.

Her story is one I've heard, in different forms, across hundreds of conversations:

fear teaches us how to survive, but courage teaches us how to live.

Racialised Fear: The Weight of Memory & Science of Inherited Caution

To talk about fear in racialised terms is to talk about *memory*, not the kind stored in the mind, but in the body. It's the tremor that precedes thought. The instinct that anticipates harm before logic can intervene.

As Resmaa Menakem writes in *My Grandmother's Hands* (2017), racial trauma is carried not only in stories but in the nervous system itself, an *embodied inheritance* of collective survival. He calls it *somatic memory*: the body's record of history.

You can feel it in the tightening of breath when authority passes by.
In the subtle self-editing in predominantly white spaces.
In the deep, unspoken fatigue of carrying ancestral caution in modern skin.

These reactions are not paranoia; they are pattern recognition.
The body remembers what the world would prefer to forget.

Emerging research supports what communities of colour have long known intuitively, that trauma does not end when violence does. Epigenetic studies, such as Rachel Yehuda's (2015) work with descendants of Holocaust survivors, demonstrate how severe stress can alter gene expression related to cortisol regulation, changes that can be passed intergenerationally. Similarly, Dr. Monnica Williams (2018) and others have shown how chronic exposure to racial discrimination creates *trauma responses* comparable to PTSD, though often unrecognised by clinical frameworks.

In this context, fear is not simply emotional; it is biological.
It's the body adapting to centuries of hypervigilance, fine-tuning its alarm systems to anticipate danger even in "safe" environments.

In William Smith's (2004) study of Black faculty, this constant vigilance was named *racial battle fatigue*, a cumulative stress response to everyday bias, microaggressions, and double standards. These professionals weren't imagining hostility; they were absorbing it, physically, neurologically, daily.

The body remains in fight-or-flight mode, even in workplaces that claim to value inclusion.
A polite meeting room can still echo with the history of exclusion.

History's Long Shadow

To live in a racialised body is to live in history's aftershock.
Every raised eyebrow, every mispronounced name, every surveillance of tone is not an isolated incident, it's a legacy

In Britain, that legacy stretches from **the transatlantic slave trade** to the **Windrush generation**, from the colour bar to the quiet codes of "fit." It extends through the policies that shaped migration, the stereotypes embedded in media, and the silences maintained in classrooms.

Post-war Britain often congratulated itself on tolerance while failing to confront its colonial melancholia .
"Multiculturalism" became a slogan, not a reckoning, and beneath it, a quieter message persisted: you can belong here, but only on our terms.

The sociologist Paul Gilroy (1993) captured this in *The Black Atlantic*:

"*Modern racial consciousness is the product of travel and displacement, of routes, not roots.*" In other words, the diasporic self is born in motion, never fully home, always half-translated. Fear, then, becomes the compass guiding, restraining, protecting, exhausting.

A Coaching Reflection: The Armour of Excellence

A client once told me, "I'm tired of being twice as good just to be seen as enough."
She was a Black senior manager, the only one in her department. Every presentation was an audition. Every mistake, a potential confirmation of stereotype.

She had perfected professionalism as armour.
The immaculate language, the poised composure, the refusal to show fatigue, all of it was survival dressed as success.

As we worked together, she realised what she called *discipline* was, in part, *defence*.
Her excellence was not only ambition, but it was also vigilance.
A form of fear turned functional.

"I've been holding my breath for years," she said.
That sentence broke something open.
Together, we worked not to dismantle her drive, but to decouple it from danger, to teach the body that excellence could come from joy, not just proof.

This is the subtle but vital work of racial healing: teaching the nervous system that safety does not always require control.

The Language of Fear

As **Frantz Fanon** wrote in *Black Skin, White Masks* (1952),

"To speak a language is to take on a world, a culture."
To live in a racialised body is to carry a language of caution, resilience, defiance, that speaks before you do. Your very presence becomes communication.

But that communication is often misread.
The same confidence that reads as "leadership" in one body reads as "threat" in another.
The same silence that reads as "thoughtful" for one is read as "cold" for another.

This is not about perception alone; it's about the inherited psychology of hierarchy.
And every act of courage in such a system, every moment of truth-telling, every boundary, every breath is therefore an act of defiance against history itself.

To understand racialised fear is to understand that trauma is not an event; it is an ecosystem.
It moves through time, through families, through workplaces, through language and tone.
It is the hum beneath belonging, the tension of being visible yet unseen.

But this awareness also offers a path forward.
Naming the weight of memory turns survival into self-understanding.

It invites healing not as erasure of pain, but as the integration of it, transforming what once signalled danger into wisdom.

Because racialised fear, when acknowledged, becomes evidence not of fragility, but of endurance. It is the body remembering, and still moving forward.

The Economics of Fear

The economic order teaches obedience not only through wages, but through worry.
Fear of losing stability, a home, a visa, a reputation keeps people compliant within unjust systems. It's what Maurizio Lazzarato (2012) described as *the indebted man*: a subject bound not by chains but by obligation. Debt, whether financial or emotional, becomes a mechanism of control, the psychological interest paid on survival.

For the single mother, the migrant worker, the early-career employee of colour, courage is not a slogan.
It's a calculation.
When your survival depends on stability, risk-taking looks like recklessness.
When courage is defined by those with safety nets, everyone else gets framed as timid.

This is why intersectional courage must always be contextual, it must honour the material realities that shape emotional ones.
Fear, in many cases, is not a flaw of mindset but a map of circumstance.

Precarity as a System

In *The Precariat: The New Dangerous Class* (2011), **Guy Standing** describes how neoliberal economies manufacture insecurity fragmenting work, eroding stability, and turning uncertainty into policy.
In such a world, fear is not an exception; it's an instrument.
It keeps workers productive, students indebted, and citizens cautious.

You don't have to threaten people to control them; you just have to make security scarce.

And yet, the emotional cost of precarity is rarely discussed.
Fear becomes ambient, a background hum that shapes decision-making, relationships, and creativity. It makes people choose predictability over purpose, safety over selfhood, not because they lack courage, but because they lack cushion.

As **bell hooks** wrote, *"Living simply makes loving simple."*

But simplicity, under capitalism, is a privilege.

For many, love, rest, and courage are luxuries purchased with stability.

During a workshop with a tech start-up, I met a young designer his name was *Ade*.
He was talented, ambitious, and clearly underpaid.
When I asked why he hadn't negotiated a raise, he smiled tightly: "I can't afford to make them uncomfortable."

Ade was the first in his family to work in tech.

His parents had sacrificed everything to get him to university.

"Job security," he said, "is my family's dream. I can't risk losing it."

His fear wasn't a lack of confidence, it was a form of loyalty.

It was the weight of generational gratitude colliding with economic vulnerability.

We spoke about reframing courage, not as defiance, but as dignity.

Instead of a confrontation, he drafted a value statement, outlining his contributions and the impact of his design work. Three months later, he secured a pay rise and told me,

"It wasn't about the money. It was about finally acting like I belong."

Ade's story reveals a deeper truth:

Courage under constraint isn't about being fearless; it's about negotiating fear in context.

It's about asking, *What does bravery look like when the cost of risk is unequal?*

Capitalism has turned fear into infrastructure.

It monetises insecurity, packages it as ambition, and sells it back as self-improvement.

It tells you to *be brave*, but only within the parameters of productivity.

It rewards risk-takers, but only those who can afford to lose.

In such a landscape, courage must be redefined not as rebellion against risk, but as resistance to reduction, the insistence that your value exceeds your economic utility. Because in a culture where worth is measured by output, even rest begins to feel like failure, and fear disguises itself as drive.

True courage, then, is not simply quitting the job or taking the leap.

It's the quiet decision to hold onto your humanity in systems designed to make you forget it, to resist the narrative that says your existence must always be justified through achievement.

Economic fear is not a personal defect; it is a systemic design. It reveals how material insecurity shapes emotional landscapes, how courage is always contextual, and how risk itself is a privilege unevenly distributed.

To understand this is to see that courage without justice is merely performance.

Real bravery must be collective, structural, and compassionate.

Because fear will always speak through economics, but courage, *real* courage, speaks back through solidarity.

The Intersectional Workplace: Fear in Professional Spaces

Nowhere does intersectional fear hide more quietly than in professional life.

Here, it masquerades as composure, diplomacy, or "fit."

In organisations, two patterns appear again and again:

- **Conformity fear** — the fear of deviating from dominant culture.
- **Authenticity fear** — the fear of being punished for being yourself.

Studies by **Catalyst (2019)** found that nearly half of women of colour report being "on guard" at work constantly anticipating bias, tone-policing, or misinterpretation. That vigilance, what Catalyst calls *emotional tax*, drains energy, creativity, and engagement.
The body remains alert long after the meeting ends.

As **Brené Brown** reminds us,

"Courage is contagious, but so is fear."

When fear becomes organisational culture, people stop taking risks, not because they lack bravery, but because the cost of honesty is higher than the reward for conformity.

Leadership that understands this recognises that *psychological safety* isn't a perk, it's infrastructure. It's what allows courage to move beyond motivational language and become behavioural truth.

Fear as a Feature of Organisational Design ?

Fear in workplaces isn't accidental, it's architectural.
Corporate structures often reward compliance and penalise candour.

People learn that fitting in is safer than standing out, that silence is strategic, that "professionalism" is often code for assimilation.

Organisational theorist **Amy Edmondson (1999)** introduced the concept of *psychological safety*, a shared belief that it's safe to take interpersonal risks. Her research found that high-performing teams weren't those with the fewest mistakes, but those where people *felt safe* to admit them.

Yet for marginalised employees, that safety is conditional.

As **Kahn (1990)** noted in his foundational work on *personal engagement*, people bring their "preferred selves" to work only when they believe it's safe to do so.

If belonging is fragile, authenticity becomes a gamble.

And so, fear seeps in, quiet, cultural, cumulative.

It doesn't shout; it whispers:

"Tone it down."
"Don't make this about race."
"You're lucky to be here."

Over time, those whispers become norms.
Fear becomes policy disguised as politeness.

The Cost of Cultural Masking

The emotional tax of intersectional fear is invisible but immense. Deloitte (2022) found that 59% of minority professionals engage in *covering*, downplaying elements of their identity to avoid negative judgement.

This self-editing might protect status, but it corrodes authenticity.

Employees describe lowering their voice, straightening their hair, "cutting dreadlocks" moderating their accent, or suppressing cultural references to appear "neutral."

But neutrality, in most workplaces, means proximity to whiteness, maleness, or privilege.

This creates a paradox, organisations preach inclusion while rewarding conformity.
Fear becomes the unspoken manager of behaviour, shaping who speaks, who stays silent, and who leaves quietly mid-career. As Robin DiAngelo notes, "The absence of race talk in white spaces is not harmony; it's control."

The same could be said of gender, class, and disability.
Silence is rarely peace, it's the sound of fear doing its job.

In one leadership programme I ran, a participant called Warren, a Black senior leader in finance, said something that stayed with me:

"I've spent my whole career trying to look unthreatening."

He smiled as he said it, but his tone was weary.
He spoke of learning how to "manage perception", lowering his register in meetings, never interrupting, smiling when frustrated. "I didn't even realise I was doing it," he said. "It's just survival."

His story echoed through the room.
Another leader, a white woman, looked up and said, "I never have to think about any of that."

The silence that followed wasn't guilt, it was revelation.

That's what fear looks like when it's normalised, it becomes invisible to those who don't carry it.

David's courage didn't come from pretending fear didn't exist.
It came from naming it, and then refusing to perform comfort at his own expense.

In most corporate cultures, professionalism functions as a form of *emotional choreography*.
It rewards neutrality, restraint, and intellectual detachment, qualities that appear objective but are often culturally coded.

As **Sara Ahmed (2012)** writes in *On Being Included*, diversity work often asks marginalised people to "bring difference in ways that do not make a difference."
They are invited to be visible but not vocal, symbolic but not structural.

In this environment, fear becomes self-policing.
People internalise the surveillance of their own authenticity.
They learn not only *what not to say*, but *what not to feel*.

And yet, this fear is often reframed as professionalism itself.
The person who raises a concern is "too emotional."
The one who names a bias is "making it about race."
The one who advocates for inclusion is "not strategic."

But professionalism without authenticity is performance.
And performance, no matter how polished, always cracks under pressure.

From Fear to Freedom: Redefining Leadership

Just as fear shapes culture, then courage can reshape it, but that requires leadership willing to make psychological safety structural, not performative.

It means embedding equity in *how* we hire, *who* we promote, and *what* we normalise.

It means creating systems where honesty is rewarded, not punished, where truth-telling is seen as contribution, not conflict.

True inclusion is not about representation alone; it's about re-distribution of power, trust, and permission.

As I often tell executives:

"You can't claim to value diversity and punish difference."

Leadership that dismantles fear doesn't do so with slogans, or events on cultural heritage days weeks or months, it does so with structures. It turns courage into culture.

Fear in professional spaces is rarely loud. It hides in the rituals of respectability, in the unspoken rules of belonging, in the quiet compliance mistaken for loyalty.

This section teaches that intersectional fear is not about fragile individuals, it's about fragile systems. And if systems can be built, they can be rebuilt. Psychological safety, therefore, is not a perk. It's the precondition for truth, creativity, and growth. Courage becomes culture when fear is no longer policy.

Intersectional Healing: Reclaiming the Right to Safety

If fear is intersectional, healing must be intersectional too.
It cannot be reduced to mantras, mindset shifts, or corporate wellness slogans.
Healing must confront the same structures that wounded us.

bell hooks called this *radical self-love*, not self-esteem built on achievement or approval, but the *restoration of worth stripped by oppression.*
It's the act of saying:

"My safety should not depend on my silence."

For those at the margins, healing is rarely solitary.
It happens in community, in resistance, in art and in the places where truth is shared, not hidden.

The psychological wounds of inequality are not only personal; they are structural.
Fear was never just individual anxiety — it was social engineering.
So healing, too, must be re-engineered at the collective level.

As **Kenneth Hardy (2015)** describes, *collective healing* transforms internalised fear into shared agency. When people who have been silenced find voice in each other, silence becomes solidarity. The act of witnessing itself becomes medicine.

This is why healing spaces must also be justice spaces, classrooms, workplaces, and families that confront rather than conceal difference, because what trauma isolates, community restores.

Audre Lorde reminded us that

"Caring for myself is not self-indulgence, it is self-preservation, and that is an act of political warfare."

In that spirit, rest becomes resistance, joy becomes justice, and belonging becomes protest. Intersectional healing, then, is not about fixing the self to fit the system, it's about building systems that honour the self.

The Body as Memory and Site of Repair

Fear lodges itself in the body, so healing must begin there too.
Resmaa Menakem (2017) teaches that the body doesn't just hold trauma; it holds history.
Our nervous systems become archives of what we've survived, the breath held too long, the muscles that never fully relax, the vigilance mistaken for personality.

Healing is the slow, deliberate work of teaching the body a new story:
That safety can exist without suppression.
That calm can come without compliance.
That stillness can be power, not punishment.

When the body learns safety, the mind follows.

Case Reflection: Healing in Practice

In a leadership retreat I once facilitated, a woman named *Aisha*, a Muslim manager in the public sector, shared that she hadn't taken a single full breath at work in years.

She described the constant vigilance of being "the only one": the only woman in hijab, the only woman of colour, the only one expected to educate others about "diversity."

When we did a grounding exercise, she started to cry.
Not from sadness, but from recognition.
"I didn't realise how much I was holding," she said.
Her tears weren't breakdown, they were release.

Healing for Aisha wasn't about resilience; it was about permission.
Permission to exhale.
To rest.
To exist without constantly managing perception.

That moment reminded me that healing is not found in grand gestures — it's found in the quiet reclamation of breath.

From Coping to Creating

Healing begins where fear loses its authority.
When we stop negotiating for safety and start building it.
When we replace apology with agency.
When survival shifts from merely staying alive to living fully.

Intersectional healing asks:

- What systems need to change so my peace isn't conditional?
- What communities can hold me when the world cannot?
- What practices help me recover the parts of myself that learned to hide?

Healing, then, is not the opposite of fear, it's the evolution of it.
It's fear transformed into awareness, awareness into boundaries, and boundaries into freedom.

Intersectional healing reminds us that safety is not self-help, it's self-determination.
It teaches that true recovery is never individual; it is relational, communal, and systemic.
It's not just about feeling better; it's about reclaiming the right to exist without shrinking.

Fear once taught us to survive. Healing teaches us to return home, to ourselves, to each other, to the world we are capable of rebuilding.

Because courage without healing burns out.
Healing without justice breaks down.
But healing with truth, that's where transformation begins.

The Courage to Reimagine Safety

Safety, through an intersectional lens, lives not in silence but in breath, in the space to exhale, to exist without explanation or apology. It begins where belonging is felt, not negotiated, where one's presence no longer requires performance.

True safety emerges when justice and compassion occupy the same ground.
It asks us to transform the environments that create fear, not simply to survive within them.

To make safety less a refuge from danger, and more a rhythm of daily life, woven into policy, culture, and care.

Angela Davis once declared:

"I am no longer accepting the things I cannot change. I am changing the things I cannot accept."

This is the radical heart of courage, the audacity to imagine safety as collective architecture, not personal privilege.

A world redesigned so that protection is not conditional, and freedom is not rationed.

Safety as a Collective Design

Safety has always been political granted, revoked, or rationed along the lines of power.
The ability to walk home freely, to speak without consequence, to make a mistake without exile, these are not universal rights; they are measured permissions. As Judith Butler (2004) reminds us in *Precarious Life*, some lives are grieved publicly while others are quietly deemed expendable.

Safety, then, is a mirror of collective value, a reflection of whose humanity institutions choose to protect.
To reimagine it means dismantling the hierarchies that decide whose fear matters.
It means building cultures where trust is policy, not rhetoric.
Where empathy replaces surveillance.
Where care replaces control.

This vision demands more than inclusion. It calls for redesign workplaces that prioritise wellbeing over optics, leaders who model vulnerability as strength, systems that measure safety not by the absence of complaints but by the presence of trust.

Because courage, in its highest form, is not simply surviving unsafe worlds, it is shaping new ones.

Fear, Safety, and the Politics of Control

Fear has always been a political tool, used to discipline bodies, regulate expression, and maintain order. It teaches us that silence is protection, that invisibility is virtue. But as bell hooks (1994) warned in *Teaching to Transgress*, "The classroom remains the most radical space of possibility." So too does every boardroom, community hall, and conversation where we choose truth over compliance.

When fear is unlearned collectively, safety shifts from protectionism to liberation. It stops being a private state and becomes a shared ethic, a social contract built on dignity. As **Gabor Maté (2022)** notes, "Safety is not the absence of threat, but the presence of connection." The goal, then, is not to become fearless, but to build worlds where fear is no longer necessary for survival.

Case Reflection: A Future Worth Breathing In

In one organisational session, I asked participants to describe what safety at work would *feel* like, not policies or protocols, but sensations.

One woman said, "Like unclenching my jaw."
Another said, "Like not having to translate myself."
A man said, "Like being able to admit I don't know without worrying it'll cost me respect."

These weren't demands, they were desires for basic human ease.
Safety, when reimagined this way, is not an HR initiative.
It's the architecture of humanity.

The Fear That Doesn't Belong to You

"I am deliberate and afraid of nothing." Audre Lorde

There comes a point in every healing journey where you must ask: **Which fears are truly mine, and which were assigned to me?**

The fear of being too loud.
The fear of standing out.
The fear of being misunderstood.
The fear of taking up space that was always yours.

These fears are often inherited, passed through culture, history, and expectation.
They are the echoes of other people's comfort, living rent-free in your nervous system.

Ask yourself:

- Whose comfort has my silence been protecting?
- Whose approval have I mistaken for safety?
- What would it mean to live without rehearsing permission?

Fear, once examined, loses its authority.
To name it is to loosen its grip.
To understand its context is to reclaim your power.

And to live beyond it, that is courage made visible.

Reflection: From Survival to Sovereignty

If fear once taught you to survive, courage teaches you to belong.
Safety, then, is not a space you find, it's a space you create.
With boundaries, with truth, with others who remind you that rest is not retreat, and bravery is not noise.

The future of courage lies not in the myth of fearlessness, but in the practice of collective care.
Because when safety expands, fear becomes unnecessary and when belonging deepens, courage becomes ordinary.

The courage to reimagine safety is, ultimately, the courage to reimagine society to build a world where every breath feels like home.

Summary: What This Chapter Taught Us

In this chapter, we traced fear beyond the boundaries of the self and into the architecture of society.
We saw how fear becomes a language of control, spoken through systems that decide who belongs, who is believed, and who is safe enough to be fully seen. Through the lens of intersectionality, we learned that fear is not distributed equally; it is shaped by history,

culture, and power. For some, fear whispers in microaggressions and tone policing; for others, it roars through exclusion, surveillance, and structural neglect. We uncovered how colonialism and patriarchy rewired older ways of living, turning balance into hierarchy, harmony into domination, and how those fractures still echo in our workplaces, relationships, and inner worlds. We recognised that fear wears many faces: politeness, performance, perfectionism, endurance, each a mask we've been taught to wear to survive systems that were never built for our wholeness. And ultimately, we arrived at the truth that to heal from fear, we must do more than soothe our nervous systems; we must reimagine the systems themselves. Because courage, in this context, is not only personal, it is political. It is the work of reclaiming safety, voice, and belonging on our own terms.

Core Takeaways from Chapter 3 summarised:

1. Fear is not only emotional, it is social, historical, and systemic.
2. Power teaches fear unevenly, shaping who must perform safety and who is allowed to feel it.
3. Intersectionality reveals that fear changes form across race, gender, class, and neurodiversity.
4. What we internalise as personal anxiety is often inherited from structures built to contain us.
5. Colonialism and patriarchy fractured older models of balance, replacing harmony with hierarchy.
6. Misogyny and racialised bias turn fear into discipline, policing emotion, tone, and visibility.

7. Unlearning fear requires both healing the self and redesigning the systems that sustain harm.

So, if this chapter revealed the architecture of fear, our next one invites us to move through it. Because awareness alone doesn't dissolve fear, movement does. *Courage in Action* is where theory meets the body, where reflection becomes practice. It's about learning to stay with discomfort long enough for it to teach you something, about your patterns, your boundaries, your power. Here, courage stops being an idea and becomes a behaviour, not the absence of fear, but the decision to keep showing up in its presence.

CHAPTER 4

Courage in Action: Navigating Discomfort

Along our journey in the previous chapters, we've unmasked fear, traced its anatomy, and learned to recognise the many ways it hides in perfectionism, in hesitation, in the need to please. We've come to see that fear isn't just something we feel; it's something we've been taught to manage, avoid, even perform around. It lives not only in our thoughts but in our posture, in our tone, in the subtle ways we shrink ourselves to fit.

Understanding fear gave us language. It allowed us to name the patterns that once controlled us in silence. But naming fear is not the same as moving through it. Awareness reveals the door, walking through it is another act entirely.

This next stage of our journey is about embodiment turning understanding into action. Because knowledge without practice is comfort dressed as progress. To transform fear, we must learn to stay present in the very places it used to make us flinch.

Courage doesn't begin with confidence; it begins with contact. With that trembling moment when we stop avoiding what unsettles us and decide to stay. True growth doesn't bloom in still water, it rises through resistance. Discomfort is the friction that shapes us into who we're meant to become.

We spend our lives trying to avoid that friction, mistaking comfort for peace and uncertainty for danger. Yet every meaningful transformation begins with unease, the tension between who we've been and who we're becoming. The real work is learning to hold that tension without retreating.

So as we move forward, let this chapter be your invitation to stay. To sit in the mess of becoming. To stop waiting until you feel fearless and start walking while still afraid. Because courage is not a destination; it's a daily practice of remaining open, honest, and awake, especially when it would be easier not to.

Discomfort Is the Ground We Grow From

The journey toward courage isn't smooth or effortless. It isn't about deleting fear, mastering confidence, or finding the perfect formula for peace. It's about learning to stay, to remain present in the places that unsettle us, to stop running when discomfort calls our name.

Discomfort is not the enemy of growth; it's the evidence of it. Every time you choose honesty over hiding, truth over performance, action over avoidance, you're engaging in the sacred work of expansion. But growth demands friction. Just as muscles strengthen through resistance, our inner lives grow through challenge. Without tension, there is no transformation.

We've been conditioned to treat discomfort as a problem to solve, a glitch in the system that needs fixing. We medicate it with distraction, drown it in busyness, silence it with certainty. But what if discomfort isn't a warning sign, but a waypoint? What if it's not punishment, but invitation?

Because the truth is, every meaningful change in life begins in unease.

The conversation you're avoiding.

The job you've outgrown.

The truth you keep postponing because it asks too much of you.

That is the edge, the space between who you've been and who you're becoming.

When we retreat from discomfort, we stay loyal to what is familiar, even if it limits us. But when we lean into it, we start to see that the tension itself is fertile ground, a kind of emotional soil where courage takes root.

Every breakthrough I've ever witnessed, whether in my own life or in the lives of those I've coached, has been born from this tension. Not from clarity, not from calm, but from chaos, from the moment someone said, "I'm tired of pretending I'm fine."

I've seen people reach that point in boardrooms and therapy rooms, in coaching sessions and kitchen tables, that quiet moment when the discomfort of staying the same finally outweighs the fear of change. That's when transformation begins.

Discomfort asks something of us: to be honest. To pause long enough to hear what our fear is trying to protect. To listen to the body before it numbs. To sit in uncertainty long enough to see that we can survive it.

Courage isn't the absence of fear; it's the decision to act within it. And that decision is rarely comfortable. It's sweaty, shaky, vulnerable, and full of doubt. But it's also holy.

This chapter is about that process, the art of staying with discomfort instead of fleeing it. It's about learning to interpret unease as information, to welcome resistance as the teacher it is, and to understand that our growth doesn't happen in the light of certainty, but in the shadow of not knowing.

In the pages that follow, we'll explore how discomfort manifests, in your thoughts, your body, your relationships, your work. We'll look at how avoidance shrinks possibility, and how leaning in, however clumsy or slow, begins to reshape everything.

Because when we learn to stand in discomfort without rushing to escape it, something remarkable happens fear stops being a wall, and starts becoming a doorway. Discomfort is the ground we grow from, not the proof of weakness, but the birthplace of wisdom.

Stepping outside your comfort zone doesn't always mean dramatic leaps like bungee jumping or climbing Everest. More often, it's the small, everyday acts that carry the most weight. Walking into a room where you don't know anyone. Speaking up when your instinct is to stay quiet. Admitting you don't have all the answers. Those moments feel awkward, the silence before a conversation starts, the fear of saying the wrong thing, the worry that you won't fit. But if you lean in rather than shrink back, you create the chance for new friendships, fresh perspectives, and a broader sense of belonging. Each small risk is like a tiny flex of your resilience muscle.

The same applies when you're learning something new. Whether it's picking up a guitar, figuring out a new piece of software, or stumbling through a foreign language, the early stages are messy. Your fingers feel clumsy, your sentences don't make sense, your mistakes feel endless. It's uncomfortable, sometimes even embarrassing. But that discomfort is the learning. Every mistake gives you feedback. Every moment of frustration points you towards progress. Without the fumbling and the friction, there's no polish, no fluency, no mastery. The struggle isn't a detour it's the path itself.

Even something as simple as voicing a different opinion in a group can feel deeply uncomfortable. When the room is leaning one way, it takes courage to say, "Actually, I see this differently." The fear of conflict, of being labelled difficult, or of sticking out as the odd one out often keeps people silent. I've been there myself nodding along while my inner voice is screaming the opposite. But the truth is, speaking up respectfully and thoughtfully can be one of the most powerful things you do. It can shift the conversation, challenge assumptions, and open space for a richer outcome. Yes, it might feel shaky in the moment, but each time you choose to honour your voice, you strengthen it.

All of these examples share one thing: they ask you to step beyond what feels safe and familiar. To lean into awkwardness, vulnerability, or the discomfort of not knowing. The richest opportunities for growth are rarely found in the familiar. They live just beyond the edges of our comfort zone, waiting for us to be brave enough to reach for them. If we always take the path of least resistance, we build our own cage one with bars made of fear and the absence of challenge.

Resilience Through Discomfort

The real gift of leaning into discomfort is resilience. Resilience isn't something you're born with it's something you build. Every time you notice the fear, breathe through it, and act anyway, you strengthen that muscle. Every time you figure out a new piece of software, you're reminding yourself of your own capacity to adapt. Walking into a new group isn't just about meeting people it's about proving to yourself that you can manage your anxieties and find your place. These aren't isolated events; they're bricks in the foundation of a stronger, more adaptable self.

And here's the bonus: discomfort often reveals new sides of you. When you're pushed to your limits, you have to find fresh ways of thinking, new strategies, and untapped strengths. Think about companies like Netflix they started out mailing DVDs, but when streaming technology emerged, the discomfort of a changing market forced them to reinvent themselves. What looked like disruption became the spark for innovation. The same is true for us: in the pressure of discomfort, we often stumble across capabilities we didn't even know we had. That's often where hidden talents emerge. An introvert forced to give a presentation might start by dreading every moment heart pounding, palms sweating. But in working through that discomfort, they learn how to calm their nerves, structure their message, and connect with an audience. Sometimes they even discover a knack for public speaking they never imagined they had. What once felt unbearable becomes the foundation of a whole new skill set.

Discomfort, then, isn't a barrier it's the teacher. It's the resistance that makes you stronger, the friction that polishes you. The very thing you're tempted to avoid is often the thing that carries you into the next version of yourself.

Avoiding discomfort might feel safe in the moment, but over time it shrinks your world. If you always stick to the familiar, the easy, the predictable, you never get to discover what lies beyond it. You don't find out what you're capable of, nor do you develop the resilience and confidence that come from wrestling with challenge. What begins as comfort soon turns into stagnation a nagging sense that life has more to offer than the small slice you're allowing yourself. The comfort zone, tempting though it feels, can become a gilded cage: it protects you from difficulty, yes, but it also keeps you from growth, from discovery, from the full vibrancy of life. Real living begins when you allow yourself to feel the sting of uncertainty, the ache of effort, and the unease of the unknown and move forward anyway. Courage is not about eliminating discomfort; it's about choosing action in the middle of it.

Courage Is Not Fearlessness

The essence of courage, then, isn't a serene inner calm, untouched by nerves or anxiety. It's not about waiting until fear disappears. Courage is the deliberate act of engaging with the world while fear is present. Bravery isn't the absence of butterflies in your stomach it's stepping onto the stage, speaking your truth, or taking the leap with the butterflies fluttering wildly.

Think of a seasoned speaker standing in front of a packed hall. From the outside, they look composed steady voice, strong presence. But inside? Their stomach might be turning, their pulse racing, their inner critic whispering doubts. Their courage isn't in being free of those feelings; it's in choosing to speak regardless. They don't wait for the nerves to vanish. They acknowledge them, maybe even channel that energy into their delivery, and then they carry on. Their bravery lives in the act of speaking, connecting, delivering doing not in an imagined absence of fear.

This distinction is crucial. Too often we tell ourselves, "If I feel afraid, I must not be courageous enough." That belief keeps us stuck, waiting for a mythical moment when fear won't exist. But that moment never comes. Courage means refusing to let fear disqualify you from acting.

Take the entrepreneur launching a new business. Their days are full of uncertainty markets shift, competitors emerge, money runs thin. They don't wake up every morning brimming with certainty about success. More often, they lie awake at night worrying about payroll, doubting their decisions, staring at projections that don't quite add up. And yet, they write the business plan. They pitch for funding. They hire their first employee. They make the first sale. Each of those steps is taken in the presence of fear, not the absence of it. Their courage is measured in action in the doing, building, trying, even when failure is a real and constant possibility.

That's what courage looks like in practice: not waiting until the fear fades, but moving forward while it's still there. The whisper of doubt doesn't mean you're not brave. Acting anyway that's where bravery lives

Everyday Acts of Bravery

This way of seeing courage, not as a state of fearlessness but as action in the presence of fear makes it far more accessible. You don't have to wait for the day you "feel brave enough." You build courage by doing. Every time you speak up when you'd rather stay silent, try something new instead of retreating to the familiar, or keep going when everything in you wants to quit you're practising courage. These aren't necessarily headline moments of heroism. They're the small, everyday decisions that shape your character and expand what you believe is possible for yourself.

Take the act of admitting you don't know something. In many workplaces, there's an unspoken expectation to always appear competent, to have answers on demand. Saying "I don't know" can feel terrifying like exposing a crack in your armour. The fear of looking foolish or unprepared often leads people to bluff, deflect, or stay quiet. But the truly courageous response is to say, "I don't know but I'll find out," or "That's a great question; let me get back to you." That moment of honesty, however uncomfortable, builds trust and credibility. It shows you're more committed to learning and truth than to ego. That's bravery in action.

Or think about setting boundaries. Saying "no" can feel like standing on a cliff edge, especially if you've been conditioned to keep others happy. The fear of disappointing someone, of causing conflict, or of being judged as unhelpful, can be overwhelming. And yet, courage lives in the quiet act of saying, "I can't take that on right now," or "That doesn't work for me." Not because you're immune to the discomfort, but because you value your wellbeing and integrity enough to protect them. Boundaries aren't about shutting others out; they're about respecting yourself enough to draw the line even if your voice shakes when you do it.

When you redefine courage as action rather than feeling, you reclaim your agency. Fear doesn't have to paralyse you. You can notice it, name it, and still decide: "What's the action here that lines up with my values?" That choice to move towards what matters even while fear is present is courage at its core. It's the difference between waiting for conditions to feel "just right" and learning to keep moving while the storm is raging.

WHAT ARE YOU SO AFRAID OF?

Think about the last time you had to learn something difficult a language, a new piece of software, a skill that felt alien at first. The early stages are messy. You get things wrong. You feel clumsy, inadequate, maybe even embarrassed. The fear of not being good enough lurks in the background: "Maybe I don't have the talent. Maybe I'm wasting my time." But the people who eventually master those skills aren't the ones who never felt doubt. They're the ones who carried on anyway. They kept practising the awkward sentences. They pressed the wrong keys until they got it right. They stuck with the frustration long enough for it to turn into fluency. That persistence that decision to keep showing up in the face of discomfort is courage. Courage, then, isn't the absence of nerves, doubt, or resistance. It's the choice to act anyway, again and again, until your world expands to fit the person you're becoming.

This way of looking at courage helps strip it of its mystery. It's not some rare, heroic quality reserved for a chosen few it's a learnable skill, available to all of us. And it doesn't just appear in dramatic moments. Courage is just as present in the ordinary as in the extraordinary. It's there when you strike up a conversation with a stranger, when you push through a tough workout, when you own up and apologise for a mistake, or when you speak up for what you believe in, even if your voice shakes. Each time you act in the presence of discomfort, you're practising courage.

The shift comes when we stop waiting to *feel* brave and instead focus on the *doing*. Every deliberate choice to move forward despite nerves, despite doubt builds your capacity for bravery.

Over time, it turns courage from some lofty, abstract ideal into a lived reality. Fear doesn't disappear it never does. But you learn that fear doesn't have to dictate your actions. You can notice it, acknowledge it, and still choose to move. That consistent, deliberate forward motion, no matter what the internal weather feels like, is where true strength is forged.

Rejection and Resilience

And yet, there's one fear that touches almost everyone: rejection. It's part of the human experience, unavoidable if you're living, working, and taking risks in the world. It comes in many forms the job you didn't get, the proposal turned down, the harsh critique of your work, or the awkward silence when someone doesn't respond the way you'd hoped. Rejection hurts. It can make you want to retreat to safety, to stop putting yourself out there. But hidden inside that sting is also an opportunity, a chance to grow tougher, clearer, and more resilient.

The first step is dismantling the story we often attach to rejection. Too often, we take it personally. We make it mean something about our worth. A job rejection becomes proof that we're not good enough. A romantic rejection feels like confirmation that we're unlovable. A critique morphs into a verdict on our talent or intelligence. This is where rejection wounds us most deeply when we confuse an external outcome with our intrinsic value.

But rejection doesn't define us. It only ever reflects a mismatch of timing, of needs, of preferences. When we uncouple rejection from our self-worth, we create a sturdier foundation to stand on. Instead of collapsing under the weight of "not good enough," we can start to see rejection as information, as redirection, as part of the process. And with each experience, we can build what I call rejection resilience the ability to bounce back stronger, clearer, and more determined than before.

The real shift comes when we begin to detach our self-worth from external validation. Who you are, your value as a human being, is not decided by how many people approve of you, how many times you're accepted, or how often your work is praised.

Your worth is inherent.

It's a birthright.

No rejection can take it away.

That said, knowing this in theory and living it in practice are two different things. It takes conscious effort to build an inner compass strong enough to guide you, even when the outside world is full of noise. It means cultivating a deep belief in your own goodness and capability, one that doesn't collapse at the first sign of criticism or disapproval. When that belief is steady, rejection loses much of its power to wound.

I learned this lesson the hard way when I set up my company, **Diversify World**. In the beginning, I thought the hardest part would be building systems, finding clients, or figuring out the finances. I thought success was about structure, spreadsheets, strategy, and solid plans. But I was wrong.

The real battle was with **rejection**.

I sent countless emails that never got answered.
LinkedIn InMails sat unopened, sometimes from people I knew personally.
I had doors closed on me that I was certain should've been open. There were days it felt humiliating, like I was invisible in rooms I knew I should be seen in.

That's when I realised something no business course ever teaches you:
rejection is a mirror. It reflects back what you believe about your own worth.

At first, every "no" felt like a verdict, proof that maybe I wasn't good enough, that maybe I'd overestimated myself, that maybe this whole idea was too ambitious. I'd spend hours replaying conversations, trying to decode what I could've said differently, how I could've presented myself better. I'd overthink, over-edit, over-apologise.

But here's what I eventually learned: the discomfort wasn't punishment, it was training.

Every unanswered message was an invitation to detach my confidence from other people's responses.
Every ignored email was a quiet test of whether I could stay committed even when the world wasn't clapping. Every "sorry, not now" was a prompt to build patience where I used to crave instant validation.

Slowly, I began to see rejection differently.

It wasn't evidence of failure, it was feedback from life, nudging me to strengthen what was weak, to refine what was unclear, and to keep showing up even when it stung.

I started noticing patterns.

The rejections hurt most when they touched an old nerve, when they echoed childhood moments of being overlooked, when they confirmed the old story that success for people like me had to be twice as hard. That's when I understood: **discomfort doesn't just expose weakness; it exposes wounds.**

And that's the work, not to run from that sting, but to stay with it long enough to hear what it's trying to say. Because when you can sit in that space, the space between what you wanted and what you received, you start to realise something powerful: every "no" can become a new direction.

Each time I faced rejection, I learned to respond differently.

Instead of spiralling, I reflected.

Instead of personalising, I analysed.

Instead of retreating, I rebuilt.

That shift didn't happen overnight, but over hundreds of small, private moments where I chose to keep going. I'd close my laptop after another ignored message, take a breath, and remind myself: *this is the work*. This discomfort the silence, the doubt, the waiting, is the ground I'm growing from.

Eventually, something shifted. My outreach got clearer. My confidence steadier. My boundaries stronger.

And in time, doors that once stayed shut began to open, not because I chased them harder, but because I stopped seeing "no" as proof of my inadequacy.

That's what discomfort does if you let it: it forges resilience that no success can teach you.
It strips away the need for approval and replaces it with something quieter but far stronger, conviction.

Now, when I mentor founders or coach leaders, I tell them the truth no one told me:
discomfort isn't the obstacle, it's the curriculum.
It's the stretch that shapes you.
The silence that strengthens you.
The resistance that refines you.

Because the real growth didn't happen when the business started to flourish, it happened in the seasons when no one was answering.

Think of a seasoned salesperson. Their job is built on the possibility of hearing "no." Every call, every pitch, every meeting carries rejection risk. If they let each lost deal define them, they wouldn't last long. But successful salespeople learn not to see rejection as proof of personal inadequacy. They treat it as data. Was the product the wrong fit? Was the timing off? Did something go wrong in communication? Each "no" becomes feedback, information to refine their approach, improve their pitch, and strengthen their chances of landing the next "yes." They aren't defined by the doors that close, but by their persistence in seeking the ones that open.

The same is true in the creative world. Writers, artists, musicians, anyone who puts their work out there, quickly becomes familiar with rejection letters, unreturned calls, or dismissive critiques. It can feel brutal, personal, soul-crushing. But those who thrive learn to separate the work from the worker. A publisher turning down a manuscript isn't saying, "You have no talent." More often, it's about fit, timing, or market trends. An artist might be told their work is "too avant-garde" for one gallery, only to find another that celebrates it. Rejection of the work is not rejection of the self. The difference lies in mindset: do you interpret "no" as a verdict on your worth, or as a signal to adapt, refine, and keep creating?

This is the heart of rejection resilience: developing emotional detachment from outcomes. It doesn't mean becoming cold or indifferent. It means recognising the limits of your control. You can control your effort, your preparation, and your intent, but you can't always control how others respond. Disappointment is natural, but it doesn't have to break you.

You can feel the sting, process it, and still move forward.

A helpful reframe is to see rejection as redirection. Every closed door pushes you somewhere else. The job you didn't get might have tied you to a path that wasn't really right for you. The relationship that didn't work out might have spared you years of struggle. This isn't to deny the hurt rejection always stings but it's an invitation to trust that sometimes what feels like a setback is actually a step towards a better fit.

Another strategy, one that reshaped how I move through life and leadership, is to **diversify your sources of validation.**

When I first started Diversify World, I didn't realise how much of my self-worth was tied to outcomes, to external recognition, to other people's approval, to visible success. Every unanswered email felt personal. Every "no" carried weight.

I'd send proposals into the void and refresh my inbox every hour. When responses didn't come, I'd replay my outreach in my head: *Was the tone off? Did I sound too confident? Not confident enough? Should I have written to someone else?* I wasn't just waiting for opportunities, I was waiting for affirmation.

And the truth is, when your sense of worth depends on one source, a job title, a client, a relationship, a single "yes", rejection from that source feels catastrophic. It's like leaning your whole life against one pillar and watching it crack.

At some point, I had to confront an uncomfortable truth: I wasn't really building a business; I was building an approval system. My sense of progress, even my peace, was outsourced.

So I started doing the hard work of reclaiming it. Not through grand epiphanies, but through small, grounded practices that slowly taught me to anchor myself in something deeper and wider than external validation.

1. Redefining Progress

In the early months of building Diversify World, my idea of success was brutally binary: win or lose, deal or no deal, email reply or silence. I measured my worth through metrics. If I didn't get a client that week, I felt like I was failing, not just as a founder, but as a person.

That kind of thinking is poison. It makes you blind to everything you *are* achieving simply by staying the course.

So, I started to redefine what "progress" meant. I began tracking effort instead of outcomes.

Instead of asking, *Did I win today?* I started asking, *Did I show up fully? Did I send that proposal? Did I push through the discomfort?*

I created a small notebook I still keep, part gratitude journal, part progress log. Every evening, I'd write down three things that reflected growth, not results:

- "Followed up even though I felt nervous."
- "Delivered value in a conversation, even if it didn't lead to a sale."
- "Stayed calm after hearing 'no.'"

It sounds simple, but it was revolutionary. Those tiny acknowledgements reminded me that the real growth wasn't happening in the outcomes it was happening in *me*.

2. Reconnecting with Community

Entrepreneurship, especially when you're breaking new ground, can be lonely. When you're building something from nothing, people don't always understand your vision. You can start to feel like you're shouting into the wind.

For a while, I withdrew. I told myself I was "focused," but really, I was protecting myself from vulnerability, from having to admit how hard it all felt. But isolation feeds insecurity.

So I made a decision: I would stop pretending I had it all together.

I started reaching out to peers and mentors, other founders, leaders, and creators who understood the silent weight of trying to build something meaningful. Sometimes we talked strategy, but mostly, we just shared truth. We swapped stories of failed pitches, ignored emails, sleepless nights.

Those conversations were medicine. They reminded me that rejection wasn't unique to me, it was universal. That normalised the discomfort. And once something is normalised, it loses its power to humiliate you.

Community doesn't make the pain disappear, but it makes it bearable. It reminds you that resilience isn't a solo sport.

3. Creating Outlets for Meaning

There was a period where Diversify World was *everything* to me. Every success felt euphoric; every setback felt existential. My whole identity was tangled up in the business so when it struggled, so did I.

That's when I realised: when your life has only one source of meaning, you're one setback away from collapse.

So, I started to build more layers into my life, more spaces where I could exist without performance. I got back into reading not just leadership books, but poetry, history, fiction. I started mentoring young professionals, not because it brought business, but because it gave me purpose beyond profit. I reconnected with family, prioritising unstructured time Sunday dinners, phone calls, small moments that reminded me of who I was outside of work.

These things didn't just "balance" my life; they anchored it.

They taught me that purpose isn't a project, it's a presence. And when your life has multiple wells of meaning, rejection from one doesn't drain you completely.

4. Learning to Validate Myself Out Loud

For years, I thought self-validation was arrogance. I worried that saying "I'm proud of myself" would sound like ego. But the truth is, self-validation is not ego, it's maintenance. It's how you refill the tank when the world is silent.

I started practising it in small ways. After difficult meetings, I'd literally say out loud, *You handled that well.* After a long day of sending proposals that went nowhere, I'd remind myself, *You're still here. You're still trying. That counts.*

At first, it felt awkward, like I was talking to myself in someone else's voice. But over time, that voice softened. It became familiar. Supportive. Mine.

Eventually, I didn't need external applause to know I'd done well. I knew it in my bones, because I'd witnessed my own effort.

That's what real confidence is: not arrogance, but quiet ownership of your own growth.

5. Finding Joy Without Transaction

When your identity is tied to achievement, joy becomes conditional, something you have to earn. I had to unlearn that.

I started allowing myself moments of joy that weren't connected to productivity or progress. Walking without my phone. Cooking just for pleasure. Listening to reggae and remembering home. Laughing with my kids without checking emails between smiles.

Those moments grounded me in something bigger than ambition: *aliveness*.

And when you start to experience joy as something that doesn't have to be justified, you become less dependent on the world's approval to feel whole.

6. Giving Back

When Diversify World began to stabilise, I started mentoring others, people earlier in their journey. Not to teach, but to share. I realised that the act of helping others navigate their uncertainty helped me process my own. It shifted my focus from *What do I need?* to *What can I give?*

Contribution heals the ego. It reminds you that you're part of something larger. That even when doors close for you, you can hold them open for someone else.

Over time, these practices reshaped me. I became less reactive, less desperate for validation, more centred in who I was.

Rejection still came, it always does but it no longer shook my foundation. I stopped needing the world to validate my worth, because I'd already built a system that did it from within.

That's what resilience really is. It's not about becoming unbreakable, it's about building enough anchors in your life that no single storm can sink you.

The more roots you grow in purpose, in people, in presence the less you need any one branch to hold you up.

Because the truth is, *validation isn't something you chase; it's something you cultivate.* It grows wherever you water consistency, authenticity, and self-respect.

And when it blooms, rejection stops being a wound, and starts being weather. Something that passes. Something you can stand through without losing yourself.

Think of someone learning a new instrument. At first, every attempt is full of wrong notes and awkwardness. It's tempting to think, "I'm just not musical." But the ones who keep going don't see mistakes as a verdict on their ability, they see them as part of the process. Each fumble is simply a signal: practise again, refine, repeat. In the same way, each rejection in life can be reframed as a step in the learning curve, not as proof of unworthiness.

Rejection resilience, then, is about perspective. It's about separating your identity from outcomes, turning each "no" into information rather than condemnation, and building enough inner strength and outer anchors that you can keep moving forward. The goal isn't to avoid rejection that's impossible. It's to meet it, withstand it, and rise stronger because of it.

Celebrating the small wins is vital. When you're chasing a goal that carries the risk of rejection, it's easy to fixate on the end result and overlook the courage it took just to show up. But every act of effort matters. Did you make the phone call you were dreading? Did you press "send" on that application despite your doubts? Did you receive feedback and actually sit with it instead of shutting down? These are victories in themselves. They're proof that you chose action over paralysis, resilience over avoidance. Acknowledging them builds momentum and reminds you that your worth is measured in your willingness to engage, not just in whether the outcome lands in your favour.

Alongside this, self-compassion is the bedrock of rejection resilience. Too often, when we face rejection, our instinct is to turn inward with blame. We replay mistakes, magnify flaws, and berate ourselves in ways we would never dream of doing to a friend. Self-compassion flips that script. It asks you to meet yourself with kindness. To say: "Yes, this hurts. Yes, I'm disappointed. But this doesn't make me any less worthy." Offering yourself empathy rather than criticism creates a buffer against the sting of external judgement. It doesn't remove the pain, but it allows you to rebound rather than crumble.

Think about how progress works in fields like software development or scientific research. A failed experiment or a crashing programme isn't seen as proof that the scientist or programmer is useless. It's data. It's a signal to refine, adjust, try again. In these worlds, setbacks are expected, part of the process, not the end of it. Imagine if we brought that same mindset to our personal lives: treating rejection not as a verdict on our worth, but as information guiding us forward.

This is where Carol Dweck's idea of a growth mindset becomes so powerful. With a fixed mindset, rejection feels final: "I'm just not good enough." With a growth mindset, rejection becomes fuel: "This time didn't work out but what can I learn from it?" The rejection is no longer about who you are, but about where you are in your development. It shifts the story from failure to learning, from limitation to possibility. True resilience doesn't come from building an impenetrable shield, as if you could somehow deflect every "no." It comes from building an inner strength that allows you to absorb the sting, learn what you can, and keep going. That's the difference between being broken by rejection and being shaped by it.

The Fear of Being Seen

And yet, beneath all of this lies another deep, often unspoken fear: the fear of being seen.

This fear runs quietly through so many of our choices. It's not usually about wanting to deceive people it's about the dread of being fully visible, quirks, flaws, vulnerabilities and all. We worry that if others see us too clearly, they'll find us wanting. That we'll be judged, dismissed, or left behind.

So we hide. Not dramatically, but subtly. We bite our tongue in meetings, even when we have something to add. We laugh off mistakes instead of owning them, terrified of what it might mean if we admit fault. We keep our real feelings under wraps in case they're labelled "too much." These aren't lies; they're acts of self-protection. But over time, they create a gap between who we really are and the version of ourselves we put on display. And in that gap lives a quiet ache, the ache of inauthenticity.

I remember one of my first big speaking opportunities. I had spent weeks preparing, carefully drafting a script that ticked all the professional boxes. It was polished, safe, the kind of talk that would sound impressive without revealing too much of me. But as I stood backstage, notes in hand, I felt that familiar conflict: Do I hide behind the polished version of myself, or do I risk telling the truth?

The truth was messy. It involved setbacks I'd rather forget, doubts I hadn't fully shaken off, and moments that made me feel small. None of that felt "professional." I worried that if I shared it, I'd lose credibility. People would think less of me.

But something inside me pushed back. Playing it safe would protect my image, yes but it would also keep me invisible. So when I stepped up to the microphone, I veered off script. I told the polished parts, but I also told the story of failure, of being underestimated, of carrying the weight of not belonging in certain rooms.

I braced for silence. Instead, people leaned in. And when it was over, the comments I received weren't about the polished points I had worked so hard on. They were about the raw story. People came up to me and said, "I thought I was the only one," or "That part about doubting yourself that's exactly what I feel."

That day, I learned something that has stayed with me ever since: people don't connect with perfection. They connect with what's real. The very parts I thought would diminish me were the ones that built trust and connection.

The irony is that our fear of being seen is rooted in our deep human need to belong. We crave connection, but we worry that if we show our true selves, we'll be rejected by the group. So we polish, we mask, we hide. And while this can give us a temporary sense of safety, it also keeps us at arm's length from the deeper connection and fulfilment we long for.

At the heart of this fear of being seen lies vulnerability. To show up authentically is to risk being misunderstood, criticised, or rejected. For many of us, that feels unbearable. Vulnerability is often mistaken for weakness, something to be hidden or avoided, but in truth, it's the birthplace of courage, connection, and creativity. Without it, we never give ourselves the chance to be fully known or to truly connect with others. Shield yourself from vulnerability, and you may protect yourself from hurt, but you'll also block out intimacy, belonging, and the richness that comes from being real.

What Research Tells Us About Being Seen

This fear of being seen is not just a personal quirk; it has been studied, named, and wrestled with by researchers across psychology, sociology, and leadership.

Brené Brown, whose work on vulnerability has shaped the conversation globally, argues that vulnerability is not weakness but the birthplace of courage, connection, and creativity. In her studies, people who allowed themselves to be seen imperfections, doubts, fragility and all were the ones who built the strongest bonds of trust and belonging. She notes that our instinct to armour up and hide is understandable, but it keeps us from experiencing the intimacy and fulfilment we long for.

Other researchers point to the toll of what psychologists call self-concealment: the act of hiding distressing or shame-laden parts of ourselves from others. Far from protecting us, research shows it increases anxiety, depression, and even physical health problems. In other words, hiding doesn't just silence us in meetings; it weighs down our whole being.

Then there is the well-documented evaluation-apprehension effect the way our performance shifts when we believe others are judging us. That knot in your stomach before speaking up? That's your body reading visibility as risk. Social psychologists have shown how this fear of evaluation can suppress creativity, inhibit learning, and distort our natural voice. It explains why we hold back, polish endlessly, or default to safe answers not because we lack ideas, but because we're afraid of what visibility might cost.

Jennifer Crocker's research on contingencies of self-worth adds another layer. She found that when our sense of worth depends on external approval being liked, praised, validated we live on shaky ground. Rejection then feels existential, because it threatens the very basis of our identity. But when we root self-worth in internal values and compassionate goals, we become freer. We can take risks, show up more fully, and see "no" as data rather than a verdict.

Leadership research confirms this too. Studies of authentic leadership show that leaders who admit uncertainty, acknowledge mistakes, or share personal struggles are often seen as more credible and trustworthy. Far from undermining authority, measured vulnerability deepens it. As one recent study put it: trust is not built on polish, but on honesty.

Even in the public sphere, commentators are noticing the same thing. The Financial Times recently noted that vulnerability, when expressed authentically and at the right moment, humanises leaders and strengthens connection. Time Magazine went further: "The best leaders are not those who project invincibility, but those who allow themselves to be vulnerable with others." And The Guardian captured what psychologists call the "beautiful mess effect" the paradox that others often find our confessions of imperfection more endearing and trustworthy than the polished front we work so hard to maintain.

The research is clear: being seen feels risky but hiding costs far more.

The challenge isn't to banish this fear completely, that's almost impossible, but to learn to navigate it with courage. And you don't have to leap headfirst into radical authenticity. In fact, it's far better to build confidence gradually through what I call micro-steps of authenticity. These are small, deliberate acts of showing up as yourself in daily life, manageable moments that chip away at the walls of fear, one brick at a time.

One example is sharing a small personal story in a professional setting. Let's say you're in a meeting discussing a tricky project and it reminds you of a challenge you faced in a previous role. Instead of keeping that experience to yourself, you might say, "This is similar to something I worked on before, what helped us then was X, and we learned Y from it." It's not oversharing; it's simply offering part of your lived experience. Yet even this small disclosure humanises you, makes you more relatable, and often strengthens the conversation. It's a tiny act of authenticity with the potential for a big payoff: connection and trust.

Another powerful step is admitting a mistake openly. Many of us instinctively deflect blame or try to cover up errors, terrified of how they'll be received. But in reality, owning up builds far more respect than pretending to be flawless. Imagine saying, "I realise I made an error with [briefly describe], and here's what I'm doing to fix it." It's uncomfortable in the moment, but it shows integrity, accountability, and a willingness to learn. Paradoxically, it's often the very act of admitting imperfection that makes people trust you more. It says: "I'm human, but I'm committed to growing."

Voicing a different opinion is another everyday act of authenticity. In group settings, we often hold back for fear of disrupting harmony or being labelled "difficult." But healthy disagreement is essential for progress. Try something like: "I see where everyone's coming from, but I'd like to offer a slightly different perspective…" or "I agree with much of this, but I'm wondering if we've thought about the impact of Y." You're not picking a fight; you're contributing value. Each time you do this, you affirm: "My perspective matters, even if it isn't the same as everyone else's."

These small acts, the anecdote shared, the mistake admitted, the opinion voiced, may not feel dramatic, but together they build a powerful habit of authenticity. Over time, they reduce the gap between who you are and who you present to the world. And that, ultimately, is the essence of being seen: the courage to let others meet you as you truly are.

Another underrated act of authenticity is being willing to show curiosity in real time. In many professional settings, there's pressure to perform as the expert, to have every answer ready, every angle covered. That pressure leads us to nod along, bluff our way through, or stay silent altogether. But what if authenticity meant dropping the façade of omniscience?

There is real strength in saying, "That's an interesting point, I'd like to understand it better," or "I haven't come across that before, could you walk me through it?" These small admissions don't diminish authority; they expand it. They show you are more interested in truth than appearance, in learning rather than pretending.

Paradoxically, it's often this openness that deepens respect. When you create space for others to share their expertise, you signal humility and confidence at the same time. You give people the gift of being valued for what they know, while modelling a culture where growth matters more than polish. And more often than not, those moments of shared curiosity become the starting point for trust, collaboration, and unexpected mentorship.

Personal interests can also be an avenue for small acts of authenticity. In work environments, there's sometimes a pressure to strip away anything "too personal," but letting glimpses of your real passions show can humanise you and deepen connection. If a colleague mentions a book or hobby you also enjoy, you might say, "I love that author, I've been reading a lot of historical fiction lately, it's how I switch off in the evenings." This isn't about oversharing, it's about offering little windows into who you are beyond your job title. Those moments of genuine exchange often spark richer, more meaningful conversations.

Simple expressions of appreciation can be acts of authenticity. Instead of the perfunctory "Good job," try being specific: "I thought the way you structured that presentation made the data so much clearer, it really stood out." Or: "Thanks for your help on that report yesterday, your input on the stats saved me hours." Genuine, detailed feedback shows you're paying attention and that you value others' contributions. These small but sincere acknowledgements don't just strengthen relationships; they signal that you're fully present.

Over time, these micro-steps add up. Each small act of openness weakens the grip of fear and builds a new story inside you: It's safe to be myself. My perspective is valuable. My voice matters. You also start to notice which spaces and relationships allow you to lean further into authenticity, and which ones might still require caution. Either way, you expand your comfort zone brick by brick.

The aim here isn't to reinvent yourself overnight, but to close the gap between who you are on the inside and who you show to the world. It's about choosing self-acceptance over constant performance, and connection over concealment. With each act of authenticity, no matter how small, you're not "faking it until you make it", you're actively creating the conditions for your real self to flourish.

There's a fear most of us carry but rarely name out loud: the fear of being seen.
Not just noticed in passing but truly *seen*.

Seen for who we are, not just what we produce.
Seen in our imperfections, our contradictions, our humanity.

It sounds paradoxical, doesn't it? We spend years striving to be visible, to get the promotion, build the business, share the work, take up space and yet when that visibility finally arrives, something inside us flinches.

That flinch has roots.

It's the same inheritance we unpacked in Chapter 1, the echoes of generations who survived by keeping their heads down, who were taught that safety lived in silence.

Our grandparents built composure as armour.

Our parents mastered endurance as protection.

And we, their children, learned to polish our light just enough to be accepted, but never enough to threaten.

That's why being *seen* feels dangerous.

Visibility, for many of us, is tangled with vulnerability. To be seen is to risk misunderstanding, envy, judgement, even rejection. It's to stand where the old rules warned us never to go.

Fear, when carried long enough, becomes culture. And culture, if left unexamined, becomes identity.

So when opportunity arrives, a platform, a promotion, an invitation to speak, it doesn't just challenge your skill; it challenges your inherited sense of safety. You can hear the whispers: *Don't draw attention. Don't make them uncomfortable. Don't forget your place.*

Those aren't your fears, they're your ancestors' survival codes, still echoing through you.

But here's the truth: what kept them safe can keep you small.

When I first began speaking publicly, sharing my story, my work, my voice. I felt that fear acutely.

Every time I posted on LinkedIn or stepped onto a stage, it felt like exposure.

Not because I doubted my message, but because I was stepping beyond the line my lineage had drawn for safety.

My grandmother's composure, my mother's caution, my father's restraint, they all lived in me.

And each act of visibility felt like betrayal, as if I was breaking an unspoken family rule: *Be grateful, be quiet, be good.*

But visibility isn't arrogance. It's inheritance fulfilled.
It's the next chapter of their story, the one where survival turns into self-expression.

Being seen asks something sacred of us: to trust that we can survive scrutiny, misunderstanding, and even rejection, and still remain whole.

It asks us to unclench from the instinct to please, to prove, to perform.

It asks us to step beyond the shadows of respectability and into the light of authenticity.
And yes, it's uncomfortable. It will always be.

Because discomfort is what happens when the old identity, the quiet one, the cautious one, starts to shed its skin.

The trembling you feel before you speak up in a meeting, the hesitation before you share your truth online, the urge to edit yourself before you hit "send", that's not weakness. That's history leaving your body.

The fear of being seen is the residue of generations who couldn't afford to be.

But we can.

And every time we allow ourselves to be visible, in our power, our pain, our truth, we do something quietly revolutionary: we heal what they couldn't.

To be seen, fully and unapologetically, is the most courageous act of all.
Because it's not just about visibility, it's about liberation.

Seen in our flaws, our contradictions, our vulnerabilities, the parts of us we keep tucked away because we're not sure the world will handle them gently.

On the surface, it looks like professionalism, composure, or humility. But beneath it, the truth is simpler: we don't want to be exposed.

I know this fear well.

I've walked into boardrooms and decided in a split second which version of myself I was allowed to be.
I've softened my accent, chosen my words carefully, tucked away the parts of my story that felt "too much."
I've posted on LinkedIn sounding like a corporate press release, while the real me, the one with opinions, doubts, and a fire in my chest, stayed quiet.
The mask kept me safe, but it also kept me small.

I remember one pitch meeting in particular, a contract that could have transformed everything for Diversify World. It was with a large financial firm, the kind where the walls gleam, the floors hum with quiet confidence, and every person in the room already knows they belong there.

I arrived early, wearing the best version of my armour, crisp suit, polished shoes, practiced smile. The receptionist offered me coffee, and I declined, not because I didn't want it, but because I didn't want to risk spilling it. Everything about me that morning was controlled. Calculated. Contained.

When I walked into the boardroom, there were six of them around the table, mostly men, mostly older, all watching with polite detachment as I set up my slides. The air was heavy with unspoken expectation. I could feel my own energy shrinking to fit the space. I adjusted my posture, straightened my tie, and within seconds, I felt myself morphing into "the version they could handle."

The professional.
The neutral.
The safe Black man.

I started the presentation strong, data, strategy, outcomes, everything perfectly framed. But halfway through, one of the directors interrupted me. He leaned back in his chair and said, "This is interesting, but do you really think organisations like ours still have that kind of problem? We're a meritocracy here."

It was the kind of comment I'd heard a hundred times before, the polite dismissal wrapped in confidence. And in that moment, I felt two voices rise inside me.

One quiet, careful, familiar, said, *Don't push. Stay diplomatic. Don't give them a reason to doubt you.*
The other, bold, honest, ancestral said, *Tell the truth.*

I hesitated for half a second, and in that pause, I made a choice, the safe one. I gave the "boardroom answer." Something polished. Something that nodded to his point without challenging it. Something that would let everyone stay comfortable.

They nodded. They smiled. They thanked me for my time. And a week later, we got the contract.

But as I walked back to the trainstation and I felt empty like I betrayed myself, not because I'd failed but because I'd succeeded at the wrong thing.

I'd been so focused on being impressive that I'd forgotten to be *authentic.*
I'd traded truth for approval. Presence for performance.
And what haunted me most wasn't the choice itself, it was how natural it felt. How easy it was to slip back into the old reflex of self-editing, the inherited instinct to prioritise safety over honesty.

That's what fear of being seen looks like. It's not always dramatic. Sometimes it's subtle, a smile held too long, a truth softened at the edges, a version of yourself you construct to stay palatable.

I told myself I was being strategic. Professional. Composed. But really, I was just afraid, afraid of confirming stereotypes, afraid of being labelled "difficult," afraid of losing the opportunity I'd worked so hard for.
And in trying to protect myself, I betrayed myself.

That moment stayed with me for years because it revealed something I hadn't wanted to see: that I was still performing, even in rooms I had earned the right to be in. I had built a business around helping organisations embrace authenticity, and yet I was still negotiating mine.

There's a unique exhaustion that comes from that kind of double consciousness, from constantly monitoring how you're being perceived, from bending and blending to fit environments that were never built with you in mind. You tell yourself it's professionalism, but deep down, it's survival. And survival always demands a piece of your soul.

It took time and a lot of uncomfortable introspection, to realise that my need to self-edit wasn't just about fear of failure. It was about fear of visibility. Because being seen, truly seen, meant risking rejection not of my ideas, but of *me*.

And yet, the irony was that the more I tried to make myself acceptable, the more invisible I became.
People liked me, but they didn't *know* me.
They trusted my expertise, but they never really felt my conviction.
I was admired, but not connected.

Respected, but not remembered.

It was only when I started allowing my full self to show up, the accent, the perspective, the stories, the truth, that things began to shift. Some rooms grew colder, but the right ones grew warmer. And I realised something profound: authenticity doesn't cost you opportunities; it filters them.

That day in the boardroom taught me one of the hardest lessons of my career: courage isn't about speaking without fear, it's about refusing to let fear edit your truth.

Because every time we hide behind the safe version of ourselves, we reinforce the very systems we're trying to challenge. The moment we stop performing for acceptance and start speaking from authenticity, something changes in us, and in the room around us. Visibility becomes not a risk, but a responsibility. And yes, it's uncomfortable. But discomfort is just truth entering the room for the first time.

Harnessing Fear's Energy

This brings us back to fear itself, that primal alarm bell = is often cast as the enemy, something to suppress, conquer, or grit your teeth through, But that framing misses a vital truth: **fear is energy.**

When a challenge looms, your body isn't betraying you; it's *preparing* you. Your heart races, your senses sharpen, your body floods with adrenaline and cortisol, not as punishment, but as preparation. This ancient "fight, flight, or freeze" response isn't evidence of weakness; it's proof of readiness. The quickened pulse, the sweaty palms, the knot in your stomach, they're not signs that you're failing, they're signs that something *matters*.

Fear is your body's way of saying, *you're alive and on the edge of something important.*
It's the electricity of potential moving through you.

We've been conditioned to read fear as "stop," when in truth, fear's message is often *"pay attention."*
It's a call to presence. A surge of energy asking to be directed, not denied.

Because that's what emotion is **E = energy, motion = movement.** Emotion is simply *energy in motion.*

The problem isn't fear itself; it's what we do with it. When we freeze or suppress it, that energy has nowhere to go, it festers, turns inward, and becomes anxiety, self-doubt, or paralysis. But when we learn to *move* with it, to give it form, direction, and purpose fear transforms from a wall into a wave.

Think about it.
That same surge of adrenaline you feel before a difficult conversation is the same energy an athlete feels before a race, or a performer before stepping on stage. The body doesn't know the difference between fear and excitement, it's the mind that decides the meaning.

So when fear rises, instead of saying *I'm scared,* try saying *I'm ready.* Instead of *I can't do this,* try *these matters to me.* You're not lying to yourself, you're reinterpreting your body's language.

When I began to reframe fear this way, everything shifted. Before keynotes, before high-stakes negotiations, before walking into spaces that once made me shrink, I'd feel that rush, heart pounding, breath shallow, palms warm. My old instinct was to fight it, to breathe it away, to hide it under a mask of composure. Now, I let it be there. I ground my feet, breathe into it, and think: *this is power, not panic.*

That physiological energy, that surge, is the same force that fuels courage, creativity, and conviction. It's the energy that turns hesitation into momentum.

Fear, when harnessed, becomes movement.
Fear, when listened to, becomes guidance.

It's not a signal to retreat, it's a compass pointing toward the very thing that will grow you. Fear says: *there's something here for you, something worth caring about, something that could change you if you're willing to stay present.*

So when you feel that familiar rush, before a big decision, before a difficult truth, before stepping onto a stage, pause and ask yourself:

What is this energy trying to help me do?
What possibility is hiding behind this discomfort?
What would happen if I used this energy, instead of resisting it?

Because the truth is this: fear is not a wall to climb; it's a current to ride.
It's the raw material of courage, the signal that you're exactly where you need to be.

Fear is not your weakness.

It's your body calling you into your next level of strength.

Courage isn't about silencing that call, it's about answering it.

One of the most effective ways to harness fear's energy is through deliberate reframing. It's about changing the story you tell yourself about what you're feeling. Instead of labelling the sensations as "panic" or "terror," try calling them "readiness" or "heightened focus." Before a presentation, for instance, those butterflies in your stomach don't have to be a warning to pull out, they can be a signal that your body is gearing up to perform. The rush of adrenaline isn't there to paralyse you; it's your system saying, "Pay attention, this matters." If you acknowledge the nerves, take a few grounding breaths, and then channel that energy into your voice and gestures, the same fear that once threatened to derail you can make you more powerful, more alive, and more engaging in the moment.

Turning Pressure into Momentum

The same principle applies to deadlines. The pressure of an unfinished project often shows up as racing thoughts, restlessness, or dread. Left unchecked, that discomfort pushes us into procrastination. But reframed, the very anxiety that feels overwhelming can become a sharp motivator. It's a signal that the task deserves your focus. By breaking it into smaller steps and giving yourself mini-deadlines, you convert that energy into momentum. Each step completed eases the weight, builds confidence, and creates the rhythm to keep going. In this way, fear doesn't block progress, it fuels it.

Awareness and Choice

The key is awareness. Rather than trying to suppress fear, which usually intensifies it, you acknowledge it and then make a deliberate choice about how to respond. Imagine you need to have a difficult conversation. The surge of nerves isn't evidence you should avoid it; it's proof it matters. Instead of spiralling into "I can't do this," you can tell yourself: "This feeling is my body preparing me to show up." You might jot down your main points, steady your breathing, and then step into the conversation using that energy to sharpen your focus and commitment. The fear doesn't vanish, but it no longer dictates your behaviour.

This approach scales up to bigger life changes too. Think of the fear that comes with a career shift. That unease isn't a sign you're on the wrong path, it's a marker that you're entering territory that matters. You can redirect that energy into research, networking, skills-building, or planning. The nerves that could have paralysed you become the very drive that pushes you to prepare thoroughly and step forward with intention.

Fear is also a surprisingly good compass.

We often feel it most intensely around the things that matter most, the people, principles, and possibilities that sit closest to our hearts. The fear of speaking up in a meeting isn't just about words; it's about the deeper need to be respected, to have your perspective valued.

The fear of rejection in a relationship points to the longing to be loved, to be seen without condition.

Even the fear of failure when starting a business isn't proof you're unprepared, it's evidence of how deeply that dream matters to you.

Fear, in its rawest form, shows you where your values live.

That's why naming your fear is such a powerful act. When you name a fear, you strip it of vagueness and turn emotion into information.

You move from *I'm scared* to *I'm scared because I value belonging.*
From *I'm nervous about failing* to *I care about doing work that matters.*
From *I'm afraid to speak up* to *I need to feel respected and heard.*

Naming isn't weakness, it's awareness. It gives form to what's been sitting in the dark.

And when you understand *what* your fear is protecting, you gain the power to redirect its energy toward what truly matters.

Here's the truth most people miss: fear is not always warning you away; sometimes it's calling you *toward* something.

That tightening in your stomach before you share an idea might not be danger, it might be desire.

That hesitation before applying for a role might not be inadequacy, it might be importance.

Fear doesn't always mean "don't do it." Often, it means "do it with care."

Once you've named the fear and identified the value it's guarding, you can transform the energy it generates. That's the alchemy of courage, taking the raw, trembling current of fear and turning it into forward motion.

So when fear rises, try this simple sequence:

1. **Name it.** Ask yourself, *What exactly am I afraid of?* Be specific. Is it rejection? Judgement? Loss? Exposure?
2. **Locate the value underneath.** Ask, *What does this fear say about what I care about most?*
   Fear of failure might reveal your value of excellence.
   Fear of conflict might reveal your value of harmony.
   Fear of speaking up might reveal your value of authenticity.
3. **Reclaim the energy.** Once you know what your fear is protecting, ask, *How can I use this same energy to move toward that value, instead of away from it?*

If you're afraid of being rejected because you value connection, use that energy to reach out anyway to nurture relationships instead of retreating from them. If you fear failing because you value excellence, use that energy to prepare, to learn, to refine but don't let it stop you from starting. If you fear visibility because you value authenticity, use that energy to speak your truth, not to hide it.

That's how fear becomes a teacher instead of a tyrant.

Fear is a messenger, not a verdict. It's the body's way of saying, *Pay attention. Something precious is at stake here.*

And when you can name it, honour the value beneath it, and harness its energy for movement, that's when fear stops being an obstacle and starts becoming an ally.

Because courage isn't born from erasing fear; it's born from understanding it.

The goal isn't to silence fear's voice, but to listen long enough to know what it's trying to protect, and then choose, consciously, what to do with that information.

When you treat fear as data, not danger, as energy, not enemy, you begin to live from a place of alignment instead of avoidance. You stop fighting your fear and start using it as fuel for what really matters.

The Body's Readiness

And when you zoom in on the body's reactions, they're not signs of weakness at all, they're signs of readiness. Trembling hands? Your muscles priming for action. A racing heart? Pumping oxygen-rich blood to keep you sharp. Dilated pupils? Letting you take in more of what's around you. These aren't malfunctions to fear, but finely tuned systems designed to help you meet the moment. Before a high-stakes conversation, for example, you can acknowledge the adrenaline and choose to let it anchor you: stand tall, breathe deeply, project your voice. The very signals you once interpreted as panic become resources for presence and power.

Practising mindfulness makes this easier. When fear rises, instead of reacting immediately or trying to bury it, pause. Notice: *Where am I feeling this in my body? What thoughts are attached to it?* That small pause creates space. And in that space, you can choose your framing: *"This is energy, not danger. This means I'm growing. This means I care."* From there, you act with intention rather than avoidance.

This is where the **TRACE Method** comes alive not as theory, but as practice. It's one thing to understand the framework in calm moments; it's another to use it when your heart is racing, when the stakes feel high, and your instinct is to retreat. TRACE gives you a language to navigate that space. The same steps we explored in Chapter 1, *Tune In, Recognise, Accept, Choose, Engage* become a map through uncertainty.

You start by **tuning in**, grounding yourself in the present moment instead of the spiral of "what ifs." You notice the subtle cues: your breathing quickens, your shoulders tighten, your palms get warm. These aren't signs of weakness, they're the body's readiness, the physical proof that something matters.

You **recognise** the emotion without letting it overtake you. "This is fear." "This is vulnerability." "This is the edge of my comfort zone." Naming it pulls you out of the blur of overwhelm and into clarity.

Then, you **accept** it. You stop arguing with reality. You stop trying to fix the feeling before you've even understood it. Instead, you breathe and allow it to exist without shame. You remind yourself, *"It's okay to feel this. It's human."*

Next, you **choose** what meaning to assign to it. Is this fear a sign to stop, or a signal to pay attention? You reframe it: *"This is energy, not danger. This is my system preparing me to perform. This means I care about what I'm doing."*

Finally, you **engage**. You take one small, deliberate action speak, write, send, step, begin and use that energy to move forward. Action becomes the bridge between fear and flow.

I've used TRACE countless times in my own life, especially before moments that carried both opportunity and pressure. Before keynote talks, before negotiations, before hitting "publish" on posts that felt too personal, I'd feel the rush, the tightening in my chest, the restless thoughts, the voice whispering, *"Not yet. Not you."*

In those moments, TRACE became my anchor. I'd close my eyes for a few seconds, feel my feet on the floor, breathe deeply, and run through it silently: *Tune in, recognise, accept, choose engage.* Every step helped me move from reaction to readiness. The fear didn't vanish, but it softened. It became motion instead of paralysis.

Over time, I realised that TRACE isn't just a response technique, it's a way of relating to fear itself. It teaches you to meet fear with curiosity instead of judgement, to stay with it long enough to understand what it's asking of you. It transforms anxiety into awareness, and awareness into action.

When you practise TRACE regularly, something shifts inside you. The distance between feeling fear and choosing action gets smaller. You stop needing fear to disappear before you move, you just move *with it* and that's the real transformation: you stop being controlled by fear, and start being guided by it.

Building a New Relationship with Fear

Fear, reframed, doesn't have to be the enemy. It can be your ally, not the force that holds you back, but the fuel that propels you forward.

Learning to repurpose fear isn't something that happens overnight. It's a practice, a skill you strengthen through repetition. At first, it will feel clumsy, maybe even forced. Old habits of avoidance or suppression will creep back in, and that's normal. What matters is noticing when you do manage to shift the pattern, even slightly. That moment where you pause, breathe, and choose to use the energy rather than freeze in it? That's a win.

Each small victory compounds. With time, your brain begins to lay down new pathways, associating fear not with danger or paralysis, but with readiness, action, and growth. Slowly, fear becomes less of a stop sign and more of a guidepost, pointing you towards the places where growth and impact live.

This change in perspective transforms your relationship with discomfort. Instead of asking, "How do I get rid of this fear?" you begin to ask, "What is this fear showing me, and how can I use it?" And that question unlocks something powerful. Fear no longer has to be a weight you drag behind you; it becomes fuel, energy you can direct towards meaningful action.

When you learn to harness it in this way, you're tapping into a resource most people spend their lives running from. The result is not fearlessness, but courage with intention, a mindset that allows you to step into challenges with energy, clarity, and a sense that fear, rather than holding you back, is actually helping to carry you forward.

From Awareness to Application

If *Chapter 1* revealed how fear disguises itself in perfectionism, procrastination, people-pleasing, and control. *Chapter 2* took us beneath the surface, dissecting fear's anatomy and showing us how it builds systems inside us. We learned that fear isn't just emotional; it's patterned, physiological, and often generational. Once we can name those patterns, we begin to take back authorship of our own story. We then moved on to Chapter 3 where we saw that fear is not only personal but political, not only emotional but structural. History, power, and identity converge to shape who feels safe, who must perform safety, and who is never allowed to forget their difference. Colonialism, patriarchy, and capitalism turned fear into governance, teaching entire groups to shrink, assimilate, or overperform just to survive. In recognising that fear operates across race, gender, class, and culture, we learned that healing it requires more than self-awareness, it demands systemic reimagining. That realisation sets the stage for what comes next.

And then came *Chapter 4*, where understanding became movement. Here, we learned that courage is not an abstract ideal, it's a living, breathing practice. We reframed discomfort not as a sign of danger, but as evidence of growth. Every tremor before we speak, every knot in the stomach before a truth, every doubt before a leap these moments are not warnings to retreat, but invitations to expand. Discomfort is the ground we grow from. It stretches us, refines us, and demands honesty. The friction you feel is not failure; it's transformation in progress.

We unlearned the myth that courage feels easy. It doesn't. True courage is often messy, shaky, and vulnerable. It's choosing to stay when escape would be simpler, to keep showing up when clarity hasn't arrived yet. Confidence isn't born in calm; it's built in tension. The gym of courage is discomfort itself.

We explored how resilience is built not through perfection, but through *repetition*, the act of staying when everything in you wants to flee. Each time you lean into something that scares you, a truth, a challenge, a conversation you strengthen your capacity to recover, adapt, and rise. The discomfort you once feared becomes the training ground for your next evolution.

We redefined courage as *movement, not emotion*. It isn't the absence of fear, but the decision to move within it. Courage is speaking while your voice shakes, applying when self-doubt whispers "not yet," telling the truth when silence would be easier. Each act of bravery expands what's possible for you. With each repetition, your comfort zone grows, and your sense of self deepens.

We revisited rejection one of fear's oldest tricks and reframed it as redirection. Rejection doesn't measure worth; it measures alignment. Every "no" holds data. When you detach your value from outcomes, you stop seeing rejection as a verdict and start reading it as feedback. Resilience grows when you stop equating failure with finality.

Through that lens, we also learned that *self-worth must be self-sourced*. When your sense of value relies on validation, your confidence will always be conditional. True assurance grows from self-recognition celebrating effort, progress, and integrity, even when applause is absent. This is how rejection becomes weather, not a wound.

And perhaps most powerfully, we confronted the fear of being seen. We traced its lineage, how invisibility once ensured safety, and how, over time, that survival instinct became a habit of shrinking. We learned that visibility, though uncomfortable, is sacred. Authenticity is not indulgence; it's leadership. To be seen as you are, accent, edges, contradictions and all is to declare that you are enough, even in your becoming.

This chapter reminded us that courage isn't built in moments of certainty but in moments of choice. It's forged in micro-moments: the boundaries you hold, the truths you tell, the pauses you take before retreating. Each one is a muscle fibre of courage being strengthened in real time.

We also learned that fear's energy is neutral until we give it direction. The racing heart, the shaking hands, the adrenaline, these are not signs of weakness, but readiness. Fear is energy asking for movement. When named and channelled, it becomes fuel for growth rather than friction against it.

At its core, *Chapter 4* showed us that courage is not a one-time act, it's a rhythm, a muscle built through repetition and recovery. Awareness opens the door, but habit keeps it open.

Because without practice, even the most powerful insights fade back into theory, admired but not embodied. The next step, then, is to make courage your *default setting*: to build the habits, structures, and rituals that make brave action your natural response, not your occasional exception.

This is the bridge between emotional insight and practical embodiment between knowing what courage feels like and training your body and mind to live it daily. It's the difference between reacting to fear when it arrives and cultivating the habits that make courage instinctive.

Core Takeaways from chapter 4 summarised:

- Discomfort isn't danger; it's development.
- Courage is not the absence of fear; it's the presence of movement.
- Rejection is redirection, not a reflection of your worth.
- Authenticity is the highest form of leadership.
- Fear is energy name it, direct it, and it becomes fuel.
- Resilience is built through repetition, not perfection.
- Courage without habit is awareness without embodiment.

In the next chapter, we'll bring this work into motion. We'll explore what it looks like to make courage tangible to build repeatable, sustainable *courage habits* that strengthen self-trust, reduce overthinking, and anchor calm under pressure. We'll also look at how courage extends beyond the self into our workplaces, teams, and leadership. Also how choosing courage collectively can transform not just how we show up, but how we lead.

Because the only thing stronger than fear itself is the routine of facing it, one act, one breath, one habit at a time.

And that's where we turn next: from courage as a moment to courage as a method. From knowing what fear feels like to practising what freedom requires.

CHAPTER 5

Leading with Courage: Actionable Habits

Every journey of transformation eventually meets a turning point. The moment where insight must become action. Up until now, we've learned to name fear, understand its patterns, and stay with discomfort long enough to see what it's really saying. But knowledge, on its own, doesn't change us. It prepares us. The shift happens when what we *know* becomes what we *do*, when courage stops being an idea and starts becoming a rhythm.

That's where this chapter begins: the practice of courage. Not the big, cinematic kind that changes everything overnight, but the quiet, repeatable kind that changes you over time. Because courage isn't built in a moment of inspiration; it's built in the consistency of choice one conversation, one decision, one honest step at a time.

From Reaction to Practice

Up to this point, we've looked at how fear shows up in the body and mind the racing heart, the restless energy, the tightening in the chest and how reframing these sensations can turn them from enemies into allies. Fear, when acknowledged and redirected, becomes fuel: energy we can use to act, grow, and stretch into our potential. But there's another step. Once we learn to work with fear in the moment, the challenge is to go beyond reacting to it. The real shift comes when we begin *cultivating courage* deliberately, not as a one-off performance, but as a daily practice.

This is where the idea of *courage habits* comes in. We often imagine courage as dramatic, once-in-a-lifetime moments, standing up to injustice, quitting a job, making a life-altering choice. And yes, those moments matter. But lasting courage is rarely built in a single leap. It's forged in the small, repeated acts that slowly change how we see ourselves. When courage stops being an occasional exception and starts becoming a steady practice, it reshapes the way we meet life.

Think of it in terms of habits. Our brains thrive on repetition. Every time we repeat an action, especially one tied to intention or positive reinforcement, we strengthen the neural pathways that make it easier next time. Courage is no different. Each small act of bravery rewires us, making it more natural to step forward rather than shrink back when fear rises. It's not about wiping fear out (that's neither realistic nor desirable); it's about training ourselves to act *with* it.

This is the quiet power of consistency. Facing discomfort regularly, even in small doses, begins to normalise it. What once felt like a mountain gradually becomes a hill. A difficult conversation, a public comment, a request you'd usually avoid, every time you choose to act instead of retreat, you chip away at fear's hold. Over time, your nervous system recalibrates. The old panic response softens, replaced by growing evidence that you *can* handle the challenge.

And that evidence is gold. Each act of courage plants a seed of self-trust. It tells you: I've been here before. I've felt this fear. And I moved anyway. That inner validation is far more powerful than fleeting praise or external approval. It's the quiet, resilient confidence that builds when you consistently show up for yourself, again and again.

Building Courage Through Consistency

So how do we actually begin weaving courage habits into daily life? The key is to start small, to look for manageable acts of bravery that sit just beyond your current comfort zone. These don't need to be grand gestures. In fact, they work best when they're repeatable, small, steady steps that stretch you without overwhelming you. Think of it as working in the "stretch zone": not so comfortable that it costs you nothing, and not so extreme that it paralyses you.

Public speaking is a prime example. If the thought of standing on stage with a microphone fills you with dread, your first courage habit shouldn't be signing up for a keynote talk next week. A more realistic habit could be committing to speak up once in every team meeting, perhaps by asking a thoughtful question or sharing one clear idea. By doing this consistently, you build the muscle of voicing your perspective, you learn to ride out the nerves, and you start to experience the positive feedback of being heard. Over time, those small contributions stack up into confidence that makes bigger speaking opportunities feel more achievable.

Procrastination is another area where courage habits can have a huge impact. Often, avoidance stems from fear, fear of failing, fear of judgement, or fear of tackling something that feels too big. Instead of aiming to conquer the entire task in one go, set a micro-habit: fifteen minutes a day, no excuses, spent working on the thing you've been putting off. You don't need to finish the project in that time. The point is to prove to yourself, daily, that you can begin. That repeated act of starting chips away at the intimidation factor and builds momentum. Before long, fifteen minutes becomes thirty, then an hour, and the project that once felt unmanageable starts to shrink to size.

The same principle applies to difficult conversations. Many of us shy away from giving feedback, raising concerns, or expressing an unpopular opinion because of the discomfort it brings. A courage habit here could be committing to initiate just one such conversation each week. That might mean scheduling the meeting, sending a message to open the dialogue, or simply practising your opening line. The habit isn't about delivering a flawless performance every time; it's about showing up consistently to the discomfort, proving to yourself that you can handle it. Each attempt strengthens your resilience, making you less likely to avoid these interactions in the future.

What underpins all of this is a shift from avoidance to approach. Psychologists call these "approach behaviours." Instead of running from situations that trigger fear, you intentionally lean into them in small, sustainable ways. Each time you approach, you teach your brain that the situation is survivable, not a catastrophe, but a challenge you can meet. Slowly but surely, you reprogramme your default response.

One way to help these habits stick is through *habit stacking*. This simply means anchoring a new courage habit to something you already do. For example: "After I hear the agenda item in a meeting, I will prepare one question to share." Or: "After I finish my morning coffee, I'll spend fifteen minutes on the task I've been avoiding." Linking courage habits to existing routines reduces the mental effort needed to remember them and makes them part of your natural rhythm.

Over time, these small acts add up. Each repetition reinforces the belief that you can face discomfort and come through it. Courage stops being a rare event and becomes a lived practice, something you carry with you, day after day.

Celebrating Small Wins

It's just as important to *celebrate the small wins* as it is to practise the habits themselves. Every time you follow through on a courage habit take a moment to acknowledge it. This doesn't require anything elaborate. It might be jotting it down in a journal, giving yourself a quiet nod of recognition, or allowing yourself a small reward. What matters is the recognition. These small acknowledgements create positive reinforcement, gradually rewiring your brain to associate courage with growth, resilience, and self-trust.

This is why a "consistency over intensity" approach matters so much. Many of us fall into the trap of trying to conquer fear in one big push, volunteering for a huge presentation, throwing ourselves into a high-stakes challenge, or tackling a problem head-on with sheer adrenaline. And sometimes, those big leaps work. But more often, they lead to a boom-and-bust cycle: a burst of bravery followed by exhaustion, avoidance, and even more resistance the next time. Courage habits avoid this trap. They're not about once-in-a-while heroics; they're about sustainable growth. Think marathon training, not a one-off sprint.

The fitness analogy fits perfectly here. An athlete doesn't get into shape by running a marathon once a year, they train gradually. Short runs, strength sessions, recovery days. Bit by bit, their body adapts. Courage works in the same way. Each small act builds resilience and recalibrates your response to fear. Over time, what once spiked your anxiety becomes more manageable, even familiar. You're training your nervous system as much as your mindset.

And neuroscience backs this up. Thanks to neuroplasticity, the brain literally rewires itself through repetition. When you consistently choose action in the face of fear, no matter how small, you strengthen the neural pathways associated with courage. You're teaching your brain: this is what we do when fear shows up. Fear doesn't vanish, but your ability to move through it becomes second nature.

Take the way we approach networking, for instance. For many people, walking into a room full of strangers feels daunting. You might worry about not knowing what to say, about being judged, or about wasting your time. A courage habit here could be setting one simple target: "I'll introduce myself to two people," or, "I'll ask one thoughtful question to the speaker." Suddenly, the event isn't an overwhelming social minefield, it's a set of manageable steps. Each time you complete one, you prove to yourself that you can handle it. Repeat this enough, and networking shifts from a source of dread to just another professional routine.

Finally, and perhaps most importantly, courage habits require *self-compassion*. There will be days when you don't follow through, when you avoid, procrastinate, or feel too drained to try. That's normal. What matters is how you respond afterwards. Berating yourself only reinforces fear. Acknowledge the slip with kindness, remind yourself that growth is never linear, and recommit. Treat yourself the way you'd treat a close friend: with patience, encouragement, and belief that tomorrow offers another chance. This softer approach makes it far easier to sustain the practice in the long run, and its sustainability, not perfection, that builds real courage.

The real benefit of building courage through small, consistent steps goes far beyond tackling individual fears. It creates a wider sense of agency, the belief that you have a say in how your life unfolds. When you know you're deliberately working on courage, even in small ways each day, it changes how you see yourself. You begin to trust your ability to handle challenges. That sense of self-trust then spills over into every part of life, giving you more confidence, more assertiveness, and a stronger willingness to chase the goals that matter most to you.

The beauty of courage habits is that they're deeply personal. What feels like a stretch for one person may feel ordinary to another. For one, it might be as simple as raising a hand in a crowded lecture hall. For another, it could be asking for a pay rise. For someone else, it might be saying "no" to a demanding colleague or setting a boundary with a family member. The size of the action isn't what matters. What matters is that it nudges *you* beyond your current comfort zone, and that you repeat it often enough to build new reflexes.

In essence, cultivating courage isn't about waiting for lightning bolts of bravery. It's about designing small, deliberate actions that, repeated consistently, slowly reshape your comfort zone. Each act builds resilience. Each step rewires your brain. Bit by bit, you're laying down a stronger foundation of inner strength that equips you to meet life's challenges with greater steadiness. Put simply: consistency, not intensity, is the route to lasting courage. Over time, these practices transform courage from an abstract ideal into part of your everyday identity.

Shifting from Fear to Aspiration

Here's where a crucial turning point arises. Courage deepens when we stop letting fear set the direction of our lives and start letting our aspirations lead. Too often, we make choices with our anxieties in the driver's seat. Fear of failure, fear of judgement, fear of the unknown, they pull us towards the safe, the predictable, the familiar. On the surface, these choices feel secure. But underneath, they can leave us restless, unfulfilled, even quietly resentful of ourselves.

The truth is, courage doesn't mean erasing fear. It means choosing to pursue what matters most, even when fear shouts the loudest. That requires a shift in how we make decisions: moving from a defensive stance of avoiding loss to a proactive stance of pursuing growth.

This shift begins with clarity. If you don't know what you value, what you stand for, or what kind of life you want to build, fear will always dominate the decision-making process. But once you're clear, your values and goals act like a compass. They don't silence fear, but they give you a reason to walk through it.

Take a career example. Imagine you're offered a promotion in your current company. It's safe, the people are familiar, and the salary bump feels comfortable. But deep down, you've always wanted to work in a cutting-edge industry where innovation and impact drive the culture. A role in a young startup becomes available, it's less stable, less predictable, and yes, a little frightening. A fear-driven decision would push you towards the promotion: security, predictability, less chance of "failure." You'd tell yourself things like, "I need more experience first," or "It's not the right time."

But an aspiration-driven decision looks different. You'd weigh the options not by "What could go wrong?" but by "Which path will bring me closer to the life I actually want?" You'd acknowledge the risks of the startup but also see the alignment with your values of growth, innovation, and impact. The fear doesn't vanish, but it becomes part of the price of moving towards something that matters.

This is the essence of aspiration-led living: shifting the focus from what we're scared of losing to what we're determined to gain. It asks: Which choice will I look back on with pride? Which path reflects who I truly want to become? When you start making decisions this way, fear doesn't disappear, but it loses its veto power.

This process of re-evaluating opportunities demands a higher level of self-awareness, and a willingness to question the assumptions that quietly fuel our anxieties. Left unchecked, we tend to exaggerate the potential losses and downplay the potential gains, especially when those gains are intangible: things like personal growth, fulfilment, or the deep satisfaction of living in line with our values. Fear-driven decision-making often works like a skewed cost-benefit analysis: the "costs" are all the imagined embarrassments, failures, or rejections, while the "benefits" tend to be the temporary comfort of avoiding risk.

An aspiration-led approach flips this dynamic. Instead of letting fear dominate the equation, it asks: What might I gain? How could this stretch me? What opportunities for joy, learning, or alignment with my values are on the table? The risks don't disappear, but they're reframed as challenges you can prepare for, rather than as barriers that stop you.

One simple way to put this into practice is to make two lists whenever you face a big decision. I first tried this when I was deciding whether to leave my corporate job and build *Diversify World*.

On paper, it looked reckless. I had stability, a salary, a clear career path, the sort of safety so many people spend years trying to find. But something in me was restless. I could see a gap in how companies spoke about inclusion versus how they actually practised it, and I wanted to be part of closing it. Still, the fear was loud.

So, I sat down one evening and made two lists.

On the first, I wrote every anxiety, fear, and worst-case scenario I could imagine. I didn't hold back:
What if I fail? What if no one hires me? What if I lose everything I've built? What if people think I'm out of my depth? What if I regret it?
It wasn't pretty, but it was honest.

Then, I made the second list, the one that asked not what I feared, but what I hoped for.

The freedom to build something meaningful. The chance to create real change. The ability to work with purpose, not just pressure. To be present with my family. To make space for the work I was actually proud of.

When I looked at both lists side by side, something became clear. The fear list was full of things that could happen.
The aspiration list was full of things I *wanted* to make happen.

One represented survival; the other represented growth.
And the truth hit me: one day, I could recover from failure, but I could never recover from regret.

So, I made the leap. Not because the fear disappeared, but because the second list, the one rooted in hope, values, and vision, was the life I actually wanted to build.

That moment taught me something I've carried ever since: **you don't need to silence fear to move forward; you just need to give your dreams equal volume.**

Whenever I face big decisions now, I still return to those two lists. It's not about pretending fear doesn't exist, it's about giving your aspirations as much airtime as your doubts.

Because when you write it down, when you see your fear and your vision on the same page, you realise something powerful: the fear is always smaller than the future you're capable of creating.

Imagine the fear of social judgement. Let's say you've written a book, composed music, or started a new artistic project. The anxious voice pipes up: What if people hate it? What if it's not good enough? What if they laugh? That fear can keep your work hidden in a drawer. But an aspiration-led mindset shifts the focus: I want to create. I want to share. I want to connect with others through my work. The courage, then, is in prioritising the joy of expression and the possibility of connection over the fear of criticism. Sharing your work becomes not just an act of exposure, but an act of alignment with your truest self.

This requires a recalibration of what we see as "risk." Too often we treat the risk of embarrassment or failure as catastrophic, while ignoring the risk of regret, the cost of never trying. But the deepest risk in life is not in failing; it's in turning away from opportunities altogether. An aspiration-led decision framework helps guard against this by asking, not what could go wrong? but What could I gain? Who could I become if I lean into this?

And this doesn't only apply to creative pursuits. It might mean volunteering for a project at work that scares you but aligns with your career goals. It might mean carving out time for a passion project at weekends, even if it eats into your downtime. It might mean having a difficult but necessary conversation with a partner or friend, fuelled by your aspiration for healthier, more honest relationships.

In every case, the principle is the same: choose the path that nourishes your growth and reflects your values, even if it feels uncomfortable. The act of choosing becomes the act of courage. And when hesitation creeps in, try asking yourself: Is this hesitation coming from a real, insurmountable obstacle, or is it just fear of discomfort, failure, or judgement? More often than not, you'll find the fear is the only real barrier. And in that moment, your aspirations can become the compass that leads you forward.

It's important to stress that this isn't about recklessness or blindly ignoring genuine risks. Responsible decision-making will always involve assessing potential downsides, planning carefully, and putting measures in place to reduce them. The key distinction is that the *primary driver* of your choice should be your aspiration, not your anxiety. An example of this is the startup founder: they'll research the market, write a business plan, secure funding, and plan contingencies. All of these are sensible, practical steps. But what keeps them moving through the long hours, the rejections, and the uncertainty is the deeper aspiration, to create something meaningful and innovative. Without that aspirational core, the sheer weight of the risks would likely hold them back.

The power of focusing on aspirations lies in the energy it generates. When you pursue something, you truly care about, your motivation runs deeper. It's intrinsic, not borrowed from external pressures. This kind of motivation makes it easier to bounce back from setbacks, learn from mistakes, and keep showing up with energy and focus. Anxieties, by contrast, are draining. Managing them, suppressing them, or constantly negotiating with them takes a toll. Aligning your decisions with your aspirations taps into a more sustainable, empowering fuel source.

Think of it in simple terms. You're choosing between two holidays: an all-inclusive resort where everything is predictable, or a trek through a remote mountain range. The anxious voice highlights the risks of the trek, bad weather, physical exertion, the absence of familiar comforts. But your aspirations might yearn for adventure, for a deeper connection with nature, for the sense of accomplishment that comes from stretching yourself.

A fear-based decision would take you to the resort: comfortable, safe, and predictable. Nothing wrong with that, but it leaves the part of you that craves growth untouched. An aspiration-led decision, however, would honour the pull towards adventure. You'd still plan carefully, check the route, pack the right gear, and prepare responsibly, but the guiding principle would be your desire to experience something new, not your desire to avoid discomfort. The very things that seem daunting become the ingredients that make the experience richer.

This way of deciding creates a powerful feedback loop. Each time you make a choice that prioritises aspiration over anxiety, you reinforce your own belief that you can handle challenge. With every step, you're building evidence for yourself: *I can do this. I can stretch further than I thought.* That growing self-trust then fuels the confidence to make even bolder choices in the future. Courage begins to generate more courage.

The opposite is also true. When we allow fear to steer the wheel, we gradually narrow our horizons. Each time we avoid an opportunity because of anxiety, our comfort zone shrinks a little more. Over time, the world feels smaller, less inviting, and our own sense of possibility diminishes. What might have been a landscape of opportunities becomes a confined, safer space, but one that starves us of growth and fulfilment.

Choosing to let aspirations lead is not simply about reaching a single goal. It's about expanding the canvas of your life. It's about deciding to be the architect rather than the bystander, creating breadth, depth, and richness by allowing courage to shape the story rather than fear.

The practice itself is deceptively simple: when faced with a choice, pause. Tune into both your anxieties and your aspirations. Then ask yourself: *which story do I want to author?* Do I want my life's narrative to be defined by what I avoided, or by what I pursued? Do I want to be remembered for playing it safe, or for having the courage to chase what set my soul alight? Each time you choose the aspirational path, you're not just making a decision in the moment, you're actively constructing a more courageous, fulfilling life, one deliberate step at a time. Your aspirations, when clearly named and consciously followed, become a compass that consistently points you towards your most authentic and courageous self.

Courage in Leadership

But when it comes to leadership, this principle is often tested under the harsh glare of scrutiny. Leadership can feel like living under a spotlight, where every decision, every word, and every perceived flaw is magnified. This constant sense of being observed and evaluated is the essence of the *fear of judgment*. And for leaders, it can become one of the most paralysing barriers to courage.

There's immense pressure to project an image of certainty, always competent, always confident, always in control. Yet this very pressure often drives leaders into inauthenticity. Instead of fostering trust and genuine connection, they become consumed by performance. The mask of perfection, worn long enough, doesn't just distance them from their teams, it distances them from themselves.

Take the leader who, when confronted with a novel challenge, feels compelled to conjure an instant answer rather than admit they need time to explore or consult. On the surface, they avoid embarrassment. But over time, the cost is steep: a culture of silence. Team members, seeing that uncertainty is masked rather than embraced, learn to conceal their own doubts. Innovation falters, problems remain buried, and the opportunity for collaborative solutions slips away.

The irony is stark: in trying to protect themselves from judgment, leaders often create an environment where everyone is afraid of it. And in doing so, they sabotage the very conditions that make leadership effective, empathy, openness, and shared humanity.

To counter this, leaders must cultivate a different kind of bravery: the courage to be imperfect. That begins with reframing strength itself. Real strength isn't about projecting invulnerability; it's about choosing honesty over image. It's about saying: I don't need to know everything, but I am committed to finding a way forward.

Vulnerability, when practised with intention, is one of the most powerful tools at a leader's disposal. It doesn't mean oversharing personal struggles or confessing every doubt. It means selectively and authentically showing your humanity. For instance, a leader might say in a team meeting:
"I don't have all the answers on this yet. I'd like us to think it through together."

Or after a project falls short:
"This one didn't land the way we hoped. I misjudged the timing, and here's what I've learnt. Let's figure out together how to adjust."

These moments of openness don't diminish credibility, they deepen it. They signal that honesty, accountability, and learning are valued more than ego. And when leaders model this, teams respond in kind. People become more willing to speak up, to admit mistakes, to share ideas that are half-formed but potentially brilliant.

This is where the paradox of vulnerability reveals its power: far from weakening leadership, it strengthens it. Because when leaders allow themselves to be seen as human, they give their teams permission to be human too. And in that space, where judgment loosens its grip, trust, innovation, and collective courage begin to thrive.

Another powerful way for leaders to loosen the grip of the fear of judgment is to invite it in. Seeking feedback proactively, rather than waiting for criticism to arrive unannounced, shifts the dynamic completely. When you ask, "What could I be doing differently to better support this team?" or "How did you experience my handling of that challenge?" you demonstrate not only humility but a deep commitment to growth. Feedback becomes less of a threat and more of a resource. By building it into one-to-ones, anonymous surveys, or dedicated feedback sessions, you normalise evaluation as part of the learning process. This way, criticism is not an ambush; it's anticipated, framed, and far less likely to sting in destructive ways.

Of course, not all feedback will be constructive, and not all criticism will be fair. The mark of courageous leadership is knowing how to filter. It takes emotional regulation: the ability to feel the sting without letting it spiral into self-doubt. It also requires anchoring yourself in a strong internal compass your values, your purpose, your long-term goals. That way, you can sift the gold from the grit: keep what's useful, discard what isn't, and move forward with clarity.

Take, for instance, a leader who's told that their communication style is too abrupt. A defensive leader might shrug it off or blame the sensitivity of the person raising it. A courageous leader pauses. They reflect, recognise that their habit of interrupting comes from wanting to drive meetings forward, but also acknowledge how it may silence contributions. They then thank the colleague for their candour, explain their intent, and commit to practising more active listening. What could have been a moment of shame or friction becomes a demonstration of integrity, accountability, and growth. The team sees that mistakes can be acknowledged without fear, and that lesson spreads.

The fear of judgment also shows up in risk-taking. Leaders may stick to the safest path, magnifying unlikely worst-case scenarios until they convince themselves that bold ideas are reckless. But courage in leadership is often about taking calculated risks, the ones that involve uncertainty, yes, but also the possibility of real progress. Think of the leader with a disruptive idea for a new product. Fear whispers: "What if this fails? What will people say about me?" Courage reframes it: "What if this works? What impact could it create for our customers, our market, our future?" They still do their homework, due diligence, business case, contingency plans but their driver is aspiration, not anxiety. And when setbacks inevitably come, they model resilience: adapting, learning, and keeping the team aligned to the larger vision.

But here's the crucial part: the responsibility doesn't rest with the leader alone. Yes, leaders set the tone, but the culture of psychological safety is a collective project. When a leader is willing to show vulnerability, admit mistakes, or invite feedback, it encourages the team to do the same. Over time, this creates an environment where authenticity is valued over performance, where mistakes are mined for lessons rather than punished, and where constructive challenge is given with empathy, not fear. In such a culture, people take initiative, share bold ideas, and grow beyond what they thought possible, because the fear of judgment has lost its power to silence them.

Leading with courage, then, is not about being impervious to criticism or chasing approval. It is about shifting the driver of your decisions: from external validation to internal conviction. When you lead from values, clarity, and a commitment to what serves your team and organisation best, you free yourself from the paralysing grip of judgment. And in doing so, you invite others to step into that same freedom, creating a ripple of authenticity, trust, and bold action that transforms not just you, but the culture around you.

The ultimate antidote to the fear of judgment in leadership is cultivating a deep sense of self-worth that isn't tethered to external approval. This strength comes not from constant applause, but from acting in alignment with your values, pursuing goals that matter, and recognising that growth is a lifelong process rather than a finish line. Leaders who are anchored in this inner confidence don't become immune to the opinions of others, but those opinions lose their power to dictate behaviour. They can then lead with greater authenticity, conviction, and the courage to make the difficult choices that drive progress. Such leadership is not only more effective; it is far more inspiring. It shifts the leader from being a distant figure of apparent perfection to a relatable, human presence, someone others can trust and rally behind.

The fear of judgment, left unchecked, can narrow our horizons. It nudges us towards the familiar, to the "safe bet," and away from the risks that hold the possibility of meaningful impact. It convinces us that it's better to avoid potential embarrassment than to pursue bold ideas. Yet the kind of leadership that changes things, that inspires innovation, adapts to complexity, and breathes life into teams, is rarely born from comfort. It requires the courage to embrace risk. Not recklessness, but calculated, deliberate risk.

It's worth drawing a line here: a gamble and a calculated risk are not the same. A gamble is impulse-driven, often reckless, fuelled by wishful thinking or desperation. A calculated risk, by contrast, is informed and intentional. It weighs potential gains against realistic downsides. It considers probabilities, explores mitigation strategies, and accepts that some uncertainty will always remain. Leaders who embrace calculated risks understand a simple truth: inaction often carries the greatest cost. The world doesn't stand still, and organisations that refuse to move forward eventually fall behind.

Preparation is the first cornerstone of calculated risk-taking. Preparation doesn't remove uncertainty, but it reduces the fog around it. Take the entrepreneur preparing to launch a new product. Instead of rushing to market, they research customer needs, analyse competitors, pilot-test an early version, and refine it based on real-world feedback. The fear of failure is still there, but so is the confidence that comes from groundwork. The leap remains, but now it is a planned leap, not a blind one.

Scenario planning strengthens this foundation. Leaders who explore a range of "what if" outcomes, from best-case to worst-case, build resilience before the first step is even taken. If projections fall short, if a competitor disrupts the space, if a supplier collapses, what then? By thinking ahead and rehearsing responses, they reduce the shock of surprise and the panic that often paralyses decision-making. Not every eventuality can be anticipated, but having a map, however rough, gives direction when the terrain shifts.

Mitigation is the next layer. For every risk identified, a leader asks: how do we reduce its likelihood, or soften its impact if it lands? That might mean diversifying suppliers, building redundancies, investing in training, or launching in stages rather than all at once. These aren't guarantees of success, but they tip the balance in favour of it. The courage here lies in taking the risk seriously, not pretending it doesn't exist.

What separates courageous leaders from anxious ones is the story they tell themselves about risk. Fear-driven leaders catastrophise: they zoom in on worst-case scenarios until paralysis sets in. Courageous leaders reframe: failure isn't the end, it's feedback. Every misstep, every experiment that doesn't go as planned, is a lesson that refines strategy and builds resilience. This mindset shift, from *risk equals ruin* to *risk equals growth*, is transformative.

When I first started my coaching and speaking career, I thought the hardest part would be the logistics, finding clients, refining my message, building a brand from scratch. But the real battle was internal. It was fear, the kind that whispers, *"Who's going to listen to you?"*

I remember one of my first keynote invitations. It wasn't a huge event, fifty people in a mid-sized room but to me, it felt monumental. I almost said no. The imposter voice was loud: *You're not ready. You're not qualified enough. You haven't done this long enough to stand on that stage.*

But somewhere beneath the noise, a quieter truth persisted: *You've spent years living what you're now teaching. That's enough to begin.*

So, I said yes.

The night before the talk, I barely slept. I went over my notes, restructured my slides, questioned every sentence. But when I stepped on stage and started speaking, *really speaking*, something shifted. I wasn't performing; I was connecting. My voice shook a little, my pacing wasn't perfect, but people leaned in. Some nodded, others smiled. A few even cried when I spoke about belonging and fear.

I walked off that stage trembling, not from nerves, but from the realisation that courage doesn't arrive before action. It arrives *through* it. That moment became a turning point for me. It taught me that courage rarely feels like confidence. Most of the time, it feels like showing up while your hands still shake.

It's the same energy I bring into my coaching practice now. When clients tell me they're not ready, I tell them what I learned that day: readiness isn't a feeling; it's a decision. You become ready by moving, not by waiting. Courage doesn't announce itself, it's revealed in the act of showing up.

Years earlier, in my corporate career, courage looked completely different. I was leading recruitment for a large financial firm, a world of sharp suits, sharper politics, and unspoken hierarchies. One afternoon, we were reviewing candidates for senior leadership roles, and the conversation turned to "fit." It was said casually, almost like an administrative detail, but I felt the weight of it.

I'd seen too many brilliant people filtered out under that label. "Fit" had become a euphemism, not for skill or capability, but for comfort. For sameness. For maintaining the invisible template of who was deemed leadership material.

I remember sitting there, heart pounding, torn between staying silent and saying what I knew needed to be said. Eventually, I leaned forward and asked, *"Can we just unpack what we mean by 'fit'? Because if we can't define it clearly, we might be gatekeeping talent without realising it."*

The room went still. Someone shifted in their chair. A senior director glanced up, eyebrows raised. It was a tense moment, but a necessary one.

Slowly, the conversation began to shift. People reflected, questioned, reconsidered. It wasn't a grand revolution, but it was a spark. Months later, that company began revisiting its hiring framework and redefining what "potential" meant.

That day, I learned a different kind of courage, the courage to confront comfort. To speak not for recognition, but for integrity. To risk disapproval in service of something greater than ego: equity, fairness, truth.

Both experiences, standing on that stage and speaking up in that boardroom, shaped how I understand leadership today. They're two sides of the same coin. One was about stepping into visibility; the other, about using that visibility for change. One demanded that I overcome fear of failure; the other, fear of conflict. Both required faith, not in the absence of fear, but in the purpose behind the action.

These moments taught me that courage isn't situational, it's structural. It's not reserved for crises or breakthroughs. It's a framework for how you live, lead, and relate. Courage is the decision to stay aligned with your values, even when it costs you comfort. It's the willingness to ask questions that disrupt silence. It's the ability to choose integrity over image, and long-term impact over short-term approval.

And most importantly, courage is contagious.
When leaders choose to engage with uncertainty instead of avoiding it, they send a clear message: *It's safe to try. It's safe to speak. It's safe to care.*
Teams learn courage by watching it.
If you shrink from uncertainty, they will too.
If you take thoughtful risks, they'll begin to do the same.

This is how cultures of trust and innovation are built, not through slogans, but through example.
When a leader dares to be human, it gives everyone else permission to be.

Courage in leadership isn't bravado. It's not about being the loudest in the room or pretending to be fearless. It's about standing in truth prepared yet open, grounded yet daring, a quiet discipline to engage with uncertainty rather than run from it.

Because while fear and uncertainty are inevitable, paralysis is optional.

When you model that truth consistently, something profound happens: your courage becomes a mirror. It reflects back to others their own capacity to rise, to speak, to lead. It's the moment your team takes initiative without waiting for permission. The moment a colleague finally voices an idea they've been sitting on for weeks. The moment someone else stands taller because they saw you stand first.

That's the real work of leadership, not perfection, but permission. Not commanding confidence, but cultivating courage.

Because leadership isn't about having all the answers. It's about showing others what it looks like to keep moving forward, with preparation, resilience, and heart, even when the outcome is uncertain.

When you lead from that place, courage stops being personal. It becomes cultural, it stops being something you perform. It becomes something you *practice.*

You see this dynamic play out in every great organisation. Consider a technology company deliberating on whether to invest heavily in a new software platform. The fearful leader shrinks from the idea, settling for minor tweaks to the existing product line. It feels safe, but it also stifles potential.

A more courageous leader convenes a diverse team, explores feasibility in detail, pilots a minimum viable product, and tests the waters with trusted clients. Step by step, they reduce uncertainty, learn, adapt, and build confidence.

The difference isn't bravado, it's a disciplined willingness to engage with uncertainty rather than run from it. This willingness to take calculated risks doesn't just move projects forward; it shapes *culture*.

Teams learn by watching. When leaders step into uncertainty with preparation and resilience, they signal that experimentation is not only tolerated but encouraged.

That's how you build organisations that are adaptive, resilient, and innovative, because their leader's model those same qualities. Fear shrinks horizons; courage expands them. Ultimately, calculated risk-taking is the practical expression of courage in leadership. It demonstrates that while fear and uncertainty are inevitable, paralysis is optional.

And when leaders choose courage consistently, in meetings, in decisions, in how they respond to failure, they don't just lead well. They lead others to believe that courage is possible for them too.

Living Forward with Courage

And this is the essence of living courageously. It isn't about climbing a single peak and declaring victory. It's an ongoing practice, a daily training ground. Each moment of discomfort, each decision weighed, each step into uncertainty is an opportunity to strengthen the muscle of bravery. You don't need to slay dragons to become courageous. It might mean speaking up in a meeting when you'd rather stay silent. It might mean making that phone call you've been putting off. It might mean taking one step towards a long-term aspiration instead of waiting for the fear to vanish.

Each small, deliberate act is a chiselling of character. Each choice to move forward, however modest, is a statement: fear does not dictate the limits of my life. Over time, those choices accumulate into a new identity, not someone who never feels afraid, but someone who has learned, again and again, to act anyway.

Crucially, this continuous practice must always be tempered with self-compassion. There will be days when the fear feels heavier than usual, when old doubts creep back in, and when the energy to engage simply isn't there. On those days, the instinct might be to criticise yourself, to interpret the struggle as weakness or failure. Resist that urge. Setbacks are not signs that you've fallen short, they are part of being human. They are pauses, not endpoints. The courageous response is to meet yourself with the same patience and understanding you'd offer a close friend. Acknowledge the difficulty, validate the feeling, and gently remind yourself of the progress you've already made. Even the decision to begin again tomorrow is an act of courage.

Persistence is the fuel that keeps courage alive. It's the willingness to keep showing up, even when results aren't immediate or obvious. Think of a sculptor working with stone. The masterpiece doesn't appear after the first strike of the chisel, it takes thousands of careful, patient cuts. What carries them through isn't a single burst of effort, but the discipline of returning to the work, again. Courage is no different. It's shaped through the steady application of your values and intentions, even when progress feels invisible. Speaking up for an idea, staying open during organisational change, continuing to back a cause you believe in, these small, repeated acts gradually carve out trust, resilience, and strength that others can depend on.

Redefining Courage

As your practice deepens, you'll also notice that your definition of courage evolves. At first, you might measure it by dramatic, outward feats, confronting big challenges or pushing through obvious fears. Over time, you'll begin to recognise courage in quieter moments: admitting you don't have all the answers, delegating a task you've always guarded closely, or simply being fully present in a conversation without preparing your reply in advance. These internal victories are no less significant. They reflect maturity, self-awareness, and a willingness to live more authentically.

Equally important is the choice to learn from every outcome, whether it feels like a success or a setback. When something goes well, take time to analyse why. What worked? Which decisions or behaviours contributed? Which assumptions proved right? This builds a clearer sense of your strengths. When things don't go as planned, resist the urge to call it "failure" and close the book.

Instead, treat it as data. Ask: What didn't work? What might I try differently next time? What external factors shaped the outcome? This analytical honesty, the willingness to face reality squarely and adapt, is a profound act of courage in itself.

Alignment and Inner Courage

At its core, courage is about alignment: bridging the gap between what you value most and what you do each day. Fear of judgment or failure can tempt you into compromise, nudging you towards choices that keep the peace but don't speak to your soul. The ongoing practice is to pause, check in, and ask: Am I acting in line with what truly matters to me? Am I shaping a life that reflects my aspirations, or one that bends to other people's expectations? This is inner courage: the refusal to betray yourself for the comfort of conformity. And when you choose it consistently, your actions carry a natural conviction that inspires others too.

Reframing decisions is a powerful part of this. Rather than chasing the elusive "perfect" choice, begin to see every decision as part of a process, an experiment that provides information. You make the best call you can with the knowledge you have, knowing you can adapt if the outcome surprises you. This takes pressure off and builds agility. Perhaps you launch a project expecting a certain response, but the market reacts differently. Courage is not stubbornly defending your first plan; it's listening, learning, and pivoting. Adaptability, not rigidity, is the hallmark of courageous leadership.

The Ripple Effect of Courage

As a leader, your own practice of courage becomes contagious. When you model openness, take intelligent risks, or admit mistakes without shame, you create psychological safety. Your team learns that it's not only acceptable but valued to try, to speak, to stretch. Courage stops being an individual performance and becomes a collective strength. It fosters innovation, trust, and resilience across the group.

Ultimately, living forward through courage is about an ongoing mindset of engagement. It's about recognising that the future isn't something that simply happens to us; it's something we co-create, choice by choice. Fear and judgment will always be present companions, but they don't have to drive the bus. With self-compassion, persistence, alignment, and a commitment to learn, you transform fear from a cage into a catalyst.

Every small step you take in the presence of fear is a statement: I am choosing courage over comfort. I am building a life that reflects my values, my aspirations, and my truest self. Over time, those steps accumulate into a powerful declaration, that your life will not be defined by avoidance, but by the steady, courageous practice of becoming who you were always meant to be.

Summary: Leading with Courage: From Reaction to Practice

Chapter 4 has been about movement, the shift from reacting to fear to consciously practising courage as a way of life. It's where theory becomes muscle. Where courage stops being an idea and starts becoming a rhythm, built through consistency, clarity, and compassion.

We began by understanding that courage doesn't emerge in grand gestures; it's cultivated in the small, repeatable acts that teach the nervous system to stay steady under pressure. Every time you face discomfort and act anyway, however small the step, you're rewiring yourself to see challenge not as danger, but as opportunity. You're teaching your brain: *I can handle this.* Over time, those repetitions accumulate into quiet confidence. Courage becomes less about the absence of fear and more about the presence of trust.

We explored how *courage habits*, small, deliberate, daily actions, build resilience. Speaking up in meetings. Asking the question you'd normally avoid. Starting the task, you've been procrastinating on for just fifteen minutes. Each action is a training ground. Each repetition a vote for your stronger self. And when you fail to follow through (as we all do), self-compassion becomes the key that keeps the practice alive. Because courage isn't about perfection, it's about persistence.

We then examined the deeper shift from *fear-based* to *aspiration-led* living.
Fear asks, What if I fail?
Aspiration asks, Who could I become if I tried?
That difference changes everything. When fear leads, we play small, choosing safety overgrowth. When aspiration leads, we

move toward meaning, even when uncertainty still walks beside us.

I shared the night I stood on a stage for one of my first keynotes, terrified that my voice would shake, and it did. But in showing up anyway, I discovered that courage isn't found before the act; it's found *through* the act. Later, I shared the boardroom moment when I asked, "What do we mean by 'fit'?" and felt the silence stretch across the table. It wasn't comfort I was chasing then, it was integrity. Those moments reminded me that courage wears many faces: sometimes it's speaking up, sometimes it's standing still, sometimes it's simply deciding that silence is no longer an option.

Through those experiences, I learned that courage is not situational, it's structural. It's not a performance for rare moments, but a framework for everyday living. Courage is the decision to stay aligned with your values even when it costs you comfort. It's asking the difficult question when silence feels safer. It's choosing integrity over image, and long-term purpose over short term approval.

We then looked outward, to leadership, to culture, to the spaces where fear and courage intertwine. Leadership, at its core, is a mirror: teams take their cues from the emotional posture of their leaders. When a leader hides behind certainty, the team hides behind silence. When a leader dares to be real, to admit uncertainty, to model vulnerability and learning, the entire culture begins to breathe. Courage cascades downwards. It becomes less about commanding confidence and more about creating permission, permission to try, to fail, to innovate, and to grow.

We explored what this looks like in practice: the difference between fear-driven leadership that clings to control, and courageous leadership that invites collaboration, curiosity, and risk. The fearful leader shrinks horizons, the courageous one expands them. The fearful leader demands perfection: the courageous one builds trust. One protects the status quo; the other transforms it.

At the heart of this chapter was a truth: *calculated risk-taking is the practical expression of courage in leadership.* It's not recklessness; it's the discipline to engage with uncertainty intelligently, through preparation, reflection, and purpose. It's what allows innovation to thrive and teams to feel safe taking bold steps of their own. Because courage in leadership isn't bravado; it's grounded bravery, the quiet conviction to lead with clarity even when the path ahead isn't guaranteed.

And finally, we returned to the personal. Because leadership, before it is ever public, is internal. Living forward with courage means learning to carry fear without letting it dictate your direction. It means recognising that fear is energy, *E-motion* = energy in motion. It can paralyse, or it can propel, depending on how we use it. By naming our fears, identifying the values beneath them, and acting in alignment with what truly matters, we transform fear from a wall into a wave, a current that carries us toward purpose.

To live courageously, then, is to build a life that reflects your highest values in the smallest actions. To meet discomfort not with avoidance, but with curiosity. To see rejection not as failure, but as redirection. To let aspiration set the compass, not anxiety. And to remember that courage is contagious, that every act of bravery, however quiet, expands what's possible for others too.

Courage is not a single act; it's a lifestyle. It's what turns self-awareness into self-trust, and self-trust into influence. It's what builds not just resilient individuals, but resilient cultures.

When we move from reaction to practice, from theory to rhythm, from isolated courage to integrated habit, we don't just lead differently, we live differently.

We lead with clarity, grounded in purpose.

We act with conviction, guided by values.

We inspire others, not through perfection, but through presence.

And that is the ultimate measure of courageous leadership: not how fearlessly we act, but how faithfully we live, day after day, decision after decision, in alignment with who we truly are.

Healing Through Integration: A Reflective Practice

Before courage can become a way of living, it must first become a way of being with ourselves. Healing begins in that quiet space between breath and awareness, the space where the body finally stops anticipating harm and begins to remember ease. For many of us, fear has been our first language. We learned it through silence, through vigilance, through the unspoken lessons of survival passed down like heirlooms. Healing, then, is the process of translation, teaching the body to speak safety again.

This practice is a gentle invitation to return to yourself. It asks for no perfection, only presence. It is an act of remembering of meeting the parts of you that learned to brace, to hide, to hold your breath, and letting them know they are safe to rest now. Healing doesn't arrive as a sudden revelation; it unfolds slowly, like dawn, reminding you that safety is not something distant to be reached, but something felt, reclaimed, and lived in the present.

Over time, fear can harden into architecture. It shapes how we move, how we breathe, how we trust. This exercise invites you to soften those structures, to loosen what vigilance has tightened, to allow warmth where tension once lived. Every small release, every steady breath, becomes a quiet declaration: *I am safe enough to exist fully here.*

Think of this moment as an integration, a weaving together of everything you have learned throughout these pages. Theories of fear and courage take root in the body only through practice. Reflection becomes sensation. Insight becomes embodiment. Healing becomes a lived dialogue between memory and possibility. It is here, in this stillness, that you begin to recognise the difference between surviving and living.

Take your time. Move slowly. Let the body set the pace. Healing has its own rhythm — steady, subtle, and sacred. And as you breathe through this exercise, remember: courage does not always roar. Sometimes, it sounds like a sigh of relief. Sometimes, it feels like peace finally returning home.

Healing Through Integration: A Reflective Practice

Healing is not about deleting the past, it's about giving it new meaning. The goal isn't to become fearless; it's to build a life where fear no longer drives the decisions. Where your nervous system learns that what once was danger, is now memory.

As trauma researcher Ruth Lanius (2020) notes, recovery from trauma is a process of *reconnection*: restoring integration between the body, mind, and self that trauma once divided. When we learn to feel again slowly, safely the fragments of identity start to return home.

Fear fragments.
Awareness reassembles.
Safety stitches us back together.

Part 1: Mapping the Body's Memory

"The body keeps the score, but it can also keep the story of recovery."
Bessel van der Kolk

Before the mind can release fear, the body must first be heard.
Somatic awareness, or *interoception* is the practice of noticing sensations without judging them.
It's how you begin to translate the body's language of tension, breath, and pulse.

Exercise 1: The Body Map

Take a quiet moment. Sit or stand comfortably. Breathe.
Now, without analysing, bring gentle awareness to your body.
Where does fear live? Where does safety live?

Sensation / Area	What I Feel	What It Might Mean
Jaw / Neck	Tight, clenched	Holding back words or emotion
Shoulders	Heavy	Carrying responsibility or guilt
Chest	Tight, shallow breath	Fear of exposure or vulnerability
Stomach	Knotted	Anticipation, uncertainty, shame
Legs / Feet	Restless, tense	Urge to escape or perform
Hands	Cold, fidgety	Readiness or anxiety

Now add your own.

Then, write one sentence completing this reflection:

"When fear visits my body, it usually feels like _____, and it's asking me to _____."

This is not about control, it's more about communication.
The body speaks in signals. Listening is the first act of healing.

Part 2: Rewriting the Internal Script

Fear speaks in stories, old ones, often borrowed ones.

Psychologists call these *core beliefs*: unconscious assumptions formed early in life.

They sound like:

- "If I'm not perfect, I'll be rejected."
- "I'm safest when I'm invisible."
- "If I stop trying, I'll fail."

These stories once kept you safe. But they no longer serve you. To reclaim your voice, you must rewrite the script.

Exercise 2: The Story My Body Still Believes

Draw a line down the middle of a page.

On the left, write your fear-based belief.

On the right, write a truth you're learning to live by.

Fear-Based Belief	Reclaimed Truth
"I'm too much."	"My fullness is my gift."
"If I speak, I'll be punished."	"My voice deserves to be heard."
"If I slow down, I'll fall behind."	"Rest is resistance. Rest is repair."
"I can't trust anyone."	"I can learn trust again, slowly and safely."

Then, close your eyes and speak one of your new truths out loud, slowly, with breath.
Notice how your body responds.
This is not affirmation. It's neural rewiring.
Every repetition tells your nervous system: *The threat has passed.*

Part 3: The Practice of Safety

Healing is not a single revelation, it's a rhythm.
A daily practice of teaching your body that safety is available, right now, in small, consistent ways.

As **Stephen Porges (2011)** reminds us, safety is not a thought; it's a state. The *ventral vagal system,* our social engagement system, calms the body through tone, touch, and connection. That's why courage can't be built in isolation.

We learn it in relationship, through **co-regulation**, when someone else's calm helps stabilise our own.

Exercise 3: Building a Safety Ritual
Choose one or more daily anchors, small actions that tell your body: *You are safe now.*

Ritual	Why It Works
Deep, slow breathing (6 seconds in, 8 seconds out)	Activates the vagus nerve, lowering heart rate

Ritual	Why It Works
Gentle stretching or shaking	Releases adrenaline, restores mobility
Warm water (bath, shower, tea)	Regulates sensory system, signals comfort
Connecting with a trusted friend	Co-regulates emotional state
Journaling before sleep	Processes intrusive thoughts safely

Then, design your own:

"My body feels safest when I _____."
"I will practice this at least once each day."

Each act of safety is a rebellion against the old neural blueprint. You are literally reprogramming your nervous system for peace.

Part 4: Reflection & Closing Ritual

"Safety is not the absence of threat; it is the presence of connection."
Gabor Maté

Before closing this chapter, take a final moment of stillness. Place a hand over your chest. Feel your heartbeat — steady, alive. That rhythm has carried you through every moment you thought you couldn't survive.

Write down three things you now know to be true:

1. _____

2. _____

3. _____

Then complete this sentence:

"Fear taught me how to survive.
Now I'm teaching myself how to live."

That is the essence of integration, not the erasure of fear, but the transformation of its purpose.
Every breath, every boundary, every honest word is a signal to your body that safety is no longer conditional.
It's yours now.

And when safety becomes your baseline,
courage becomes your second nature.

When you finish this exercise, don't rush to name what has changed. Healing rarely announces itself; it hums quietly beneath the noise of habit. Sometimes the shift is as subtle as a slower heartbeat, a deeper breath, a thought that lands more gently than before. These are the quiet proofs that courage has found its way into the body.

Fear will still visit, it always does but perhaps now you'll recognise it differently. Not as an enemy to conquer, but as a messenger reminding you of what matters. And when it comes, you'll know how to meet it: not with resistance, but with breath; not with armour, but with awareness. Because the opposite of fear was never fearlessness, it was understanding.

This is what the journey has been leading you toward: not a life without fear, but a life no longer ruled by it. A life where courage feels less like a performance and more like a posture, something that lives in your body, in your choices, in the way you speak to yourself.

So, as you step back into the noise of the world, carry this stillness with you. Let it remind you that you have already faced what frightened you most: your own doubt. And you're still here. Still breathing. Still becoming.

That is the answer to the question this book began with, *What are you so afraid of?*
Perhaps, now, the answer is: *nothing I can't meet with courage.*

CHAPTER 6

Conclusion
- The Only Way Out Is Through

Fear never really leaves us.
It just changes its shape.

When I began this book, I described how fear enters quietly, polite, persuasive, disguised as caution or professionalism. It doesn't announce itself with chaos or panic; it whispers logic, offering you a hundred reasons to wait.

And for a long time, I listened.

I thought if I planned enough, prepared enough, proved enough, one day I'd finally feel ready.

But readiness never arrived.

Because fear doesn't dissolve with time, it dissolves through action.

And that's what this journey has been about.

What This Journey Has Been

When you first opened this book, I asked a question: *What are you so afraid of?*

Not to provoke, but to invite, because behind that question lives another: *What would your life look like if fear no longer led it?*

The truth is, fear lives in all of us. It's universal, intimate, and intelligent.

It takes on different shapes: the fear of failure, of being seen, of disappointing others, of losing what we've built, or of never quite living up to what we know we could be. Even paradoxically and ironically the fear of succeeding and being successful. But fear, when left unexamined, becomes the silent architect of our limits. It draws invisible boundaries around what feels safe. It convinces us that hesitation is wisdom, that busyness is purpose, that silence is strength.

So, we began this journey by bringing fear into the light.

In **Chapter 1: Unmasking Your Hidden Fears**, we started at the surface with the masks fear wears. We learned that fear rarely shows up shouting; it whispers, it blends in. It dresses itself as perfectionism, people-pleasing, control, or busyness, behaviours the world often rewards. We peeled back those disguises and began to understand that what we've long labelled as "habits" or "traits" often began as survival strategies.

I wrote that chapter because I've lived those masks.
For years, fear shaped how I spoke, how I worked, how I moved through the world. It taught me to perform competence while

doubting myself. To over-prepare instead of risk being unready. To stay quiet when speaking might have changed everything. It took me years to realise those weren't personality quirks, they were forms of protection. That's why we begin here, with awareness. Because you can't heal what you can't see.

Then, in **Chapter 2: The Autopsy of Fear**, we went deeper, beyond the masks and into the mechanisms. If the first chapter was about seeing fear, this one was about understanding it. We examined how fear doesn't live in moments, but in patterns, how it builds systems inside us: cycles of overthinking, avoidance, control, and self-criticism. We dissected the anatomy of fear, how it thinks, hides, and heals. We discovered that fear is not irrational; it's logical but outdated. It was designed to keep us alive, not fulfilled. Once we understand that, we stop treating fear as the enemy and start seeing it as information. As data about what matters most. This chapter existed because I wanted you to know that fear isn't weakness, it's wiring. You're not broken; you're just running an old program, and awareness is how we start rewriting the code.

In **Chapter 3: Fear and Intersectionality — The Masks and Architectures of Survival**, we widened the lens. We explored how fear isn't only psychological but political; how it becomes gendered, racialised, and institutionalised, shaping who feels safe and who must perform safety to survive. We traced its evolution through colonialism, patriarchy, capitalism, and the social hierarchies that taught us to fear visibility, ambition, emotion, and even belonging itself. We examined how identities intersect to produce different kinds of fear, how Black women and those living between cultures experience the world through layers of vigilance and conditional acceptance. This chapter existed because I wanted you to see that fear isn't only personal, it's inherited, enforced, and sustained by systems that reward silence and punish authenticity. When we name those systems, we begin to reclaim power. Because awareness of structure is the first step to liberation, and liberation begins the moment we stop mistaking survival for safety.

In **Chapter 4: Courage in Action: Navigating Discomfort**, we crossed the bridge from understanding to embodiment. This is where knowledge becomes practice and where the theory of courage meets the reality of living it. We learned that discomfort isn't the opposite of growth; it's the evidence of it. Every meaningful transformation begins with tension, the moment you feel torn between the comfort of who you were and the calling of who you're becoming. This is where courage lives. Not in grand gestures or big leaps, but in the quiet choices. Like speaking up when it's easier to stay silent, saying no when your fear wants you to please, showing up before you feel ready.

I wanted this chapter to be a mirror of real life, the moments where courage feels awkward, inconvenient, human. Because that's the truth I learned in my own journey: courage isn't glamorous; it's gritty. It happens in the small acts that no one claps for, but that slowly change everything.

And finally, in **Chapter 5: Leading with Courage: Actionable Habits**, we turned the lens outward, from the individual to the collective. We explored what it means to lead with courage in our work, our relationships, and our communities. Because fear doesn't vanish as you rise; it just changes shape. It hides behind control, behind overcommitment, behind the performance of certainty.

We learned that leadership is not about being fearless; it's about modelling courage in real time. It's about creating spaces where others can show up fully, fail safely, and speak honestly.
That chapter was written for anyone who's ever thought, *"I can't lead until I have it all figured out."* Because true leadership doesn't come from perfection, it comes from presence. The willingness to be real, to be wrong, and to keep growing in public.

When I first began writing this book, I didn't want to create another self-help manual. I wanted to create a mirror. Something you could hold up to your own life and see yourself more clearly, not the curated, polished version, but the version that's still learning, still afraid, still trying.

The structure of this book from *unmasking*, to *autopsy*, to *action*, to *leadership* — was intentional. It follows the same path every human transformation takes: awareness → understanding → embodiment → integration. We start by seeing the pattern, then we study it, then we practice something new, and finally, we teach it through how we live. That's how change sustains itself, not through information, but through repetition, community, and modelling.

My hope is that somewhere in these pages, you found permission, permission to be honest about what scares you, to meet fear with compassion, and to move forward even when it still lingers. I hope you've learned to see fear not as the full story, but as the opening line of a much larger one, the story of your becoming.

Because fear will still visit you. It still visits me.

But now, you know its patterns. You can name its disguises. You can feel its presence without letting it drive. You can thank it for its concern and still move forward.

That's what courage is. Not the disappearance of fear, but the decision to walk with it, deliberately, gently, again and again, until self-trust becomes your new safety.

And maybe that's been the quiet goal of this entire book: not to make you fearless, but to make you free. Free enough to speak truth even when your voice shakes. Free enough to stop performing for approval. Free enough to choose purpose over perfection.

If fear taught you to shrink, then courage must teach you to expand, into the fullness of your potential, your power, and your presence. Because courage, when practised consistently, becomes something greater than self-development; it becomes service. When you embody it, you give others permission to do the same. That's how families shift. That's how organisations evolve. That's how cultures change, one honest, trembling act of courage at a time.

This work doesn't end here. It's a cycle, an ongoing relationship between fear, awareness, and action. So when fear returns, as it will, I hope you don't see it as failure. I hope you see it as a sign that you're stretching again. That you're still growing. That you're still alive to what matters.

If you take one thing from these pages, let it be this: courage is not a personality type. It's a daily practice. Some days it roars, some days it whispers, but every day it's available to you. In the way you show up for yourself. In the way you show up for others. In the way you choose truth over performance, progress over perfection, meaning over fear.

So as you close this book, remember:
Fear may have written the first draft of your life,
but you hold the pen now.

The question that began this journey still stands: *What are you so afraid of?*
But this time, I hope your answer is not retreat, but readiness.
Not silence, but movement.
Not survival, but freedom.

Because courage isn't the end of the story.
It's how you begin again.

What We've Learned

Across these chapters, we have unlearned a few myths.

We've learned that fear is not weakness; it's wisdom in disguise.
That discomfort is not danger; it's evidence of growth.
That confidence isn't the prerequisite for courage; it's the result of it.
That failure isn't the end; it's feedback.

That leadership isn't about perfection; it's about permission, giving others the courage to try, to speak, to be.

We've learned that fear doesn't go away as we succeed, it evolves. Every new level of visibility, responsibility, or love comes with a new edge of vulnerability. But each time we walk through fear, we build resilience, the quiet, unshakable confidence that whispers, *I've been here before. I can handle this.*

And maybe most importantly, we've learned that courage is not an event, it's a lifestyle.
It's built through daily acts of integrity, compassion, and curiosity.
It's sustained by self-compassion.
It's strengthened through community.

Because no one walks through fear alone.

A Personal Reflection

I've had moments in my own life where fear won, where I stayed quiet, stayed small, stayed waiting.
I've had moments where I chose differently, moments when I spoke up, stepped forward, and risked failure for the sake of alignment.
Those are the moments that shaped me.
Not because I was fearless, but because I was faithful, faithful to what I valued, even when it cost me comfort.

That's what I want for you.
Not fearlessness.
Faithfulness.

Faith in your ability to face discomfort.
Faith in your right to take up space.
Faith in your capacity to rise again and again, no matter how many times fear knocks you down.

Remember this courage is not the absence of fear, it's the presence of faith.

The Practice Ahead

So, when fear visits you, as it inevitably will, as it does all of us. Here's what I hope you'll remember:

When it tells you you're not ready, remember, readiness is a decision, not a feeling.
When it tells you you're an imposter, remember, you've already earned your place by showing up.
When it tells you silence is safer, remember, silence serves the status quo, not your soul.
When it tells you perfection is protection, remember, connection lives in imperfection.
And when it tells you you're alone, remember, every courageous person you admire has felt exactly what you're feeling now.

Fear may still knock on your door, but you no longer have to invite it in.

Because now, you know its voice, the rhythm of its logic and the shape of its disguises. You can feel it rise and still choose movement. You can hear its warnings and still follow your purpose. You can carry fear without letting it steer.

That is the practice, not the elimination of fear, but the mastery of response.

Each time you act in alignment with your values, you reinforce the truth: *I can do this.*

Each time you show up even slightly braver than before, you retrain your nervous system to see discomfort not as danger, but as data.

In my consulting and coaching work across more than a hundred organisations and with thousands of individuals, I've seen this principle unfold again and again. From senior executives facing imposter syndrome in the boardroom, to graduates afraid to use their voice in their first team meeting, the pattern is universal. Fear thrives in silence and isolation; it loses its power in conversation, in understanding, in practice.

The people who transform aren't the ones who never feel afraid, they're the ones who learn to recognise fear's arrival, pause, breathe, and respond differently. They build habits of courage, small, daily acts that compound into confidence.

One boundary held.

One truth spoken.

One step taken in the direction that once felt impossible.

That's what courage looks like in real life. Not cinematic heroism, but quiet, consistent honesty. Not the absence of trembling but the decision to keep walking even whilst your heart races.

So when fear visits tomorrow, you'll know what to do.
You'll know that fear's presence doesn't mean you're on the wrong path, it means you're on the edge of growth.
You'll know that feeling exposed is part of expansion.
And you'll know that courage isn't waiting to find you, it's waiting to be chosen, again and again, in the smallest, simplest ways.

Fear will still visit you, but courage now calls this place home.

Epilogue: The Work Continues

The journey doesn't end on this page. It begins here, in the space between what you know and what you'll do next.

Fear will return, wearing new clothes, whispering familiar lies. But now, you'll recognise its tone. You'll meet it with calm instead of chaos, compassion instead of shame. You'll remember that fear is only proof that something meaningful is at stake, that you're standing at the threshold of something that matters.

And when that moment comes, at work, in love, in leadership, I hope you pause and remember this:
You've already done the hardest part. You've learned to see yourself clearly.

So, take what you've learned here and bring it into your world, into your meetings, your parenting, your art, your leadership, your life. Let the awareness turn into action, and the action turn into influence.

Because the work of courage is never finished.

It evolves with you. It expands as you do.

And with every act of honesty, kindness, and conviction, you make it a little easier for someone else to do the same.

The work continues in you, through you, and beyond you.

The Only Way Out Is Through

We spend so much of our lives trying to negotiate with fear. We bargain with it, outsmart it, disguise it. We tell ourselves, "Once I feel ready, then I'll act. Once the timing is perfect, then I'll try." But readiness never arrives. Perfection never comes. Fear doesn't dissolve on its own. The truth I've learned sometimes painfully is this: the only way out is through.

I've had moments where I waited too long. Ideas that could have shifted my career, opened doors, or changed lives, I kept them hidden. I told myself I needed another qualification, more experience, another sign of validation, another nod of approval before I was "enough." The delay cost me more than the risk ever would have. Fear won those days. And I've also had the opposite moments. Times I moved forward trembling, pitching an idea in a room where I wasn't sure I belonged, stepping on stage with my voice shaking, launching a project that could have stayed on my hard drive forever. I was scared in each of those moments. But those are the choices that shaped me. Not because I was fearless, but because I acted while afraid.

That's the paradox of growth. Fear doesn't shrink as you rise, it grows. Bigger opportunities bring bigger anxieties. But courage grows too. Every time you walk through fear, you prove to yourself that you can. And eventually, the fear may still whisper, but it no longer gets a vote in your decisions.

Fear is not your enemy. It is the raw material of courage, the trembling hand, the racing heart, the voice of doubt that reminds you this moment matters. Vulnerability is not weakness. It is the doorway to authenticity, the place where trust and real connection are born. Judgment will always whisper that you're safer hiding behind masks, but authenticity reminds you that your worth is not on trial. Risk will always loom, tempting you to retreat to the familiar. But comfort has never been the birthplace of progress.

Courage is the decision to move through fear. To show up, imperfect, human, and willing. To admit what you don't know, to voice what you believe, to own your mistakes, to take calculated risks when silence or stagnation feels easier. It is choosing to build a life authored by your aspirations rather than dictated by your anxieties or societal expectations and constructs. And it is not reserved for the heroic or the exceptional few. It is available to you, here and now, in the small habits of bravery that, repeated daily, rewire the way you see yourself and the world. Courage is built in small moments. Over time, those choices create a life defined not by what you avoided, but by what you dared to face.

This cycle of fear, courage, and growth is available to you every single day. Fear arises. You feel it in your body. Courage is the choice to act anyway. Growth is what happens on the other side. That cycle isn't just for moments of crisis or opportunity; it lives in the ordinary. The conversation you finally initiate. The boundary you hold. The project you put out into the world. Every act of walking through fear is a declaration: I refuse to live small.

Your Invitation Forward

So, as you close these pages, I want you to remember this:
You are not behind.
You are not unqualified.
You are not too late.
You are exactly where courage begins. Here, on the edge of uncertainty, holding the choice to move.

Start small.
Speak the truth.
Ask the question.

Take the risk.
Write the email.
Share the idea.
Say the thing.

You don't have to roar to lead. You just have to move, faithfully, consistently, one act at a time.

Courage will not make the fear vanish, but it will make you unshakable. In time, your life will stop being a negotiation with fear and start being a declaration of freedom.

Because courage, practised daily, becomes character.
And character, practised daily, becomes legacy.

Full Circle

You began this journey by asking, *What am I so afraid of?*
Maybe, at first, the answers felt heavy, failure, rejection, exposure and loss.
But now, at the end, perhaps the question has changed shape.
Maybe it's no longer about what you fear, but what you're ready for.

Ready to say.
Ready to build.
Ready to become.

Fear will still visit you softly, persistently, like an old language your body once spoke fluently.
But now, you'll know how to translate it.
You'll know that fear's presence doesn't mean *stop* it means *step with care.*
It means you're standing at the edge of something sacred, something that matters enough to tremble for.

So ask the question again, one last time not in doubt, but in devotion:
What are you so afraid of?

And this time, let the answer sound different.
Let it sound like *readiness.*
Let it sound like *freedom.*
Let it sound like *you.*

Because this is where every quiet revolution begins, not in noise or certainty, but in stillness, in awareness, in the moment you choose to walk forward anyway.

A Quiet Revolution

Perhaps that question *What are you so afraid of?* began this book, but maybe now, it's also the answer.

Because whatever your fear points to, there lies your calling.

The place where fear shouts loudest, that very place is often your soul is asking you to step into.

The only way out is through, and every time you walk through, you teach others they can too.

That's how change happens, not through the loudest voices, but through the steady ones.

The ones who lead with heart.

The ones who live with integrity.

The ones who refuse to let fear decide who they become.

May you go forward with courage in your bones and compassion in your heart.

May you speak when it's hard.

May you risk when it's uncertain.

May you lead when it's lonely.

And may you never forget that the quiet voice that says *"maybe I can"* is the beginning of every revolution.

Because courage doesn't always roar.

Sometimes, it just whispers *keep going.*

And if you do, you'll find that fear was never there to stop you.

It was there to shape you.

To sharpen you.

To lead you home to yourself.

So here is the charge I leave you with:
When fear rises pause. Recognise it as energy, not enemy.
When judgment threatens remember your worth is not on trial.
When risk appears measure it, then step forward anyway.
When vulnerability feels unbearable lean in, because it is where your power lives.
And when courage feels too big make it small: one act, one word, one choice at a time.

Carry this with you: courage is not what you feel, it's what you do. Let that truth be the compass you return to, again and again, as you move into the next chapter of your life.

From Me to You

If you've reached this page, it means you've done something extraordinary, you've stayed. You've leaned in, you've allowed yourself to see the parts of you that fear tried to silence. That alone is courage.

When I began writing this book, I didn't want to offer perfection. I wanted to offer permission, permission to feel afraid and still move forward, permission to be unfinished and still enough.

I've seen what happens when people choose courage. In conversations, in classrooms, in boardrooms, the same quiet transformation repeats itself: a shift in posture, a steadier breath, a softening into self-trust. It's subtle, but it's real and it always begins the same way, with honesty.

So if there's one thing I hope you carry from these pages, let it be this:
You are not behind. You are becoming.
Every act of honesty, every boundary, every truth spoken, they're all acts of courage.

And one day, you'll look back and realise that every moment you thought fear was breaking you, it was building you.
Into someone braver.
Someone freer.
Someone more you.

Author's Note

I wrote this book because I needed it once and if I'm honest I still do. I needed a language for the silence that fear creates the quiet, heavy kind that makes you doubt your worth, your readiness, your right to take up space.

Through my work with leaders, teams, and individuals across more than a hundred organisations. I've seen how universal that silence is. Fear shows up in different forms, but it speaks the same language everywhere. And yet, so does courage.

Over time, I learned that fear isn't something we outgrow it's something we outlearn. We learn to meet it, manage it, and move with it instead of against it. That's what this book became: an invitation to see fear differently, and to live differently because of it.

So, thank you for reading, for reflecting, for staying with these pages even when they asked you to look inward. If these words have met you where you are, may they also carry you where you're meant to go with clarity, compassion, and courage in equal measure.

With courage, gratitude and strength,
R.M.

Glossary of terms

A

Active bystander: Someone who intervenes safely when witnessing harm or bias.

Affect labelling: Putting feelings into words to reduce their intensity.

After-action review (AAR): Short, structured debrief of what happened, why, and what to change.

Agency: The felt capacity to act and influence outcomes.

Anchoring bias: Early information unduly shapes later judgements.

Anti-Blackness: Specific systemic devaluation of Black people in culture and institutions.

Anti-racism: Active work to identify and dismantle racist policies, practices and norms.

Appraisal (primary/secondary): Initial threat/benefit check and "can I cope?" evaluation of a situation.

Approach vs. avoidance goals: Moving toward desired outcomes versus away from feared outcomes.

Assimilation: Pressure to conform to dominant norms at the expense of identity.

Attentional bias: Tendency to notice information that confirms expectations or threats.

Availability cascade: A claim seems true because it's widely repeated.

Availability heuristic: Judging likelihood by how easily examples come to mind.

B

Backlash effect: Penalties when people from marginalised groups defy stereotypes.

Base-rate neglect: Ignoring general probabilities when judging specific cases.

Behavioural activation: Doing valued actions first to lift mood and momentum.

BIC (Brief–Impact–Change) feedback: "Brief" observation, "Impact" felt, "Change" requested.

Bias blind spot: Seeing others' bias more readily than one's own.

Blameless post-mortem: Analysing failures without shame to find systemic fixes.

Belonging: Feeling accepted, valued and safe to be oneself within a group.

Belonging cues: Signals (names, norms, rituals) that say "you are valued here."

Belonging uncertainty: Persistent doubt about whether one is accepted in a setting.

Boundary spanning: Connecting across teams/functions to solve complex problems.

Boundary statement: Respectful line that clarifies limits and alternatives.

Boundaries: Clear limits on time, energy or responsibilities to protect wellbeing and performance.

Burnout: Chronic workplace stress causing exhaustion, cynicism and reduced efficacy.

Bystander effect: People are less likely to intervene when others are present.

C

Catastrophising: Habit of imagining the worst-case and treating it as likely.

Choice architecture: How options are presented to steer decisions.

Choice overload: Too many options reduce decisions and satisfaction.

Code-switching: Adjusting language/behaviour to fit dominant norms; often costly.

Cognitive dissonance: Tension when actions and beliefs don't align, prompting rationalisation or change.

Cognitive load: Mental effort required to process information; high load impairs performance.

Colourism: Preferential treatment based on lighter skin tones.

Compassion fatigue: Emotional depletion from prolonged caregiving or high-empathy roles.

Confirmation bias: Seeking/weighting evidence that fits existing beliefs.

Conformity pressure: Tendency to align with group norms even when inaccurate.

Contact hypothesis: Structured, equal-status contact can reduce prejudice.

Counter-narrative: A story that challenges dominant explanations, restoring context and dignity.

Counter-stereotype exposure: Deliberate contact with examples that violate stereotypes.

Covering: Downplaying aspects of identity to avoid stigma or penalty.

Cue design: Making the prompt obvious where the behaviour should happen.

Cultural add (vs. fit): Hiring for new strengths that enrich culture rather than sameness.

Cultural humility: Lifelong self-reflection and power-aware learning across difference.

Cultural tax: Extra, often invisible labour expected from staff of colour to "fix" culture.

D

Decision fatigue: Decision quality drops after many choices.

Decision rights: Clarity on who decides what, and how input and vetoes work.

DEI (Diversity, Equity & Inclusion): Practice of representation, fairness and culture design so all can thrive.

Default effect (status-quo bias): Preference for existing options even when better ones exist.

Discretionary effort: Energy people choose to give when trust and purpose are high.

Dunning–Kruger effect: Low skill breeds overconfidence; high skill breeds underestimation.

E

Ego depletion: Idea that self-control can temporarily run low with effort.

Emotional contagion: Emotions spread through groups via cues and mimicry.

Emotional granularity: Ability to distinguish finely between similar emotions.

Emotional labour: Managing feelings to meet job expectations; hidden workload.

Equal pay / Pay equity: Same pay for same work / fair pay accounting for structural gaps.

Equality duty (public sector): Requires public bodies to consider equality impacts.

Equality vs. equity: Equal treatment versus fair outcomes that account for different starting points.

Evaluation criteria: Agreed standards used to assess performance; clear and consistent.

Expectancy / Pygmalion effect: Performance shifts to meet others' expectations.

Exposure hierarchy: Stepwise plan to face feared tasks.

Exposure ladder: Graduated steps for facing feared tasks to reduce avoidance.

F

Fair process leadership: Tough calls land better when the process is transparent and dignified.

False consensus effect: Overestimating how much others share our views.

Feedback: Information intended to improve performance; specific and timely.

Feedback culture: Norms where feedback is routine, reciprocal and safe.

Feedforward: Future-focused advice about what to try next.

Flow: Absorbed, focused state where challenge meets skill.

Focus time: Protected blocks for deep work, free of meetings/alerts.

Framing effect: Different wording changes choices (gain vs. loss frames).

Friction audit: Identifying/removing unnecessary steps blocking desired behaviour.

Fundamental attribution error: Over-assigning others' behaviour to traits rather than context.

G

Gaslighting: Manipulating someone to question their reality or sanity.

Glass ceiling: Invisible barriers blocking advancement for marginalised groups.

Glass cliff: Tendency to appoint marginalised leaders to crisis-prone roles.

Goal cascade: Linking team goals to strategy so effort compounds.

Growth mindset: Belief that ability can be developed through effort, strategies and support.

H

Habit friction: Environmental factors that make a behaviour harder than needed.

Habit stacking: Linking a new behaviour to an existing routine to make it stick.

High-contrast message: Clear yes/no or stop/start that prevents ambiguity.

Hindsight bias: Seeing past events as "obvious" after the fact.

Hostile Environment (UK policy): Approach that increases everyday barriers for migrants.

I

Identity safety: Confidence that one's identity will not be devalued or penalised.

Identity threat: Fear that one's social identity will be judged or punished.

Implementation intentions (if–then plans): "If X happens, then I will do Y" to automate action.

Imposter syndrome: Persistent self-doubt despite evidence of competence.

In-group bias: Systematic favouring of one's own group over others.
Inclusion: Designing norms, decisions and spaces so all can contribute and progress.
Indirect discrimination: Neutral-looking rules with unequal impact on protected groups.
Inner critic: Internal, self-judging voice that amplifies doubt.
Interoception: Sensing internal bodily states (breath, heartbeat, tension).
Intersectional invisibility: Overlooked experiences at intersections of multiple identities.
Intersectionality: How overlapping systems of power shape experience and outcomes.

K
Keystone habit: One habit that triggers multiple positive changes.

L
Learning debt: Skills/knowledge gaps that build when development lags change.
Learning organisation: A culture that experiments, shares error data and improves continuously.
Legitimacy (leadership): Perceived right to lead based on fairness, expertise and care.
Listening: Attentive, non-defensive hearing of words and intent; foundation for trust.
Locus of control: Belief about whether outcomes are driven by self or circumstance.
Loss aversion: Losses weigh more heavily than equivalent gains.

M

Masking (neurodiversity): Hiding traits to meet social expectations; draining over time.

Meeting hygiene: Clear intent, agenda, airtime balance and decision record.

Meeting norms: Agreed ways we run meetings (airtime, decisions, challenge).

Mental contrasting (WOOP): Visualising the goal *and* obstacle to trigger action.

Micro-affirmations: Small behaviours that recognise, include and encourage.

Microaggressions: Everyday slights or exclusions that cumulatively cause harm.

Minimum viable habit: Smallest version that's too easy to skip.

Minoritised: Groups made marginal by systems/practices (focus on process, not numbers).

Model minority myth: Stereotype that flattens Asian experiences and hides inequities.

Neurodiversity: Natural variation in cognitive functioning (e.g., ADHD, autism, dyslexia).

Nonviolent Communication (NVC): Observe, feel, need, request; judgement-light dialogue.

O

Occupational requirement: Narrow, lawful role criterion linked to duties (strict test).

Optimism bias: Underestimating risks; overestimating positive outcomes.

Organisational debt: Accumulated process/culture gaps that slow progress and harm people.

Organisational justice: Fairness in processes, outcomes and interpersonal treatment.

Othering: Casting people as fundamentally outside the "we."

Over justification effect: External rewards crowd out intrinsic motivation.

Overwork: Excessive hours/effort that harms health and performance.

P

Performance bias: Systematic differences in how similar performance is judged across groups.

Perfectionism: Rigid standards and evaluation anxiety that block learning.

Planning fallacy: Consistently underestimating time/cost for tasks.

Polyvagal (polyvagal theory): Links safety cues and autonomic states to behaviour.

Positive action (UK): Lawful measures to offset disadvantage (not quotas).

Positive discrimination (UK): Unlawful selection based solely on protected traits.

Power distance: Degree to which hierarchy and unequal power are accepted.

Present bias: Overvaluing immediate rewards versus future gains.

Protected characteristics (UK): Traits legally safeguarded by the Equality Act 2010.

Psychological capital (PsyCap): Hope, efficacy, resilience and optimism as trainable resources.

Psychological contract: Unwritten expectations between worker and organisation.

Psychological safety: Shared belief that it's safe to speak up, ask for help and admit errors.

Psychological safety signal: Behaviour that broadcasts safety (admitting error, inviting dissent).

R

RACI (Role clarity grid): Responsible, Accountable, Consulted, Informed.

Reasonable adjustments (UK): Changes to remove barriers for disabled/neurodivergent people.

Recency bias: Over-weighting the most recent events in evaluation.

Representation debt: Compounded absence of marginalised groups in roles and decisions.

Repair attempt: Early cue to de-escalate tension and rejoin respectfully.

Rest-recovery cycle: Planned micro-rest to sustain performance and learning.

Restorative conversation: Structured dialogue to understand harm and agree repair.

Retrospective: Regular review of ways-of-working to improve flow and morale.

Root cause analysis (5 Whys): Iterative questioning to find underlying drivers, not just symptoms.

Rumination: Repetitive, unproductive dwelling on problems.

S

Safe-to-fail experiment: Small, bounded test where failure is informative, not harmful.

Self-affirmation: Reconnecting with core values to buffer threat.

Self-compassion: Treating oneself with kindness, common humanity and mindful awareness.

Self-efficacy: Belief in one's capability to execute actions for desired outcomes.

Self-silencing: Withholding views to preserve belonging or safety.

Shadow decision-making: Informal power outside documented processes.

Shadow work: Unseen mental and emotional labour required to "fit in."

Somatic marker: Bodily feelings that guide decisions under uncertainty.

Sponsorship (vs. mentoring): Senior advocacy that opens doors and shares power.

Stakeholder mapping: Identifying influence/interest to tailor engagement.

Status threat: Fear of losing standing, attention or respect in a group.

Stereotype content model: Groups judged along warmth and competence dimensions.

Stereotype lift: Performance bump when a positive group stereotype is salient.

Stereotype threat: Performance drops when a negative stereotype is salient.

Structural discrimination: Routine policies/practices producing unequal outcomes.

Sunk cost fallacy: Continuing a losing course because of past investment.

T

Talent velocity: Speed at which people grow into scope and responsibility.

Temptation bundling: Pair a must-do with a want-to to increase adherence.

Tokenism: Symbolic inclusion without voice, power or pathway to influence.

Trauma-informed: Recognises trauma's impact; prioritises safety, choice and pacing.

Trigger stacking: Accumulation of stressors that lowers tolerance and amplifies reactions.

Trust repair: Acknowledge harm, explain, apologise, offer remedy, and change behaviour.

V

Values–behaviour map: Converting values into specific, observable actions.

Voice climate: Shared belief about whether speaking up is welcomed and acted upon.

W

White fragility: Defensive reactions that stall racial dialogue and learning.

Whiteness (systemic): Norms that centre white experience as default or "neutral."

Window of tolerance: Optimal arousal zone for learning and connection.

Windrush: The generation invited to rebuild post-war Britain and their descendants.

Workload design: Structuring capacity, priorities and trade-offs to make work sustainable.

Z

Zero-sum thinking: Belief that gains for one group mean losses for another.

Bibliography & Further Reading

Trauma, Neuroscience, and the Body

van der Kolk, B. A. (2014). *The Body Keeps the Score: Brain, Mind, and Body in the Healing of Trauma.* New York: Viking Press.

Felitti, V. J., Anda, R. F., Nordenberg, D., Williamson, D. F., Spitz, A. M., Edwards, V., ... & Marks, J. S. (1998). *Relationship of Childhood Abuse and Household Dysfunction to Many of the Leading Causes of Death in Adults: The Adverse Childhood Experiences (ACE) Study.* American Journal of Preventive Medicine, 14(4), 245–258.

McEwen, B. S. (2007). *Physiology and Neurobiology of Stress and Adaptation: Central Role of the Brain.* Physiological Reviews, 87(3), 873–904.

Yehuda, R., et al. (2016). *Holocaust Exposure Induced Intergenerational Effects on FKBP5 Methylation.* Biological Psychiatry, 80(5), 372–380.

Tobi, E. W., et al. (2009). *DNA Methylation Differences After Exposure to Prenatal Famine Are Common and Timing- and Sex-Specific. Human Molecular Genetics, 18*(21), 4046–4053.

Porges, S. W. (2011). *The Polyvagal Theory: Neurophysiological Foundations of Emotions, Attachment, Communication, and Self-Regulation.* New York: W. W. Norton.

Dana, D. (2018). *The Polyvagal Theory in Therapy: Engaging the Rhythm of Regulation.* New York: W. W. Norton.

Lanius, R. A., et al. (2015). *Restoring Large-Scale Brain Networks in PTSD and Related Disorders. European Journal of Psychotraumatology, 6*(1), 27313.

Levine, P. A. (1997). *Waking the Tiger: Healing Trauma.* Berkeley, CA: North Atlantic Books.

Ogden, P., Minton, K., & Pain, C. (2006). *Trauma and the Body: A Sensorimotor Approach to Psychotherapy.* New York: W. W. Norton.

Fisher, J. (2017). *Healing the Fragmented Selves of Trauma Survivors.* New York: Routledge.

Perry, B. D., & Winfrey, O. (2021). *What Happened to You?* New York: Bluebird.

Psychology, Cognitive Dissonance, and the Self

Festinger, L. (1957). *A Theory of Cognitive Dissonance.* Stanford: Stanford University Press.

Winnicott, D. W. (1965). *The Maturational Processes and the Facilitating Environment.* London: Hogarth Press.

Miller, A. (1981). *The Drama of the Gifted Child.* New York: Basic Books.

Barrett, L. F. (2017). *How Emotions Are Made.* Boston: Houghton Mifflin Harcourt.

Schore, A. N. (2012). *The Science of the Art of Psychotherapy.* New York: W. W. Norton.

Herman, J. L. (1992). *Trauma and Recovery.* New York: Basic Books.

LeDoux, J. (2012). *Rethinking the Emotional Brain. Neuron,* 73(4), 653–676.

Feeney, J. A., & Noller, P. (1996). *Adult Attachment.* Thousand Oaks, CA: Sage.

Sociology, Culture, and Collective Trauma

Menakem, R. (2017). *My Grandmother's Hands.* Las Vegas: Central Recovery Press.

Fanon, F. (1952). *Black Skin, White Masks.* Paris: Éditions du Seuil.

DeGruy, J. (2005). *Post Traumatic Slave Syndrome.* Portland, OR: Joy DeGruy Publications.

Collins, P. H. (2000). *Black Feminist Thought.* New York: Routledge.

Alexander, J. C. (2012). *Trauma: A Social Theory.* Cambridge: Polity Press.

Eyerman, R. (2001). *Cultural Trauma: Slavery and the Formation of African American Identity.* Cambridge: Cambridge University Press.

Brave Heart, M. Y. H. (1998). *The Return to the Sacred Path. Smith College Studies in Social Work,* 68(3), 287–305.

Gender, Intersectionality, and Power

Crenshaw, K. (1989). *Demarginalizing the Intersection of Race and Sex.* University of Chicago Legal Forum.

Crenshaw, K. (2017). *On Intersectionality: Essential Writings.* The New Press.

Butler, J. (1990). *Gender Trouble: Feminism and the Subversion of Identity.* New York: Routledge.

Butler, J. (2004). *Precarious Life: The Powers of Mourning and Violence.* London: Verso.

Oyěwùmí, O. (1997). *The Invention of Women.* Minneapolis: University of Minnesota Press.

Oyěwùmí, O. (2011). *What Gender Is Motherhood?* New York: Palgrave.

Amadiume, I. (1987). *Male Daughters, Female Husbands.* London: Zed Books.

Connell, R. (1995). *Masculinities.* Cambridge: Polity Press.

Gilligan, C. (1982). *In a Different Voice.* Cambridge, MA: Harvard University Press.

Hochschild, A. R. (1983). *The Managed Heart.* Berkeley: University of California Press.

Manne, K. (2017). *Down Girl: The Logic of Misogyny.* Oxford University Press.

Manne, K. (2020). *Entitled: How Male Privilege Hurts Women.* Penguin / Crown.

Bailey, M. (2021). *Misogynoir Transformed: Black Women's Digital Resistance.* New York University Press.

Nanda, S. (1990). *Neither Man nor Woman: The Hijras of India.* Wadsworth.

Nanda, S. (2014). *Gender Diversity: Crosscultural Variations.* Waveland Press.

Amadiume, I. (2020). *Reinventing Africa: Matriarchy, Religion and Culture.* Zed Books.

Mullings, L. (2005). *The Sojourner Syndrome: Race, Class, and Gender in Retrospect. Journal of African American Studies.*

Neurodiversity, Anxiety, and Adaptation

Kapp, S. K. (2020). *Autistic Community and the Neurodiversity Movement.* London: Palgrave.

Armstrong, T. (2010). *Neurodiversity: Discovering the Extraordinary Gifts of Autism, ADHD, Dyslexia, and Other Brain Differences.* Cambridge, MA: Da Capo Press.

Beardon, L., & Edmonds, A. (2007). *Executive-Function Supports and Autistic Adults. Journal of Autism and Developmental Disorders.*

Mazurek, M. O. et al. (2012). *Sleep Problems, Fatigue, and Social Isolation in Autistic Adults. Journal of Autism and Developmental Disorders.*

Craske, M. G. et al. (2014). *Optimizing Inhibitory Learning During Exposure Therapy. Behaviour Research and Therapy.*

Dunn, W. (1997). *The Sensory Processing Framework.*

Philosophy, Meaning, and Existentialism

Tillich, P. (1952). *The Courage to Be.* New Haven: Yale University Press.

Frankl, V. E. (1946). *Man's Search for Meaning.* Boston: Beacon Press.

Fromm, E. (1941). *The Fear of Freedom*. London: Routledge.
Kierkegaard, S. (1844). *The Concept of Anxiety*. Copenhagen: Reitzel.
May, R. (1975). *The Courage to Create*. New York: W. W. Norton.

Emotional Resilience, Courage, and Leadership

Brown, B. (2012). *Daring Greatly*. New York: Gotham Books.
Brown, B. (2018). *Dare to Lead*. New York: Random House.
Neff, K. (2011). *Self-Compassion*. New York: HarperCollins.
Goleman, D. (1995). *Emotional Intelligence*. New York: Bantam Books.
Siegel, D. J. (2012). *The Developing Mind*. New York: Guilford Press.
Seligman, M. E. P. (2011). *Flourish*. New York: Free Press.
Edmondson, A. (2019). *The Fearless Organization*. Hoboken: Wiley.
Grant, A. (2021). *Think Again*. New York: Viking.

Decolonial Thought, History, and Identity

Fanon, F. (1963). *The Wretched of the Earth*. Grove Press.
Gilroy, P. (1987). *There Ain't No Black in the Union Jack*. London: Routledge.
Gilroy, P. (1993). *The Black Atlantic: Modernity and Double Consciousness*. London: Verso.
Ngũgĩ wa Thiong'o. (1986). *Decolonising the Mind*. London: Heinemann.

Mbembe, A. (2017). *Critique of Black Reason.* Durham, NC: Duke University Press.

Hall, S. (2017). *Familiar Stranger: A Life Between Two Islands.* London: Allen Lane.

Olusoga, D. (2016). *Black and British: A Forgotten History.* London: Pan Macmillan.

Akala. (2018). *Natives: Race and Class in the Ruins of Empire.* London: Two Roads.

Gentleman, A. (2019). *The Windrush Betrayal.* London: Guardian Faber.

Further Reading

Amabile, Teresa M., & Kramer, Steven J. (2011). *The Progress Principle: Using Small Wins to Ignite Joy, Engagement, and Creativity at Work.* Boston: Harvard Business Review Press.

Amadiume, Ifi. (1987). *Male Daughters, Female Husbands: Gender and Sex in an African Society.* London: Zed Books.

Butler, Judith. (1990). *Gender Trouble: Feminism and the Subversion of Identity.* New York: Routledge.

Connell, Raewyn. (1995). *Masculinities.* Cambridge: Polity Press.

Dana, Deb. (2018). *Polyvagal Theory in Therapy: Engaging the Rhythm of Regulation.* New York: W. W. Norton.

Eddo-Lodge, Reni. (2017). *Why I'm No Longer Talking to White People About Race.* London: Bloomsbury.

Eastwood, Owen. (2021). *Belonging: The Ancient Code of Togetherness.* London: Penguin Business.

hooks, bell. (2000). *All About Love: New Visions*. New York: William Morrow.

hooks, bell. (2004). *The Will to Change: Men, Masculinity, and Love*. New York: Washington Square Press.

Hochschild, Arlie Russell. (1989). *The Second Shift: Working Families and the Revolution at Home*. New York: Viking.

Lorde, Audre. (1984). *Sister Outsider: Essays and Speeches*. Trumansburg, NY: Crossing Press.

Nanda, Serena. (2014). *Gender Diversity: Crosscultural Variations*. Long Grove, IL: Waveland Press.

Oyěwùmí, Oyèrónké. (2011). *What Gender Is Motherhood? Changing Yorùbá Ideals of Power, Procreation, and Identity in the Age of Modernity*. New York: Palgrave Macmillan.

Price, Devon. (2022). *Unmasking Autism: Discovering the Hidden Neurodiverse Self*. New York: Penguin.

Steele, Claude M. (2010). *Whistling Vivaldi: How Stereotypes Affect Us and What We Can Do*. New York: W. W. Norton.

Sue, Derald Wing. (2010). *Microaggressions in Everyday Life: Race, Gender, and Sexual Orientation*. Hoboken, NJ: Wiley.

Tatum, Beverly Daniel. (2017). *Why Are All the Black Kids Sitting Together in the Cafeteria?* 20th Anniversary Edition. New York: Basic Books.

www.ingramcontent.com/pod-product-compliance
Lightning Source LLC
Chambersburg PA
CBHW020349080526
44584CB00014B/952